Go for It!

be good to yourself,
and remember the positive.

Go for It!

HOW TO WIN
AT LOVE, WORK AND PLAY

Dr. Irene C. Kassorla

DELACORTE PRESS   NEW YORK

Published by
Delacorte Press
1 Dag Hammarskjold Plaza
New York, N.Y. 10017

Manufactured in the United States of America
First printing

Library of Congress Cataloging in Publication Data

Kassorla, Irene.
  Go for it!

  Includes bibliographical references.
  1. Success. I. Title.
BF637.S8K36 1984   158'.1
ISBN 0-385-29329-1
Library of Congress Catalog Card Number: 83-23942

I dedicate this book to my mother, Bertha, whose positive approach to life has served as a constant source of energy and motivation for me.

Acknowledgments

The genesis of this book dates back to London, when I was a graduate student. It was there that I began writing and conducted my first research project on how to make a "win out of life." I investigated the behaviors and thinking patterns of a number of extremely successful people. My study was called "Twenty of Britain's Most Famous Men." My grateful thanks go to the exceptional group of people who helped me and sponsored that study: George Perry, Senior Editor of the London *Sunday Times;* Susanne Puddefoot, Women's Editor of the London *Times;* Dr. Robert Reid, Science Director, BBC Television; Lord John Wakehurst, former Governor General of New South Wales and Ireland; and Sir Hue Weldon, who later became Director of BBC Television. I especially want to thank George Perry for the many talks we had in which I discussed my ideas on "winners and losers" and how they would be presented in this book.

With affection and gratitude I want to acknowledge my appreciation to the loyal group of friends and helpers who have stayed

viii ACKNOWLEDGMENTS

beside me through the months and years of writing this book: to Johanna Dick for the interviews she had with some of the "super-stars" and her patience and excellent skills as my editor; to my office managers Vicki Hiney and Dalia Weiss and their co-workers Susan Canzoneri and Tami Applegate; and to Joe Loesch, for his devotion and accuracy on the word processor; and to Denise Demong for her fine work on reorganizing the manuscript.

My thanks also go to my beautiful daughters, Ronnie and Jackie, whose hugs, kisses and caring words kept me feeling safe and loved when exhaustion and tears blurred my vision. They were my inspiration when I became discouraged. A special thanks go to my dearest friends, Judi Williams and Lani Alpert, whose caring and encouragement has nurtured me through my writing.

The endless source of meaningful data for my books has been my patients, who are my friends and part of my raison d'être. It is their miraculous progress which continues to fuel me. Their dramatic lifestyle changes and ability to learn new winning skills serve as the magic which prompted me to go to my desk and write *Go for It!*

Contents

PREFACE

Winning Beats Losing

If the day and the night are such that you greet them with joy, and life emits a fragrance like flowers and sweet-scented herbs, is . . . more starry, more immortal, —that is your success.

—HENRY DAVID THOREAU

What do you want out of life?

If you could make your dreams come true, would you be living in comfort, with all the material possessions you ever wanted? Adored by the opposite sex? Enjoying a stable and loving family life? Acclaimed in your work? Traveling to untamed corners of the earth in search of adventure? Sought after by exciting people for your wonderful companionship?

WHAT WOULD YOUR CHOICES BE?

In working with hundreds of patients over the years, I think I've probably heard all of the possible dreams, the longings and the hopes. And in treating these people, it pleases me that I've been able to make so many of their dreams come true. Ever since I began my practice as a psychologist, this has been an important part of my therapy.

I've seen remarkable transformations occur over and over again. The patients have called them "miracles" . . . but I prefer to call them "new skills that can be learned." My techniques embody the behaviors and methods that I recommend every day on the media and in my office. They are the simple, easy-to-understand procedures that lead to success . . . the skills that I teach for living and winning.

YOU CAN LEARN THESE SKILLS, TOO.
AND YOU CAN BECOME A WINNER.

One of the special dreams I had when I first started treating patients was to write a book that would help people to change their fantasies into realities and realize their fullest potential. This has been the therapeutic cornerstone of my work.

I am convinced that all of us have the power to stretch ourselves . . . to accomplish more . . . and to expand our horizons. Unfortunately, few of us know just how to tap into the vast storehouse of talent, ingenuity and imagination that we possess. We use only a fraction of our abilities because too much of our potential lies dormant . . . buried in the unconscious . . . and waiting to be discovered.

But how can we unearth this payload of creativity . . . and where can we begin?

We are filled with visions of what we would like to achieve in our lifetimes. But we are afraid to reach out for our dreams. Instead, we rationalize our ambitions away convincing ourselves we are better off without them. Beaten before we ever get started, the hopes we cherish lie quietly, dying within us.

You can learn how to EXPAND your hidden capacities . . . you can favorably alter your personality and make remarkable, POSITIVE transformations.

EVERYONE READING THIS BOOK HAS THE
POWER TO CHANGE.
EVERYONE . . . AND ESPECIALLY *YOU*
CAN DEVELOP WINNING BEHAVIORS.
YOU CAN START RIGHT NOW!

In my experience as a psychotherapist I have treated many exceptionally successful people. What is particularly interesting is that I have found that they *all* have behaviors in common . . . and that these traits are LEARNABLE and TEACHABLE.

I've also treated a vast number of patients who have been labeled "losers" by their families and society. These people have shed oceans of tears in their sessions with me, confessing that they really *do* feel like losers as lovers, parents, friends or businesspeople. They, too, have a common denominator of behaviors weaving through their life patterns, which are also learned. Fortunately, these loser patterns can be changed to winning skills.

MY GREATEST JOY IS TO HELP LOSERS
TO BECOME *WINNERS!*

YOUR PERSONAL DEFINITION

What do *you* consider to be winning in life? What will make *you* joyous and satisfied? It doesn't matter if the "win" you are seeking is in a career, sports or the arts . . . or if it is a personal win, such as earning the respect and admiration of your spouse, children, friends or the world. However you are spending your time now, you can learn to be happier, to improve your life and to experience more success in your interpersonal relationships and at work.

REALIZE YOUR DREAMS AND FIND OUT
WHAT *YOUR* MEASURE OF SUCCESS AND
ACHIEVEMENT WILL BE.

Will it be increased feelings of self-confidence, dignity and self-esteem? Will it be more approval from others . . . fame, wisdom, awards, promotions, money? Or will it be some kind of service to the community . . . or all or none of the above?

Whatever the hopes and aspirations are that lie deep inside of you, they are good if *you* value them.

LEARN HOW TO GO FOR THEM!

You are the only person who knows what will stir a tempest in your heart. YOU ARE THE BEST JUDGE of what will put a smile on your face and make your life more meaningful. It doesn't matter what your personal concept of winning may be, YOU DESERVE TO HAVE IT . . . shaped by your history and stamped with your signature . . . according to your own standards and desires.

There are only a few of us who will be able to make a mark on mankind like the great leaders of history, or develop vaccines that will save lives or create sophisticated technology that can put men into space. With such lofty models as criteria, however, perhaps you have wondered: Does one need to be an exceptional genius to become a winner? Is there any room for the more common "everyday" brand of a success story? Can "regular folks" who worry about paying bills, having a good relationship with their spouses or getting a small raise move into the winning circle, too?

ABSOLUTELY!
THIS BOOK IS DESIGNED TO SHOW YOU
THE WAY.

Within the parameters of your particular world, you can get more of what you want . . . the most possible! No dream you cherish is too grand or too insignificant . . . no arena you strive to excel in is too impressive or too small.

IT IS NOT THE SIZE OF THE ARENA IN WHICH
YOU FIND YOURSELF THAT COUNTS;
IT IS WHAT YOU *DO* WITH IT.

Whether you are responsible for only yourself or for a business employing thousands of people, you can positively affect the lives of your family, your neighbors, your colleagues and your friends. Most importantly, you can actively and positively direct the course of your own life.

Learning to become a winner starts when you accept that regardless of your social status, physical endowment, income or education, you can:

- become the person you could greatly admire.
- make a difference in your world.
- be increasingly creative and innovative.
- balance a healthy combination of warmth and assertiveness.
- infuse a sense of joy into your daily activities.
- get the appreciation and approval of those you value.
- develop more endurance and energy.
- explore the full extent of your personal magnitude and power.

BECOME THE STAR

We have all cheered for the heroes in epic films who have rightfully recaptured their thrones, have won on life's battlefields and have been victorious in defeating wicked villains. We have known the elation of vicariously identifying with these winners as well as with the other stars in sports, the arts and the media.

BUT IMAGINE HOW MUCH MORE GRATIFYING
IT WILL BE
FOR YOU TO STOP IDENTIFYING AND
FANTASIZING . . .
AND BECOME THE STAR *YOURSELF!*

I believe that winning beats losing and that winning is worth every effort you can make. *You* can be the hero who triumphs over adversity, solves difficult problems and learns how to excel.

AND WAIT UNTIL YOU GET A TASTE OF THIS
KIND OF JOY!

In my experience with treating exceptionally creative and productive people, I have found that there are additional advantages to succeeding: Winners are FAR HAPPIER and much MORE FUN to be with than people who are less productive and accomplished.

> I never met anyone in my whole life who is as happy as I am, and at ninety that is a very big declaration. I'm wildly interested in everything.
>
> —ARTHUR RUBINSTEIN

DECIDE FOR YOURSELF

I know that successful people share very similar thinking and behavioral patterns . . . and that people who suffer repeated failures share habits and thinking patterns that are similar, too. You can learn to understand how these differences are established and maintained. This information will give you more choices, as well as the freedom to decide for yourself the many directions you may want to take.

In the chapters to come, we will take a close psychological look at winners and losers. By examining their extremes, the dramatic polarities in thinking and action that set them apart from each other will become obvious to you.

You will also find many interviews in this book with fascinating super-achievers from the fields of entertainment, athletics, politics and industry. They will offer you models to emulate and give you an intimate look at excellence. Then you can better understand and absorb how winners reason to themselves and behave. Running through the personal philosophies of these superstars you will find common threads . . . valuable ideas that you can incorporate into your own framework and approach to winning.

Get ready now, with your eagerness, pencil and paper, because there will also be interesting homework for you to practice and easy exercises for you to do.

TAKE MY HAND

I want you to take my hand now, so we can get started on our journey into developing the MAGIC OF YOU. Miraculous changes can happen in the thrilling adventure that lies ahead, as you discover how extraordinary YOU WILL BECOME.

You, too, can be the winner that you and others will admire . . . you, too, can be the person that people will want to emulate . . . you, too, can add winning skills into your life.

It is time now for you to acquire your own philosophy, methods and techniques that will carry you closer to your desires and personal victories.

As you read my words, imagine that we are sitting together, talking. I want to fill your mind with new information, simple formulas and ideas that will enhance your daily living and increase your feelings of joy.

Success has no limits: After winning comes more winning, and after more winning comes even more. The frontier is infinite, and your dreams really can come true, once you get one important person to believe in you.

THAT PERSON IS YOU!

As you practice the exercises and attitudes outlined in this book, you will experience new self-confidence and a greater sense of your own worth. You will learn the psychological importance of "falling in love with yourself" as you develop the assets that are uniquely yours.

Your feelings of love and respect for others will also grow. Friends and family will notice the difference in you. They will sense the healthy, positive messages that you are sending out. Imitating you, they will return feelings of warmth, appreciation and respect.

YOU WILL FEEL GREAT . . . AND SO WILL THEY!

Winners do feel great! And they have the "sweet smell of success" that attracts others. Now is the time for *you* to become a more interesting, dynamic and attractive personality.

YOU HAVE THE POWER WITHIN YOU TO:

- make a difference;
- bring about changes in your life;
- transform your losing patterns into winning skills.

YOU HAVE THE POWER WITHIN YOU TO:

- improve yourself;
- positively affect others;
- better the conditions around you.

YOU HAVE THE POWER WITHIN YOU TO:

- double your feelings of self-esteem;
- triple your feelings of self-respect;

• quadruple your feelings of self-confidence.

You have the power to attain your dreams and capture your own brand of excitement and fulfillment. You will be happy, happier, the happiest . . . experiencing the surging excitement of winning. Happiness and winning are contagious, and they are within your reach. I can show you how to make it happen.

EXPERIENCE THE JOY OF WINNING.
GO FOR IT!

PART ONE

Winners Get Going

CHAPTER 1

You've Got to Do It for You

Is not life a hundred times too short for us to bore ourselves?
—FRIEDRICH WILHELM NIETZSCHE

Often the patients I treat say things like "My mother always wanted me to be a doctor," or "My father hoped I'd be like him and take over his business," or "My sister thought I should be like her and become a teacher." Then my patients add, "But what about me? My feelings are completely left out! Even my neighbors think they have the best ideas about the way I should spend my time! No one seems interested in knowing what I want to do."

WHAT ABOUT YOU?
WHO PLANS *YOUR* LIFE?

Who is making *your* important decisions? Who is running *your* show? Following the advice of others will probably make you feel very inadequate. If you listen to them, someone will be happy . . . but it WON'T BE YOU. If *you* want to be happy, and feel adequate and successful, *you* will need to be the one who designs your life.

THE FIVE-HUNDRED-YEAR PLAN

Do you have five hundred years to live? Are you one of those immortals who has almost unlimited time? If so, the first hundred years on this planet you could afford to spend your time according to your parents' needs and desires . . . you can "do it" for them.

The second hundred, however, I think you ought to "do it" for
your neighbors; they're nice people . . . find out what they
would like you to be. The third hundred, "do it" for your children
or family . . . they're important, too. And by the fourth hundred,
you can "do it" for some other pressure group that you value . . .
that would be very generous of you. By the fifth hundred year . . .
which would be your last century of life . . . I think you ought to
"do it" for you!

When you are mortal, you don't have unlimited time and you
can't sacrifice your dreams and ideals for others, or you will hate
yourself . . . and them.

All any of us have is *now* . . . our *todays*. Everyone you know is
dying; no one gets out of this beautiful world alive. The "win" in
life is enjoying every precious moment of *your* days in *your* way.

WHAT DO *YOU* VALUE?
WHAT PUTS A SMILE ON *YOUR* FACE?

Ask yourself: "If I had just one year to live, and I was told I had to
do forty hours of work a week and forty hours of 'play,' how would
I spend those hours? Would I continue to live my life in the same
way I am now?"

If the answer to this last question *isn't* "Yes" . . . wake up! You
are mortal, sweet friend! The clock is ticking and *your* years are
numbered!

Every now and then, I hear someone say, "I hate my work, but
it's a living." And I think to myself, "Are you kidding? You must be
one of those people who has five hundred years!"

Me? I'm limited to this first hundred . . . or less. I can't afford
to spend my life doing anything that I hate. I've got to find the
work arena, the friends, the activities, that put joy in my life.

"It's a living" isn't reason enough. Suppose you're doing work
you hate so much you can hardly get up in the morning, or are
bored, or have bleeding ulcers. But it pays for your rent, your car
and buys your necessities. Remind yourself: If you're smart
enough to have learned how to support yourself in the job you
can't stand, you're smart enough to do it another way. You don't
have to be miserable and stay where you are. If you're doing well
in one particular area, you will do equally well in work that you
prefer. Dare to experiment with life and find *your* place in the sun.

DON'T STAY STUCK.
DON'T BE UNHAPPY.
DON'T WASTE AWAY YOUR *ONLY* LIFE.

WHAT *DON'T* I WANT TO BE?

Convincing people to "do it" for themselves usually isn't too difficult. The problem begins when they start: "How? I want to 'do it' for me, but I'm not sure what *I* want."

When they first come in to see me, some of my patients are what I call "big losers." They have never "made it" at anything, except being very negative. They don't know what they want to do. So I use that.

I give them a pencil and paper and say, "Start making a list: 'WHAT *DON'T* I WANT TO BE?' "

They respond very quickly. Many people haven't a clue about what they *want* . . . but they *do* know what they *don't* want . . . because they are so skilled at being negative. "I don't want to be a garbage collector," one writes. "I don't want to be a servant." They write and write, but finally they start to run out of ideas. Negatives don't work after a while.

Then . . . still working with their negatives, because that is what many people are comfortable with . . . I say, "Now start a second list. This list begins: 'I *MIGHT* NOT MIND BEING.' " And they start writing again. They mention things they might do part-time. By the time they run out of ideas for that list, they are slowly becoming more positive.

Now I ask them to write a third list, "I *THINK* I MIGHT LIKE." The heading is still very tentative, because people who are accustomed to being losers are afraid to make decisions or be responsible for definite statements. They fear that decisions mean action and ultimately failure. And their worries about failure are often greater than their hopes to succeed.

To help patients move into a winning posture, my goal *isn't* to get them to say "I *definitely* want to be a _____." Rather, I want a nonthreatening jumping-off spot for them to examine new alternatives and start thinking. Once patients have at least a vague picture of things they "might like" to do, we are moving toward a winning frame of mind.

START PRACTICING NOW

Perhaps you have thought you "might like to" get into a particular field or occupation. You can start by looking at the want ads for job offers. Search out schools or training centers . . . talk to peo-

ple who are already working at this . . . become more familiar
with the opportunities. Eventually you may decide to enroll in a
course. Then you may find that you don't like it at all! Fine! You
"took a look" . . . you tried. Doing this kind of intelligent research DOESN'T mean that you will be stuck for life in that work.
It only means that you are EXPLORING . . . and that's a wise
thing to do.

By getting more information you will be in a better position to
evaluate WHETHER OR NOT to pursue it further. Knowing that
you "might be" interested will give you a "jumping-off" place
from which to start, because . . .

WINNING MEANS "GET STARTED . . .

GO FOR IT!"

Sometimes people who long for accomplishment and success
seem to get stuck before they begin . . . they're not sure where
they want to go. Without a clear goal in mind, they find it difficult
to decide what to do next. So they sit and wait for that magical bolt
of "knowing *exactly* how they want to spend their lives" to strike
them.

But I've learned that many of the exceptional winners I've
treated don't have a lot of clear goals in mind, either. Rather, they
are achievers who move so fast, sometimes they don't even *know*
what their goals are. They just keep trying new things until they
become more satisfied with their choices. They do a lot of "trial-
and-error" behaviors. They are like blind batters who swing so
often they hit lots of homeruns.

Winners are so ACTIVE . . . so MOVEMENT-oriented . . .
they experiment with so many new avenues . . . that they can't
help but accomplish something worthwhile by the end of their
busy days.

YOU HAVE TO SEARCH

I began college as a music major. I had never considered any
other alternative. Everyone in my family was musical . . . it was
a very important part of our home life. We even had two pianos,
one upstairs and one down, so that my older sister Charlotte and I
could practice simultaneously without disturbing each other.
Charlotte's major in college was music and my parents and friends
expected me to follow her example. It seemed very natural for me
to choose music as my major.

I had been a "star" at Fairfax High School because my music had opened many doors for me. I was in every "aud" call playing the piano, accompanying the choir, performing solos and writing musicals. This helped me to become very popular, and I felt special. But there were fewer than twenty-five *hundred* students at Fairfax, and more than twenty-five *thousand* at UCLA where I enrolled. The music students came from all over the world. There was a freshman pianist from Switzerland whose playing was close to flawless, his mastery was brilliant; and a senior from Russia whose technique was even more extraordinary.

Slowly it dawned on me, "This is not high school, and you are not so special here." I didn't have the intense devotion or the great love for music the others had . . . nor the skills! But all my life, everyone had assumed my career would be in music. It took me another two years before I realized, "I don't want to be what my mother wants me to be. I'm lousy at it. My friends think I'm interesting when I play the piano and that I write good songs. But I know I'm mediocre."

I made a wise decision and left the music department. I wasn't disappointed because I had spent my time well . . . it took me only two years . . . instead of a lifetime to realize that music was not the career I wanted.

I began hunting for what I *did want*, but I still relied heavily on others' choices for me. I had one friend who was in economics and wanted me to follow his lead, so I changed my major to economics. *He* loved our being in class together. But *I* understood very little and was in a constant fog in class. I even fantasized one day about throwing the dreary textbook at the professor, who was also the author. The only thing that kept me going was my friend's approval. But finally I realized again, "This isn't the career for *me.*"

Then I tried what another friend was doing. I liked the idea of designing my own clothes and had a job one summer as a sportswear designer. So I decided to change majors to marketing and fashion design.

And so it went. I switched my program so many times that the counselors would start smiling whenever they saw me coming. Almost every semester I would try a new major.
BUT THAT IS FINE.

By exploring, failing and trying, I finally discovered what gets *my* pulse racing . . . what keeps *my* energy soaring . . . what has *me* surging with excitement. It is my work in psychology.

If life were a fairy tale, I would have awakened one morning, heard violins and seen a light flashing to me: "You should become a psychologist; you would be wonderful." In a daze, I would have floated off to UCLA on my flying carpet. I would have arrived at all the correct classrooms, magically whizzed through all the best courses, aced every exam and instantly popped out as a highly experienced and insightful psychologist. In three more seconds, I would have become famous and respected on six continents.

But that is not how it happened for me or anyone else! What did occur was that after many foolish decisions and errors, I stumbled into a psychology course because it was required. It appeared to be a miraculous accident when I fell in love with the material, the research, the department, the professors . . . the entire field of psychology. Perhaps even more of a miracle was that often, when I would say something in class, a hush would come over the room. I was always surprised: "They all get quiet when I speak! Usually nobody seems too impressed when I talk, except my family and closest friends."

Inspired, I enrolled in a second psychology course and studied as hard as I could. I would spend weeks in the library on papers that took other students only hours. Then I began working at hospitals. I found myself doing therapy with a psychotic child who slapped me in the face, and another who bit me. I thought, "What am I doing here? I must be crazy!" But there were great moments, too . . . and I continued taking course after course.

Several professors took a special interest in me. Then I began doing research with an autistic child who improved remarkably with my therapy. People in the field came from all over the country to observe the work. *Life* magazine reported on it.

Then I was invited to Europe, where I replicated my experiments at the University of London. I did more therapy and more research. In London, I worked with a man who hadn't spoken in *thirty* years, and I was able to get him talking in *thirty* days! That became the subject of my doctoral thesis. The newspapers reported on it and I became famous. All this happened in the sixties.

As I look back on the meandering course I followed on my way to discovering my great love for psychology, I feel very fortunate. Becoming a psychotherapist and helping people to lead more productive lives has given much meaning and purpose to my own life. While I am now much honored as a winner, I started out as a loser who was a mediocre music major because that is what my family wanted. I never even asked myself what I wanted. But once I embarked on my educational "hunt" and tried everything . . .

because I wasn't sure what else to do . . . my dreams began to gradually take shape the way *I wanted.*

IT IS TIME FOR YOU TO START THE SEARCH
FOR *YOUR* WANTS AND WINS.

Take the first step by using an exercise similar to the one I have already described when I was discussing my patients.

If you're just starting your career, or if you're unhappy in the work you're doing now and thinking of making a change, you can use the exercise just as it's set forth below. But maybe career isn't your concern right now. Maybe the "win" you're after is improving your relationship with your spouse, friends, parents or children. Maybe you're unhappy about your weight, your smoking or the place where you live. This exercise will still be useful. Modify it according to what your concerns are today. The purpose is the same: to help you sort out all the voices clamoring in your head telling you what you *should* do, and to help you establish the first *hints of what you want to do for you.*

EXERCISE 1: DO IT FOR YOU

This exercise is designed to help you get acquainted with *you* . . . what it is that you *really* want . . . that you *really* enjoy . . . that *really* interests you.

Sit down with a pencil and a stack of paper. At the top of the first sheet, put:

Step One: What My Parents Wanted Me to Be: Career.

Write down whatever career they hoped you would follow. For example, if your parents wanted you to get married and raise a family, the top of your first sheet would read:

WHAT MY PARENTS WANTED ME TO BE: HOMEMAKER.

If, however, your folks' dream was for you to follow in Dad's footsteps and take over the business, the top of your first sheet would read:

WHAT MY PARENTS WANTED ME TO BE:
BUSINESSPERSON.

Then list every characteristic that your parents valued, in detail. Outline what they said were "good" qualities for a homemaker or businessperson to have.

Step Two

Take another paper and begin this second category at the top: "What My Friends (or Spouse) Think I Should Be: Homemaker (Model, Beachbum, Mogul, Artist, etc.)." Again, list as many things as you can think of that this group believes are important.

Step Three

Begin a third list now, headed: "I Don't Want to Be a _____." Add as many different items as you like. Include in this list all the things you are sure you would hate to do.

Step Four

Begin a fourth list: "I Might Not Mind Being a _____." Don't worry about making a mistake. This is not decision time. You are just practicing with new techniques of thinking and action.

Write down anything that appeals to you at all. If you believe it may not be obtainable for you, write it down anyway because I want you to take a closer look at your dreams . . . just for the practice.

When you are all finished, take the first three lists . . . "What My Parents Wanted Me to Be," "What My Friends Think I Should Be" and "I Don't Want to Be" . . . and
THROW THEM AWAY.

Keep only the last list, "I Might Not Mind Being." It will represent your *own* feelings. Although they may not be well formulated yet, it will be a start for you to begin building on more positive action.

HOW WE DENY OURSELVES SUCCESS

It doesn't matter what others "think you should be doing," only your own standards will work for you. In order to become the winner that *YOU* will respect and admire . . . you must have control of the authorship of your own destiny . . . the pen that writes your life story MUST be held in your own hand. You are the one who has to GO FOR IT! If someone else does and is responsible for your successes . . . he or she will be the winner and you the loser.

You couldn't be happy watching someone else eating your food daily, nor could you be happy being robbed of your self-determination. You will miss too much joy if you cannot taste your own life.

Accepting another person's frame of reference and value systems will make you a self-destructive loser.

But most of us *are* self-destructive . . . most people miss experiencing the happiness that could be available to them in their own lives.

Why are we so self-destructive? Why do we keep losing in the same ways, year after year?

My work with psychotic patients will help you answer these questions and understand how your own losing patterns were established and why you unconsciously maintain them today.

In the early sixties, I treated only severely disturbed psychotics. Whether I was helping autistic children speak their first appropriate words or getting mentally ill adults to behave more rationally, I was grateful when my patients made progress in coping with their lives.

In 1967, I began doing therapy with normal people who were looking for "gourmet living." They wanted to improve the quality of their relationships, marriages and careers. Although these patients were healthy and usually functioned well, at times they approached their problems in ways that were not only ineffective, but without realizing it, these patients were actually *harmful* to themselves or others. I was surprised to discover how similar their actions were to the behavior of psychotics. The difference lay in the *intensity* and *frequency* with which they acted out particular behaviors.

Let me explain further: If someone sitting across the dinner table from you were to scratch his nose for a moment, you probably wouldn't even notice. If he scratched his nose for hours, however, you might think, "Why is that fool continually playing with his nose? That's so peculiar. He looks bloody crazy!"

And you would be correct. Such a person would be diagnosed as "crazy," or mentally ill, because of the *frequency* and *intensity* of his nose-scratching . . . not the behavior itself, which would otherwise be considered normal.

The severely regressed psychotics whom I worked with early in my career often used normal behavior patterns, but they did so in a peculiar and repetitive manner. You couldn't miss how obvious their disturbed behavior was because they moved in "slow motion" and it was impossible to ignore. An untrained observer could easily see that their actions would lead to failure and self-destruction.

But even people whose behavior is well within the normal

bounds use patterns that result in repeated failures and emotional pain. It is easy for a trained therapist to see them. Whether their vehicles for stopping the wins in life are overeating, alcoholism, smoking, not achieving, losing money, fighting with those they love . . . or whatever . . . most people continually repeat behaviors that are harmful to themselves. Looking back to early childhood experiences can offer more insight into these self-destructive patterns.

THE LOSER'S VICIOUS CYCLE

How many times have you left a situation angry with yourself, knowing when it is too late exactly what you should have said or done? Have you pondered why you get in your own way and prevent yourself from enjoying the very things you want?

BECAUSE YOU'VE LEARNED TO, THAT'S WHY!

We all *learn* to be winners . . . or losers and failures. It is not in our bloodstreams or in our genes. Our styles of behaving have been shaped by our parents, who learned from their parents.

NO ONE IS TO BLAME.

Each of us is using patterns now that trace back to our unique history of family interactions. They were transmitted to us daily throughout our childhoods. We watched our loving caretakers in action hour by hour and unconsciously learned to imitate their methods of handling conflicts and problem solving. We incorporated everything they did or said and made it into our own model for living.

Today, regardless of the size or complexity of the dilemmas we face, we still employ our parents' modes of dealing with problems. We had studied them well by the end of our first four years: We knew when we were allowed to cry or laugh . . . when to be angry, happy, sarcastic, cruel, loving, . . . when to feel hurt and when *not* to feel or react.

All we can do as children is soak up whatever it is that our own parents have to teach us. It is during these developmental years that we become so much like them. We collect their behaviors and gather them into a little emotional satchel that we carry around with us. Wherever we go throughout our lives, we drag these patterns along.

Most parents are totally innocent about what is happening. They want the best for their families and have no idea they are causing harm. But all they can teach is what they themselves have learned. Thus, if our parents live, think and plan in a mediocre way . . . we are probably living, thinking and planning in a mediocre way, too. Like an emotional "osmosis," we absorb their ineffective methods and "crazy-making" skills . . . their *loser* techniques.

Rarely do we realize that *we are the ones* now who most often stand in the way of our own growth and happiness. It is difficult for us to fathom that we are unconsciously sabotaging our own success or the success of those we care about most. We do this unwittingly because our early training has blinded us, emotionally.

MARGARET LEARNED FROM MOTHER

Let's look at the story of Margaret, a new patient, who told me how happy she was about the raise she had just received. She was the secretary to an executive in a large computer firm. When Margaret phoned her mother and gave her the good news, her happiness vanished because she was so upset by the parent's reaction:

"My mom is very negative," she told me. "She's always laying her downers on me whenever I feel great. When I called and told her my boss gave me more money after only three months, she began crying! Then she started in with the line I've been hearing since I was a kid, 'If only your dad were alive to see that you're finally doing well after all these years!' Like always, she killed my great mood!"

Margaret was right. Her mother's comments *were* negative. The "if only your dad" and "you're finally doing well after all these years" *were* emotional downers. By turning the focus of the conversation onto her dead husband, Margaret's mother had wiped out Margaret's good feelings about herself and her raise.

"My mom doesn't appreciate how well I'm doing in lots of ways," Margaret continued. "Take my daughter Stephanie . . . she came home today with a great report card. I'm very *positive* with *my* kid.

"I gave her a big hug, and said, 'If only your grandma were here to see this card, she'd know I'm not only a good secretary, but I'm a good mother, too!' "

I quickly pointed out to Margaret that she had turned the focus of the conversation away from the report card and onto "if only-ing" her daughter, just the way her mother had done with her! Margaret was shocked at my comments. Because her behavior wasn't conscious, she hadn't realized that she had switched the center of attention from Stephanie's achievement to her own merits as a secretary and parent. She had dampened the child's high spirits about her report card, just as her mother had abruptly deflated her happy feelings about the raise.

Margaret would never have knowingly delivered emotional downers to Stephanie. But unfortunately, she had learned the family's loser patterns too well.

START CHANGING YOUR LIFE

It's too late now to rearrange the circumstances of your birth and select a new set of parents. But regardless of your early emotional training . . .

YOU CAN IMPROVE YOUR LIFE NOW.

You can become a better problem solver. *You can* transform patterns of repeated failure into more effective winning styles. *You can* become a more successful person.

IT'S NEVER TOO LATE

Perhaps you're saying to yourself now "My parents were such a mess, if I'm like them I'll never make it! I'm worried that there's been too much damage . . . that it's too late for me."

STOP WORRYING!

The work of Dr. Judianne Densen-Gerber, founder and president of Odyssey Institute of America and Odyssey Institute International, affirms my belief that it is never too late to adopt healthy, new skills and make the effort to improve your life.

For almost two decades, Dr. Densen-Gerber has offered people a haven where they can learn how to overcome life patterns that have resulted in chronic failures. She has helped countless drug addicts, alcoholics and child abuse victims at centers around the world.

When I first met Dr. Densen-Gerber, who holds degrees in both psychiatry and law, I thought to myself, "That woman is so bright and dynamic, I'll bet she could move a mountain three feet!" After getting to know her better, and hearing about the hope she has given so many people, I believe she could!

She focuses her amazing energies on helping people who have had unfortunate parental role models to start a new life. "Most of the people in the Odyssey program have been raised under the influence of alcoholic and depressed parents who have abused them physically and emotionally," she explains. "They think that they grew up under a dark cloud and are tattooed with 'Born to Lose.' They don't understand the differences in behavior and attitude that people have who enjoyed healthier childhood experiences.

"I tell them to hook onto someone successful who embodies the things they would like to be. When they find someone that they admire, I urge them to closely observe their productive actions and creative lives. 'Watch everything that person does, follow him and try to do the same things.'

"Once our patients can incorporate the winning skills they have observed from others into their *own* behavioral patterns, they also can become people that others will want to emulate."

Many of the people who have gone through her programs have been able to *completely turn their lives around*. In her offices in Detroit and Flint, Michigan, 45 percent of the clients were originally classified as illiterate. Yet 93 percent of them went on to pass their G.E.D.'s, or high-school equivalency exams, compared with a national success rate of only 45 percent. Dr. Densen-Gerber demonstrates the successful changes that are realistic, even when someone starts out under highly adverse conditions. Her work proves:

IT REALLY IS POSSIBLE TO DO IT FOR YOU.

I want to help you get the most out of your life. You really can "do it" for yourself . . . and learn to feel and behave in the ways you want to. Whether you want it to be at home, on a farm or working around the world, you have within you the power to lead a great life. Then the fun and effort that goes into winning will become a rewarding way for you to spend your precious time.

LEARN HOW TO BE JOYOUS AND FULFILLED
AND FEEL LIKE A WINNER.

WINNER SCORECARD #1

Rate yourself: When it comes to "Doing It For You," are you living like a loser, or are you ready to establish some "winning ways"?

LOSERS

1. Losers blindly follow the goals their parents set for them or the objectives their neighbors, friends or society consider worthy.

2. Losers often cling to professions they despise because they represent an income and security.

3. Losers become immobilized by a lack of clear goals. They wait to get started, thinking they must first know *exactly* what they want to do . . . and exactly where they want to go.

4. Losers are self-destructive. They continue to use the same behavioral patterns, year after year, fearing they are too old . . . or it is too late . . . to change.

WINNERS

1. Winners know their time on earth is limited: They pursue the objectives that will be rewarding for them and will give their lives personal meaning, using their own standards.

2. Winners know "It's a living" isn't reason enough and realize that if they've done well in work they *don't* enjoy, they will do equally well, or even better, in work that gives them *real* pleasure.

3. Winners know they have to search to find their niche. They experiment actively, taking many different directions, failing and trying new avenues until they finally discover where their interests and talents lie.

4. Winners believe that . . . no matter how unfortunate their training or early childhood was . . . they can positively affect the course of their lives and learn new winning skills.

5. Losers offer outside causes to themselves and others for their ineffective patterns and losing skills. They don't understand that it is they who have contributed to their own dilemmas and losing situations.

5. Winners understand they are the saboteurs who stop the joy in their lives. They don't blame others, rather they try to learn new winning skills and abandon the old self-destructive patterns they have learned during childhood.

CHAPTER 2

Blowing the Whole Thing

Nothing comes into being all at once; not even the grape or the fig. If you say to me now, "I want a fig," I shall answer, "That requires time." Let the tree blossom first, then put forth its fruit, and finally let the fruit ripen.

—EPICTETUS

When a loser tries something new and makes mistakes or runs into difficulties, he blows the whole thing: He stops. He is sure that a stronger person . . . a real winner . . . would have learned without effort on the first few trials. He thinks: "I wish I were a whole person and not so bloody stupid! If I had good stuff inside of me, if I were *really* intelligent, I would learn how to do it on the first lesson. I would stay on that diet forever with nary a slip; I would quit smoking instantly; I would become a great skier on Lesson One."

Losers' belief systems are almost childlike. They assume that winners have a special genetic endowment, a knack for perfection, and learn most things easily. According to losers, when a winner attempts something new, it's "tra-la-la" for them . . . a cinch! Losers are certain that winners are "naturals" . . . great students who can jump from lesson one straight to proficiency.

THE MOUNTAINS AND THE VALLEYS

When I was doing the research for my doctoral thesis, the walls of my office were covered with charts depicting the results of my experiments. The learning curves . . . graphic representations of the rate at which my patients were able to absorb and apply new information always fascinated me. A learning curve never climbed straight up from zero at the bottom to 100 percent learning at the top, as a steep incline might climb toward the sky. Rather, each graph looked like a series of mountains and valleys . . . reflecting how irregular learning patterns really are.

Neither humans nor animals acquire new skills easily. Usually great effort that requires extensive trial-and-error behaviors are needed. People who become winners work at it over long periods of time, failing and trying again before mastery is attained.

Learning is a slow process. Winners know that it takes time . . . that they won't be able to climb to the top of their mountains and be successful in one jump. In every type of endeavor, they understand that they may have to start out at the lowest rung of the ladder and spend years slowly moving up the hierarchy before they reach their own ideal of an executive suite.

THE LOSER THEORY OF INSTANT GRATIFICATION

Infants require instant gratification. They fill their diapers the moment they have the urge. We accept their immaturity and we don't put demands on them that are developmentally unrealistic.

Unfortunately, with losers, this pattern of requiring instant gratification continues throughout their lives. For example, if a loser decides to become an artist, his impossible expectation is that he will become a promising talent and produce a masterpiece almost immediately. If he finds that his first class is difficult, BOOM! he quits. He believes that when a person is bright and gifted, satisfaction quickly follows desire. No painful tedium, no struggle, no long hours . . . no dues to pay.

Losers want fast results in return for very little effort. When things become difficult and progress moves slowly, they soon become bored. This is how they think a learning curve should look

... straight up, easy progress ... no problems ... instant gratification and rewards:

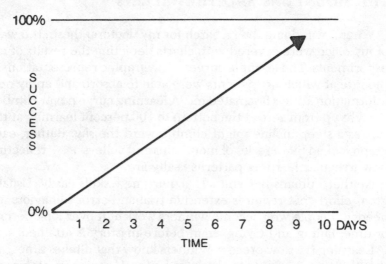

Figure 1: Loser's view of a learning curve.

Winners know that a learning curve records one struggle after another. Their curve *does* move up ... but gradually, embodying discouraging frustrations and disappointments. Sometimes it takes winners years ... with little gratification in sight until they finally reach their goals and enjoy their rewards.

FALLING OFF THE WAGON

Not only does a loser become annoyed if he doesn't learn a new skill quickly; he is equally impatient when he's trying to improve his life by changing an old habit. A loser believes that once he makes that first slip and falls off the wagon, he's finished. He gives up quickly. He thinks that if his record isn't perfect, he's a failure. The loser's formula is:

ONE FAILURE MEANS YOU WILL NEVER
MAKE IT;
ONE FAILURE MEANS YOU DON'T HAVE
WHAT IT TAKES.

Nonsense! This kind of perfectionism really does belong in a child's world of make-believe!

Winners know that the fruits of success ripen slowly and often

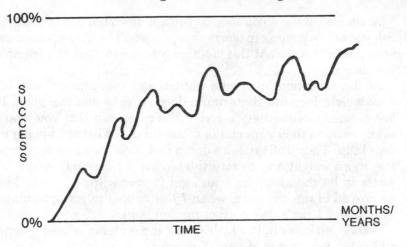

Figure 2: Winner's view of a learning curve.

after repeated errors. They know that when they make a mistake there's no reason to blow the whole thing by stopping. Rather, they learn what they can from the experience, hang in and try harder.

When a loser fails, he says to himself: "I just don't have what it takes to keep going." When a winner fails, he says to himself: "All that it takes to keep going . . . is to *keep going!*"

Because mistakes are so much a part of living, adages such as Alexander Pope's "to err is human" have become part of the winner's everyday speech.

A THINNER WINNER

I want *you* to begin to incorporate a winning outlook into your thinking patterns. The following example, which describes how an overweight loser can learn to be a thinner winner, will help you "get back on the wagon" regardless of the particular behavior you are trying to change.

Let's imagine you want to break your habit of overeating. You have made up your mind to lose twenty pounds and become a new, streamlined person. You read all of the bestsellers on how to lose weight and go on a diet.

For the first week, you do well. You resist your favorite foods: spaghetti, pie, ice cream, bread. You feel strong and in control and you lose five pounds! You are thrilled with yourself.

At the end of the second week, you are down ten whole pounds. But you are beginning to worry that you won't be able to continue your perfect record. At this juncture you are invited to a friend's wedding.

At the reception, everyone notices and compliments you on your weight loss. But their praise doesn't make you feel good. It just creates more anxiety for you. You're certain that you won't measure up to their expectations. You think, "What am I going to do if I slip? They'll all say I'm a damn fool. Everyone expects me to lose more weight and to *stay* thin! What if I can't? It would be easier to let the ax fall now and get it over with. Why should I endure all of this pressure, when *I just know* I'm going to binge eventually? I can't stay perfect forever, and . . ."

Before you know it, you have drunk three glasses of champagne and eaten four plates of hors d'oeuvres.

What happened? Your mind went blank after the second helping of stuffed mushrooms. But now you think to yourself, "What have I done? I've failed again. This diet is all over."

NO IT ISN'T!

NO IT ISN'T!

NO IT ISN'T!

As long as you are alive, it is *never* all over. Winners make mistakes . . . they binge when they are dieting, too! But they know *it isn't all over.*

SLIPPING AND ERRORS ARE A NORMAL PART
OF CHANGE.

BACK ON THE WAGON

If you are really going to break an old habit, you need to realize that you *can* get back on the wagon when you fail. Anxiety doesn't stop you . . . *you do!* When you go off your diet during an irresistible feast . . . that's understandable. You can get back to your diet at your next meal. One error doesn't mean the entire ball game is over.

Remind yourself, "I *am* a winner. I stuck to my diet for two weeks. That was *real* winning!" Mentally, give yourself a big hug and continue, "I did beautifully for fourteen days . . . that means that for forty-two meals I was sensational. And I goofed only *once!* Forty-two wins and only one loss . . . that's excellent!"

Give yourself credit for the remarkable effort you *did make*, and get back on your diet again.

Whether you are trying to master a new task or establish a healthier way of behaving, mistakes are indications that you went too far off in one direction or another. You need to get back on course.

WINNERS MAKE FRIENDS WITH FAILURE.

Failures offer valuable information about where *not to go* next time . . . and are helpful guides . . . not signals to give up.

THE CHASTISING CYCLE

A loser starts groaning, whining and beating his chest when he makes a mistake. He calls himself names like "stupid" and "foolish," feels worthless and sinks into a depression. He assaults himself with destructive questions: "Why wasn't I more careful? Why was I so gullible? Why didn't I do more checking? Why do I make so many mistakes?"

WHY? . . . WHY? . . . WHY?

The loser continues this self-punishing litany throughout his life. He berates himself mercilessly, like an overly strict parent reprimanding a helpless child. The result: With every critical jab, his ego suffers, withers and dies a bit.

A negative cycle results. The more the loser chastises himself, the more incompetent he feels. The more incompetent he feels, the more mistakes he makes. The more mistakes he makes, the more inadequate he feels, and the more inadequate he feels, the more he chastises himself, and so on. Once this cycle becomes well established, the fear of making a mistake causes so much anxiety that the loser moves into a protective immobilized state that others might view as "lazy" or "unmotivated."

By blowing the whole thing, the loser diminishes his fear of making further mistakes. This reduces his anxiety, and immediate comfort and relief follow. Now there are no more trials, no more errors, no more failures . . . and, unfortunately, no more chances for success.

EXERCISE 2: LEARNING TO GET ACROSS THE POND

In most life situations there are difficulties that we must face regularly. The methods that we use to deal with these conditions can *reduce* our probabilities for success or *enhance* our coping skills for winning.

I want to give you an example that will help you look at the significant contrasts in the approach to problems that winners and losers demonstrate. Let's assume in this example that your real-life conflicts are analogous to crossing an icy pond.

Suppose that in order to get to your job, you need to cross a pond every day. In some places, the ice is thick and safe to walk on, but in others, it is so thin that very little pressure will cause you to fall through into the freezing water.

A *Loser* Would Think in This Way:

- At all times, focus on avoiding failure rather than on getting across the pond. Proceed fearfully and with great caution.
- Carefully test the ice as you take each step: Put your foot down lightly and make certain that the surface is firm before you place your full weight on it. Then take a hesitant step. Again: Avoid failure at all costs!
- Repeat the testing process cautiously with every single move. Expect and be prepared for failure at all times.
- Never stop your worrying about making a mistake and falling into the freezing water.
- If necessary, take all day to cross the pond. Don't be overly concerned about missing work. Remember: The most important thing is *not to fail*.
- If you are foolish enough to misjudge a spot where the ice is thin and you do fall into the water, reprimand yourself unmercifully. Continue this tongue-lashing as you pull yourself out of the hole for hours afterward. As you sit there . . . shivering and freezing, beat your chest and rock back and forth, moaning loudly. With great disgust, go over a detailed summary of every wrong move you made. Repeat each item over and over. Be thoroughly annoyed with yourself, every time you repeat.
- Call yourself ugly names. Do this out loud as you sit and face the hole . . . the place where you failed and fell in. Here is a list to get you started. With practice you will be creative and think of more.

        a. stupid
        b. careless
        c. blind
        d. moron
        e. idiot
        f. fool
        g. jackass

- After thoroughly castigating yourself, rise and, with great trepidation, again start testing the ice inch by inch. Be careful. If you need to, take hours to traverse a few feet.
- Repeat all of the above steps religiously, until you reach your destination on the other side.
- When you arrive at your job, give your co-workers *detailed descriptions* of every mishap you encountered. Be very graphic.

A *Winner* Would Follow a Very Different Procedure:

- Before approaching the pond, do research on icy surfaces. Talk to experts who have had experience in similar circumstances. Read everything you can about the topic.
- When you do start out, focus on the problem, which is crossing the pond, rather than on the possibility of landing in the icy water.
- Be prepared. Since the chances for failure are so great, wear a wet suit.
- Leave for work early, giving yourself enough time to deal with mishaps and still arrive punctually.
- Don't worry about falling in. Be assured that *you will* at times, because everywhere you go in life, there are places where the ice is thin.
- Keep moving. When you do break through, pick yourself up right away and quickly start pushing forward again. Persevere.
- Because failure is your friend and teacher, mark each spot where you fall in, so that next time you can avoid those places.
- Prepare resources in advance at your job that will allow you to get comfortable with a minimum of inconvenience so that you can get to work without much delay (i.e., towels, a set of clean clothes, hair dryer, makeup, etc.).
- Regardless of how many falling incidences you encounter, *praise yourself* that it wasn't more . . . and that you made it across so fast.
- When you arrive at your job, remember that all the people there have crossed their own ponds and experienced their own traumas, so they will have limited tolerance to hearing about yours. Instead, be *interested in them* and share something mutually rewarding.

Looking at these two divergent examples, can you find yourself in either one of these camps? In my work with patients I have seen that those who *could look at* and *identify* their problems made the fastest changes.

A winner keeps sight of his ultimate objective . . . whatever pond he finds himself in. He works at facing challenges and over-coming problems in order to achieve his goals.

When he makes an imprudent decision or misjudges a situation, he reassures himself, "I did the best I could." Then he does something constructive and moves on quickly in the pursuit of his goals. Knowing that the shortest distance between two points is a straight line, he concentrates on arriving at his destination as directly and as rapidly as he can. He wants to take as few steps as possible. He tries not to waste energy or effort. He looks for short-cuts and timesavers whenever possible . . . *without* sacrificing quality or excellence.

THEY START IN THE MAILROOM

> . . . people seldom see the halting and painful steps by which the most insignificant success is achieved.
> —ANNIE SULLIVAN, Helen Keller's teacher

Goals are achieved little by little, step by step. Because learning goes slowly, and progress requires time . . . change sometimes takes years. Winners know this. They give themselves the opportunity to go step by step, trying and failing as they struggle to succeed. Their stories are much the same . . . they understand that instant gratification isn't realistic . . . but they start . . . they get going early and *keep going*.

This was true with my agent, Norman Brokaw, whose career in showbiz began in the mailroom when he was only fifteen. Now, at the age of fifty-five, Norman is considered to be one of the world's most respected agents. He is the Executive Vice President of William Morris, Incorporated, which is an international theatrical talent agency.

Today Norman talks proudly about his roster of clients whose names have included personalities as notable as former President Gerald Ford, Natalie Wood, Barbara Stanwyck, Marilyn Monroe and former Secretary of State Alexander Haig.

AND NORMAN STARTED IN THE MAILROOM!

It is important for you to see that people who hold positions "at the top" . . . frequently start "at the bottom!" They work their way up slowly, learning as they go, making mistakes and acquiring their expertise as Norman did. Throughout their lives, much like saving up pennies in a bank, their information builds and expands as they become richer in knowledge and experience.

"STICK-TO-IT-IVENESS"

Many people don't realize that in their struggles to become successful, they may encounter many frustrating and agonizing steps and challenges.

In examining the characteristics that go into making up an outstanding personality, someone who is highly successful, I have found that "stick-to-it-iveness" is one trait common to *all* of them. This quality personifies John R. Johnson.

Born in poverty in Arkansas in 1918, John R. Johnson worked his way through the University of Chicago and Northwestern. Although he was never graduated, he has since been awarded sixteen honorary degrees.

Johnson, who sits on the board of directors of several giant corporations, got his start in the business world as an office boy at Chicago's Black-run Supreme Life Insurance Company of America. Today he is chairman of the board.

In 1942, with a $500 pawnshop loan on his mother's furniture, Johnson singlehandedly launched a publishing enterprise that has become the second largest Black-owned business in the United States. It started with *Negro Digest* (now *Black World)* and includes *Ebony, Jet, Black Stars* and *Ebony Jr.* In 1961, Johnson moved into book publishing. By 1973, he had further extended his operations by purchasing Chicago radio station WGRT and founding Fashion Fair cosmetics.

Johnson speaks with humility and sincerity about his philosophy of hard work and achievement: "My mother was a primary motivator for me. She believed, and preached all the time, that 'Maybe you'll work hard and not make it. But if you don't work hard, you *know* you won't make it. So if you want to succeed, you've got to take that chance! There is always a solution of some kind to problems . . . search for it. You've got to persevere; you've got to keep searching for answers.' "

When he moved to Chicago to go to high school, Johnson got caught up in the struggle to succeed: "I had no friends, no money, and people laughed at me because I had handmade clothes. I had an extreme Southern accent and kids made fun of my bow legs. So I had to show them, and I could only show them one way—by being superior to them in school.

"I studied harder, got good grades and took classes in public speaking; I read Dale Carnegie's *How to Win Friends and Influence People* at least fifty times.

"All of the people in class were afraid to speak up except me. I had been practicing before the mirror, as it was suggested in the public speaking book that I was reading. As a result of my making a few remarks, they elected me president of the class. I also became president of the student body, editor-in-chief of the school paper and editor of the school annual."

A dramatic episode occurred in 1943 when Johnson launched a small publishing business. He wanted to boost the circulation of his magazine *Negro Digest*.

"I decided to run a series of articles called 'If I Were a Negro,' in which a white person would put himself in the position of a Black and seriously look at the issues, to decide what he would really do if he were in that position," Johnson recalls. "I felt that Eleanor Roosevelt would be the best person to write the article. So I sat down and composed a letter to her.

"Mrs. Roosevelt wrote back and said she was too busy to do it. But *she didn't say she wouldn't do it*.

"So I wrote to her again one month later. She said she was still too busy. I sent her one more letter after another month had passed, and she said she just didn't have a free minute."

Since Mrs. Roosevelt continued to indicate that her problem was a lack of time, Johnson was undeterred. "She wasn't saying she wouldn't do it. So my reasoning was that maybe, if I kept trying, one day she *would* have time.

"Finally, I read that she was speaking in Chicago. I decided to try again, and sent her a telegram asking if she would write the article for *Negro Digest* while she was in Chicago.

"It just so happened that when my telegram arrived, she had a spare moment, so she sat down and dictated her thoughts.

"The news releases went out and were picked up all over the country. The net result was that my circulation went from fifty thousand to a hundred and fifty thousand within one month. It was indeed the turning point in my career."

He discounts quick solutions. "Sometimes it takes many failures. *It always takes trying.* When people come here and they see me in these rather palatial surroundings, they say, 'Gee, you're lucky.' I remind them that it took me *thirty long, hard years* to get here. I started in one room at the insurance company. Then I moved to a little building that was literally a coal bin. I just went from one thing to another until I finally got *here* . . . but I didn't *start* here.

I think you have to be a long-distance runner. Keep going, and *don't give up.*"

AN INVINCIBLE SPIRIT

When examining notable historical figures, this characteristic of "stick-to-it-iveness" becomes an underlying theme. This was apparent in the bestselling biography of Harry S Truman, written by his daughter, Margaret. In her story she describes the tenacity her father displayed in his 1948 battle for the presidency.

A mood of defeatism surrounded Truman's candidacy, but he fought against it by announcing, "We *are* going to win. I expect to travel all over the country and talk at every whistle-stop."*

Truman's daughter affectionately portrays his invincible winning spirit. At one point, she records, *Newsweek* polled fifty veteran political writers around the country and announced their results in huge black type: FIFTY POLITICAL EXPERTS UNANIMOUSLY PREDICT A DEWEY VICTORY.

When her father saw the article he grinned and said, "Oh well, those damn fellows—they're always wrong anyway . . . let's get on with the job."

Truman's remarkable election triumph took all the pollsters, and indeed the entire country, by surprise. When he returned to Washington before his inauguration, a huge sign hung outside the *Washington Post* building: "MR. PRESIDENT, WE ARE READY TO EAT CROW WHENEVER YOU ARE READY TO SERVE IT."**

"YOU HAVE TO SET YOUR COURSE AND STICK TO IT"

In another era, this same kind of "stick-to-it-iveness" helped bring *down* the presidency. Persistence, which is part of the special fabric that winners are made of, is certainly a major trait of Bob Woodward, the Pulitzer prize–winning reporter for *The Washington Post* and coauthor of three bestselling books, *All the President's Men, The Final Days* and *The Brethren.*

In the earliest days of investigating what was at first thought to be a simple robbery at the Democratic National Headquarters in

* Margaret Truman, *Harry S Truman* (New York: Pocket Books, 1974), p. 5.
* *Ibid., p. 48.

the Watergate Building, Woodward and his partner, Carl Bernstein, tenaciously refused to give up.

"With the spokesman and leader of the free world calling us . . . a liar . . . our posture was one of being very much down. So our incentive was to get to the bottom of this.

"We had positioned ourselves factually, but by increasing the ante and denying things, the White House was really saying, 'Look, it's either up or *down.*' Our credibility and ultimately our careers were on the line."

Woodward was personally concerned, because he had been rejected for a job at the *Post* a year earlier and had not been there long. But he was particularly driven to keep going because he was sure there were a lot of facts concealed by top government officials.

His single statement—"You have to set your course and *stick to it*"—seems to summarize Woodward's approach to his career. "In my work, nothing beats research. You keep talking and talking to people. If I need to quote thirty people for a story, I'll interview sixty."

When people refused to talk to him, Woodward says, it increased his incentive. "When somebody looks pained and shuts the door in my face, it's pretty obvious that there's something he doesn't want me to see.

"Initially I had no idea that it went to Nixon. Not even an inkling of that. But you keep digging and doing your work. It's continually gratifying. There are lots of important things hidden. It is challenging. The fact that they were all so powerful made the stakes higher.

"This motivated us even more. Our curiosity was aroused, and we wanted to do the job well. It was the little guys versus the big guys. Not the good guys versus the bad guys."

For Woodward, the exhilaration in his work comes when he gets the information he's after and makes a breakthrough. *"No matter how much effort I have to put into it,* the moment of discovery is the high for me."

By *not getting discouraged,* even when faced with name calling and accusations from the nation's highest political sources, Woodward's "stick-to-it-iveness" literally changed the course of American history.

A STEP TOWARD SUCCESS

Few of us are taught as children that failure is a step toward success. There aren't many parents who understand for themselves that mistakes are part of winning . . . that SETBACKS ARE AN INTEGRAL COMPONENT OF SUCCESS.

Teach yourself new lessons, now. Here is one you can read aloud and integrate into your winning philosophy:

> A child must learn very early to realize that failing is a part of living. To lead him to believe otherwise is to deny reality, to bring him up in an atmosphere of false—and destructive—superiority . . .
>
> To love your child for his perfection is nothing. To love him for his failures is to love him well. It is that love which will form the later man —the man whom failure cannot defeat.*

It is impractical for any of us to think that we will never miss the mark when we are learning a new task, settling into a new job or developing a new relationship. Of course we will fail, at least some of the time, because defeat is an important component of the adventure.

Become a survivor when you are learning a new task and memorize this winning formula:

FAILURE . . . TRY SOME MORE.

FAILURE . . . HANG IN AND BE GOOD TO YOURSELF.

FAILURE . . . KEEP GOING UNTIL YOU SUCCEED.

WINNER SCORECARD #2

Falling short of an objective can be very disappointing. It hurts. But it can also make a positive contribution to your learning. What counts is how you deal with unsuccessful efforts, and whether you are kind and understanding to yourself.

Do you *use* the information you learn from your mistakes? Or do you abuse yourself with negatives about your errors and waste precious time scolding yourself?

---

* Louis Binstock, *The Road to Successful Living* (New York: Simon & Schuster, 1958), p. 111.

LOSERS	WINNERS
1. When losers can't master a new skill on the first effort, they blow the whole thing and stop trying. They assume that intelligent people jump from lesson one straight to proficiency.	**1.** Winners know that learning takes time . . . sometimes years of practicing and polishing. They understand that they won't be able to climb to the top of their mountains in a day.
2. When learning something new is slow and laborious, losers soon become bored. They are willing to spend very little time; they want fast action and instant results.	**2.** Winners know that learning isn't easy going; the learning curve represents one struggle after another. There are frustrations and problems along the way, but if one stays with it, learning will occur!
3. When losers hope to stop a well-entrenched habit and fall off the wagon (i.e., bingeing or having that one cigarette), they are convinced that it's all over; they might as well give up. They say to themselves, "I don't have what it takes to keep going. I'd better stop right now, before I make a fool of myself."	**3.** When winners lapse back into an old habit they had hoped to break, they get back on the wagon as soon as they can and keep trying. They focus on what changes they *have* accomplished and work at increasing the successful intervals between slips.
4. When losers make a mistake or misjudge a problem, they label themselves with names like "stupid" or "foolish." They ask self-destructive questions like "Why wasn't I more careful? Why didn't I see the obvious? Why? Why? Why?" Eventually they become immobilized by their fear of failure and stop trying.	**4.** When winners have difficulties or make errors, they try again. They know that making mistakes is part of actively doing and trying. Winners make a friend of failure . . . they use their mistakes as a source of information, so they know what to avoid next time.

5. Losers are so focused on avoiding failure that they often lose sight of their real goals. They spend much of their energy analyzing and reviewing their mistakes. This becomes a major activity and prevents them from finding the payoff they're seeking.

5. A winner keeps his eye on his ultimate objective and concentrates on moving toward it as directly and rapidly as possible. He tries not to waste time and looks for shortcuts and timesavers. When he makes a mistake, he learns what he can from it. He reassures himself, "I did the best I could," and moves himself quickly to the next phase in the pursuit of his goal.

6. Losers are impatient with trying and can be totally discouraged by a single defeat. They want instant gratification. When they are pursuing a goal and meet with problems, they can't bear the thought of further failures, so they quit . . . and never learn the pride involved in overcoming difficult situations.

6. Even when everything looks bleak, winners fuel themselves with continued optimism and determination. They persevere, knowing that it may take years to become successful. Problems and frustrations are an incentive for them to work even harder.

CHAPTER 3

Kick That Block

There are very few human beings who receive the truth, complete and staggering, by instant illumination. Most of us acquire it fragment by fragment, on a small scale, by successive developments, cellularly, like a laborious mosaic.

—ANAÏS NIN

Have you ever had an emotional block . . . a feeling that something inside was holding you back from completing a task? Has it ever seemed that just getting to a job, even though the job itself may have been small, was almost overwhelming? Or perhaps the project was major . . . it meant your livelihood . . . and still you couldn't get started.

Blocking is an unconscious device we use that prevents us from being effective, because without being aware of it, most people are afraid to experience success. Blocking is a subliminal order sent from the brain that tells us, "Watch out! Keep looking busy. But don't be too effective, because no matter what, you don't want to be too capable or powerful."

When such unconscious orders are ruling your behavior, instead of activating the winning process of going for it . . . problem solving and achieving . . . you block. Your mind seems to go blank. You tend to forget whatever you were about to do or say. Instead of getting to your task, you find yourself avoiding your job and wasting time. This can happen to you in any work situation or area when you are attempting something new or difficult.

You may encounter many tough tasks in your quest to become a winner. But no matter how strenuous they may appear to be, I want to help you understand how to *get to them* and how to *finish* them.

WAITING FOR THE RIGHT MOOD

Writers often talk about being blocked . . . unable to write a word. They complain about "hating the typewriter" or "dreading to face that empty sheet of paper." Indeed, they call this condition "writer's block." One of my patients is a writer named David, whose struggle with blocking clearly illustrates how difficult completing a task can be. By reading about David's experience, you can begin to absorb some of the techniques he learned in therapy. These skills will enable you to get on with your work.

When David came to see me, he said he was talented and didn't understand why he couldn't make a living at writing. Together we began to explore the problems he was encountering in his career.

David wanted to be inspired before he could work. He believed that good writing always began with the author experiencing high energy and creativity. In order to write well, he felt he had to "wait until the mood hit" before getting to the typewriter. Feeling depressed on a given day meant he wouldn't be able to work.

Needless to say, with these ideal standards to meet, David seldom felt good enough to accomplish anything. He was rarely productive . . . which made him depressed . . . and pushed him even farther from being "in the mood." So he wrote even less!

David's method for getting himself started contrasted sharply with that of National Book Award–winner Joyce Carol Oates, who *does* earn a living as a writer:

> One must be pitiless about this matter of "mood." In a sense, the writing will *create* the mood. . . . I have forced myself to begin writing when I've been utterly exhausted, when I've felt my soul as thin as a playing card, when nothing has seemed worth enduring for another five minutes . . . and somehow the activity of writing changes everything.*

SITTING DOWN POWER

I explained to David that the first step he needed to take was to develop "sitting down power." In order to do the job, he had to *sit*

---

* George Plimpton, (editor), *Writers at Work: The Paris Review Interviews* (New York: Penguin Books, 1981), pp. 364–65.

down at the place where something *was likely to happen* . . . the typewriter. Sounds simple enough, but often it's very difficult to do.

Normally, when David tried to write, his mind would go blank. This frightened him, so to avoid staring at that empty white sheet of paper, he would run from the typewriter. He felt better when he just forgot about writing and did a little gardening. Other escape routes for him included cleaning out his closets or trimming his beard.

The prolific writer Tom Wolfe has poked fun at this same inclination in himself:

> As I look back on it, I can see that my usual strategy has been to go over to the tailor's and have a suit made. The amount of time you can eat up simply by going through swatch booklets to choose a fabric . . . really gets the job [of avoiding work] done. After that you have at least three long fitting sessions to look forward to, plus intermediary trips to talk about darts, buttons, stepcollars, and American Bemberg linings.*

Being in the bathroom fiddling around with his beard or in the garden planting roses would not put any words on paper for David. To complete a project, you need to be in the area where it is possible to achieve your goal. In David's case, it was essential for him to *sit down* at the typewriter.

I remember once sharing a lecture podium with Neil Simon, the famous writer who has scores of successful plays and films to his credit. He described how *he* fights writer's block. He said that he makes himself "sit there." He admitted that there were days when writing didn't come easily to him. But every single day, he sat down at the typewriter and started typing. Simon explained that once he gets something down on paper, he has a chance to see how bad or good it looks and can then start editing and revising. It is the rewriting process that moves him toward his goal:

> Rewriting is when playwriting really gets to be fun. . . . In baseball, you only get three swings and you're out. In rewriting, you get almost as many swings as you want and you know, sooner or later, you'll hit the ball.**

That phrase . . . "sooner or later you'll hit the ball" . . . has stuck in my mind ever since.

* Karin Mack, Ph.D., and Eric Skjei, Ph.D., *Overcoming Writing Blocks* (Los Angeles: J. P. Tarcher, 1979), p. 18.
** Ibid., p. 148.

Actually, I first learned this technique myself when I was writing my doctoral thesis at the University of London in 1968. It was difficult for me to begin organizing the reams of my research data into a comprehensive thesis.

Treating patients was easy for me . . . it was the part of my work that I loved. But writing up every single detail of my experiments was laborious and I dreaded the tedium.

I knew there was no alternative . . . I had to get the statistical information, as well as my philosophy and methodology, down on paper. Otherwise, I would not receive my doctorate. I had spent my whole life studying, and I knew I couldn't quit.

I was afraid to start writing because I was doing something that was pioneering in therapeutic practice. I felt anxious about whether traditional British psychology would bend and accept my innovative techniques. I worried that my work would not be sufficiently scholarly to withstand my supervisor's scrutiny. I was already criticizing the words that I hadn't yet committed to paper.

Each day, when my alarm clock went off, I quickly dressed and sat down at my desk. At first, that was all that happened . . . I just sat there.

I knew I couldn't leave my desk, because the only chance I had of putting something down on paper depended on my staying there. The first day I did just that: I sat there for hours with that bloody white page staring at me. Eventually, I started typing. I can remember reading the first two pages and thinking they were awful. I felt as though my fingers (and my ideas) were anchored in cement . . . but I kept typing.

By the fourth day, I began to feel more relaxed and the words seemed to flow more easily into logical sequence.

It was five months later when my "sitting down power" paid off and I had a completed doctoral thesis in my hand. After two rewrites, which took another three months, they called me "Doctor." The comment that I valued the most came from my supervisor, Gwynne Jones. He said, "I'm most impressed with your *scholarly* approach."

GET SOMETHING DOWN

Recently, I read some advice from the noted science fiction author Frederick Pohl. His words might have helped me when fears were blocking me from getting started on my thesis:

When I find I'm having trouble now I . . . just do rough drafts for a
while . . . as roughly and crudely as necessary. Then I go back and
rewrite that part. That seems to have kept me from any prolonged
blocks in the last few years. Nobody's going to see it but me, and I
suspend criticism. I just plunge ahead . . . whatever possible avenue
occurs to me I put down on paper. If that looks bad later on, I can
always change it, but meanwhile I've managed to get a little further
along.*

This was another of the lessons that David had to learn. He
complained to me that he hated to type "just anything." He
wanted his writing to be really "fine," at least in his head, before
he put it down on paper.

"Nonsense!" I said. "Just put it down! Then you will have something tangible to work on . . . to rewrite and correct . . . to improve. Get started!"

DAVID'S WINNING SCHEDULE

Together David and I worked out a schedule for him. His alarm
clock would ring every morning at 7:30 A.M. and by 8:00 A.M. he
was to be at the typewriter. His homework was to sit there, all day
if necessary, until he got *something down on paper*.

We also established a system of rewards: David couldn't eat his
breakfast until he had completed at least one typewritten page.

On the first day, David was so anxious that he didn't finish a page
until 2:00 P.M.

On the second day, David had improved so much that only two
hours after he sat down, he had finished one page and was able to
have his breakfast earlier. On the third day, he typed his first page
almost immediately and kept going for five more pages before he
even thought about breakfast. His writing was finally taking shape.
David was learning to face his tough task by sitting down and
DOING IT.

> Knowing is not enough, we must apply.
> Willing is not enough, we must do.
> —GOETHE

Let this happen to you. You can help yourself take that first plunge in
the smallest possible way, so it won't be too frightening or anxiety provok-
ing. On your first day, you may even experience physical symptoms . . .
you may have stomach problems, headaches, nausea, a cold . . . or any of

* Ibid., p. 147.

an endless array of other minor discomforts. But don't be discouraged. The second day will be easier and a little more fun. And by the third try, you will probably be far more relaxed and even comfortable . . . using "sitting down power" with your difficult task.

It is crucial to winning to *get started* in the area in which you want to change or accomplish something new. David did just that and you can do the same . . . *you can get started.*

THE DIALS, THE SWITCHES AND THE CLOCKS

I had a problem getting started when I was asked to host *my own* talk radio program in 1982. I have been actively involved in radio starting in 1967 with the BBC in London. Since then I've often guested on someone else's program. But it was always *their* responsibility to deal with the mechanics of planning and engineering the interview. Hosting my own program, I found myself sitting in front of a complex technological maze of switches, dials, buttons, lights, clocks, phones and computers . . . with no background in how to operate them . . . and a well-established aversion to everything mechanical or electrical.

I was elated and happy to be asked to do my own program, but this emotion changed as soon as I discovered that after a brief training period, I would be expected to sit there all alone . . . facing the electronic dilemma.

I was ready to run!

I'm the kind of person who has an anxiety attack when I try to switch on my stereo. Still, my excitement about reaching countless people all over the country temporarily overshadowed my fears.

With much confusion, wet with perspiration and having stomach cramps, I took my first call on that pioneering Monday. Hearing the voices of the listeners and working with them was pure heaven for me. But facing those dials and switches was torture. I was concerned that I needed to be ready to go to commercials at 9:12:56 and anxious that I had to be finished with the caller at exactly 9:20:48. No matter what was happening I had to close at 9:56:33. By the time the program ended I had a severe headache.

The second day, I was surprised to realize how much I had learned. I had made fewer mistakes, and my headache and cramps were almost gone. Wednesday I was a bit more confident, Thursday I felt still more assured, and by Friday I was like Professor Higgins in *My Fair Lady* shouting, "I did it, I did it!" Although I

had always believed I was an electronic retardate, I had finally
mastered the tough task before me.

The program director, the engineers, the staff . . . everyone
generously helped me. And accepting help is a winning behavior
. . . so is asking questions. Losers worry they will appear to sound
stupid if they ask questions. They try to "bluff" their way through,
pretending they "know" . . . and hoping no one will discover
their ignorance.

Nonsense! I never feel inadequate when I ask questions. I know
I'm bright, and I realize that I don't always have enough expertise
in some areas. When I took the radio assignment, I certainly didn't
know about satellite equipment. But it wasn't a problem, because
I'm perfectly comfortable asking questions and gathering as much
information as I can.

This philosophy can work for you, too. Remember this formula
. . . and practice saying these words:

WINNERS ASK QUESTIONS.

WINNERS GET HELP.

WINNERS MASTER THE TASK.

EXERCISE 3: DEVELOPING NEW SKILLS

The exercise that follows offers guidelines and techniques to
help you master new behaviors and expand existing repertoires.
These steps will enable you to develop skills that can improve your
chances for success. Learn them.

Step One: Learn How to Zero In

Block out distractions . . . sounds, music or anything that will
interfere with your ability to think. Concentrate on your work. *Focus
all your attention on what you are doing.*

Turn off your radio or television set and take the phone off the
hook. Tell your friends and family the hours you will be working so
they won't interrupt you. Let them know when you *are* available to
talk to them, so they'll have something to look forward to.

Competing thoughts may pop into your head and try to divert you
from your purpose. When this happens, instruct yourself to redirect
your thinking back to the job you are doing. *Get control of your
thinking.*

Step Two: Learn to Talk to Yourself a New Way

Whenever you are tempted to forget your "sitting power" technique and escape, repeat this chant out loud several times. Do this in front of a mirror. Make certain that your voice is strong, accepting and friendly:

—"I want to *concentrate* on what I'm doing now.

—"I'm going to give this my *full attention.*

—"I *deserve* to succeed at this task.

—"I'm going to see to it that *nothing stops me from winning.*"

Step Three: Learn from Criticism

Discuss your work with knowledgeable people who have the background to comment about your abilities. Ask them to give you critical feedback about your methods and practice. Listen and learn.

Don't give these people excuses or rationalizations about why you haven't been working more. That will only slow up the interaction and keep you from absorbing important data from them. Their suggestions will offer you new insights about how to do a better job and improve your skills.

Step Four: Learn from Models

Carefully analyze the behavior and thinking of others who are *already* more experienced and successful than you. You can find books and magazine articles about them in your local library. These people can serve as good role models. By learning about them, you will pick up new tips and techniques that you can incorporate into your own behavior patterns.

It will not be enough for you to read about them or see their methods in person only once. Get more exposure. Each additional time you read about them or view them in action, you will be gathering important modeling material for you to emulate. It will take repeated observations and exposure for you to finally absorb enough of their style to be able to reshape your own practices.

Step Five: Learn to Accept New Ideas

Your career and lifestyle patterns are *not* fixed in granite. Be open to changes: Thoughtfully consider new horizons and other ways of living.

The human organism is capable of absorbing far more insights, developmental changes and intellectual maturation than most people allow themselves to experience. The amount of information that you can absorb in a lifetime is almost limitless.

Seek out new situations, human potential workshops, psychotherapeutic professionals and self-actualization groups. Extend your thinking into new areas. Expose yourself to mind-expanding and motivational seminars. Find opportunities to learn new subjects at personal-growth or night school classes.

Step Six: Learn How to Get Unstuck

As you're working, there may be moments when you'll suddenly become sleepy. You may even find yourself nodding off. This is usually anxiety . . . not fatigue. At these junctures, realize that you are *unconsciously* trying to sabotage yourself and stay a loser. Instead, take a brief time-out. Do something else for a *short* time, or you may go on to another phase of your task and work at that for a while. After this quick relief, you will return to your work with renewed vigor. When the sleepy feelings come back again, just repeat this cycle: brief time out . . . then right back to work.

Don't let your anxiety about success *control you* . . . instead, *you control your anxiety!*

Step Seven: Learn How to Follow Instructions

If you are lucky enough to have a teacher when learning a new task, listen to him. In the initial phases, don't challenge his methods or try to improve on what he is telling you. First, be a student and absorb the material he has to offer. Then when you have mastered the task, you can experiment with breaking rules and becoming an iconoclast.

The great painters at the turn of the century, who were part of the Fauvist movement that included Matisse, Derain, Dufy and Rouault, broke away from the art forms that were acceptable at that time. But first they were serious students who mastered what they were taught . . . the traditional modes of painting. *Then* they became the innovators who broke with accepted practice and experimented with ideas and started new schools of thought.

First, you will need to know how to follow instructions and learn the established ways of doing things. Then you will have the knowledge . . . a stable foundation on which to make better judgments about the "pros and cons" of breaking rules. A real winner will use the establishment, rather than fight it. He will learn how to break rules with the acceptance and approval of both his peers and society.

Step Eight: Learn How to Make It Inviting

By making your environment more comfortable and inviting, you will be adding still another way to improve your probability of success in learning new skills. Because a beautiful environment filled with flowers has a relaxing effect on me . . . I see to it that there are several arrangements where I work.

Being comfortable for me also means wearing clothes that are loose fitting and made with soft fabrics that don't wrinkle . . . and tennis socks without shoes. Feeling warm and cozy and having plenty of fruit on my desk is also essential for me, because I don't want to be distracted thinking about my physical needs or my body.

HELP YOURSELF

Whatever task you are trying to master, it is important to *help yourself* as much as possible. How to do this will be different for each individual's tastes and needs. For David, the writer, helping himself meant putting his body in front of a typewriter in a room where there were no noises or interruptions.

At the radio station I "helped" myself by asking others to help me until I mastered the dials and the intricate timing schedules. YOU WILL NEED TO GET HELP, TOO.

Even gigantic ocean liners require the assistance of small tugboats to help guide them to safe, deep waters. Find *your* best way to get guidance and help. And adjust your environment so that you will feel at ease and be more comfortable. You will learn as you work, for every hour that you are encouraged to sit there, you will be rewarded with feelings of pride and self-respect. By just being in the place where you have the highest probability of getting the job done, you will learn to become disciplined and more determined to finish *your* tough task. This is certainly not a new idea. As far back as the fourth century B.C., Aristotle counseled:

> For the things we have to learn, before we can do them, we learn by doing them.

YOU CAN BE A WINNER, TOO . . . YOU CAN KICK
YOUR BLOCKS . . .
AND DO THE TOUGH TASKS AHEAD.

WINNER SCORECARD #3

When faced with a difficult new task, winners do everything they can
to help themselves get the job done. Losers get in their own way and
"block" their own success.

LOSERS	WINNERS
1. Losers complain about how hard it is to get going and avoid starting a task until they are "in the mood." They let their emotional climate govern their level of productivity.	**1.** Winners know they can't always wait until the "mood hits" to get started. They get right to work regardless of their frame of mind or their emotional status at the moment.
2. When losers try to work and their minds go blank, they tend to leave the job and escape to unrelated distractions.	**2.** Winners develop "sitting down power" . . . they put themselves in the precise environment where winning is most likely to occur.
3. Losers hesitate to get started by producing something that is less than perfect. They expect their efforts to yield polished results instantly. They seek immediate perfection.	**3.** Winners get going with an undeveloped plan . . . a rough idea, a concept, a draft. This gives them a foundation from which to work. Once they have something in hand, they can make changes and add new material.
4. Losers are so afraid that something will go wrong or that they will look foolish that they don't even *begin* to tackle a difficult task.	**4.**Winners realize that if they *don't try,* they'll *never accomplish* their goals. When they face a tough task, they take their first plunge in a small way, so it won't be too anxiety provoking.

5. Losers think asking questions or accepting help will make them look foolish or inadequate. They insist on being do-it-yourselfers and resist getting help. In the end, they can't finish, because they become so discouraged and disillusioned.

6. Losers provide a work setting for themselves that encourages distractions and interruptions. They have difficulty concentrating because of their self-imposed interference.

7. Losers attempt to work under difficult circumstances, suffering with improper or inadequate heating, clothing, equipment or help. They divert their attention from their task by forcing themselves to struggle with problems they set up through inefficiency and lack of planning.

8. Over time, losers fail to achieve their objectives so often that negative syndromes develop. They begin to link trying with failure. Whenever new projects are presented, they predict negative outcomes, and they are forever afraid to try something new.

5. Winners ask questions and accept help in order to increase the probability that they will be successful. They know that even an ocean liner needs the help of a tugboat to guide it out into the deep waters where it can finally sail alone.

6. Winners make their working conditions as quiet and free from stress as possible. They create an atmosphere in which they can focus on their task without being disturbed.

7. Winners equip their work environments with the tools and body comforts necessary to improve the probability of their success. They want to focus on their work, not their physical needs.

8. Winners develop a history of success . . . they remember receiving rewards for trying and still more praise for finishing. They gain pride and self-respect each time they carry a tough task through to completion.

CHAPTER 4

You Can Make Your Own Luck

People are always blaming their circumstances for what they are. I don't believe in circumstances. The people who get on in this world are the people who get up and look for the circumstances they want, and, if they can't find them, make them.

—GEORGE BERNARD SHAW

"JUST GIVE ME A BREAK"

Recently, I was visited by a new patient, Sylvia. She was a member of a very distinguished family; her father was a well known orthopedic surgeon in Boston and her mother was an associate professor of English literature at a prestigious university. Sylvia had been raised with the advantages of upper-middle-class social connections and parents who were successful in their professions. With all the help and support she received from her family, she had every opportunity to make her dreams come true.

Since college, her biggest dream had been to become a television interviewer. She felt she had the talent because whenever she was with people . . . even strangers . . . they would get into long conversations with her. People seemed to trust her, and would confide secrets or reveal personal intimacies. Sylvia knew how to "get things out of" people. Her friends called her their

"friendly neighborhood shrink." Sylvia often said, "If only someone would give me a break on television, I know I could make it."

Based on our early sessions together, I, too, tended to believe
that Sylvia might have ability in this area. But what was she *doing*
about it? Nothing! She was *waiting* for someone to appear like a
genie and grant her wish: She wanted to be an immediate success
as an interviewer on a network program.

When Sylvia first described her unrealistic expectations, I was so
disturbed by her attitude I almost jumped out of my chair. "That
just isn't the way it happens!" I exclaimed. "*You* have to do something if you want a job . . . *you* have to put yourself out there
. . . *you* have to get the training and background that is necessary.

"No one is going to ask an inexperienced person to assume a
starring role as a television interviewer! And network executives
aren't interested in going out and searching for talent. People
approach them. I have patients who work on television, and they
have had years of schooling and on-the-job training, and they are
still learning. It takes time to polish and perfect those techniques."

Then I told Sylvia about another patient, Cindy, who had already realized Sylvia's dream and become a popular TV interviewer. Cindy hadn't waited around for someone to give her a
break. Because she didn't have the kind of financial security that
Sylvia had, she worked days and attended extension classes in the
evenings at UCLA in the Theater Arts Department. After graduation, she began looking for a job, visiting every radio and television
station in Los Angeles. But every station manager had told her
essentially the same thing: "We can't hire anyone unless they have
years of experience in front of the camera."

Cindy had argued with each of them: "How can I *get* any experience when everyone is telling me they can't hire me unless I
already *have* experience? It seems impossible to get going!"

But she wouldn't give up. She didn't *wait* for her break; she
went out and *found* it. After scanning all the trade journals for
months, she saw an ad for a weather girl in a very small station in
North Dakota.

Cindy was a Californian who hated snow. "I'll *die* in North
Dakota," she said to herself. But that didn't matter: sun, snow,
sleet or hurricanes . . . she wanted a job on television . . . any
job! She grabbed the opportunity to work and left for North Dakota.

After spending two years there, Cindy finally found a position back in Los Angeles at a local station. She was thrilled to return. After another five years, she finally moved up. At last she landed the network job she had dreamed of for so long.

The contrast between Sylvia's loser thinking and Cindy's winner's point of view is this: For ten years Sylvia had kept dreaming, waiting for her chance and expecting it to just *happen* . . . somehow . . . while time slipped by. Cindy took action. First, she had gotten her education, then training in North Dakota, followed by more experience in Los Angeles . . . and then that important network job.

When losers talk about the success of others, they are resentful discussing how the "next guy had pure luck" and happened to have been "in the right place at the right time." They don't act, they wait for their "someday" to happen. They see winning as a fortuitous accident that befalls the "lucky ones." Losers believe that the winner's luck is all good and that theirs is all bad . . . so there's nothing left for them to do when Lady Luck doesn't smile on them . . . except complain and be bitter.

Year after year, people play out their loser lifestyles, rarely understanding that they are active participants in setting up their self-destructive scenarios. Not seeing their hand in their own failures, they blame spouses, business partners, bad luck, the president, the economy, "the system." They spend hours discussing how the world has "done them wrong."

Winners can't afford to waste the time. They are too busy solving problems, working hard, getting the job done and developing an energetic and optimistic attitude.

SUCCESS DOESN'T HAPPEN BY CHANCE.
YOU HAVE TO GO FOR IT!

Becoming a winner takes conscious effort and work. Winners don't postpone action until "someday"; they do it today. Yesterday they were busy doing the best they knew how. And tomorrow they will be where the action is . . . trying and failing and succeeding.

Remember the old saying, "Don't put off until tomorrow what you can do today"? Winners deal with problems *as soon as they come up*. They don't spend time worrying, because worrying doesn't help lessen the problem, it just repeats and magnifies the pain. Instead, they focus on finding solutions . . . *right now* . . . with zest and drive.

I COULD HAVE BEEN . . . IF ONLY

Have you ever been trapped at a dinner party with a boring "I-could-have-been-er"? You know, someone who goes on and on, talking about vague accomplishments he just missed in his past, or equally obscure projects he is "planning" for the future?

Jill was like that. When she joined my Monday night therapy group, she began reciting a variety of tearful "I could have beens" and "If onlys": "I could have become a great opera singer *if only I hadn't* married; I could have become famous *if only I hadn't* raised so many children."

After a few minutes, the group came up with a unanimous "Nonsense!" Trying to help Jill stop the grumbling and do something about her life *right now*, one of them said: "You've heard of the famous opera star Beverly Sills? Well, she's married and has a family and has worked hard for years to build her reputation. *Work at it*, and you'll become successful, too!"

Losers can't stop procrastinating and start prospering, because they are busy with their "If onlys."

Those who *talk* about what they *could have* done are not achievers or winners, they are just talkers. This is how a "do-er" sounds:

> Some singers make it with ten roles. I learned a hundred! If mine was an overnight success, it was the longest day's journey you ever saw!
>
> —BEVERLY SILLS

Don't wait for your "ship to come in," and feel angry and cheated when it doesn't. Get going with something small.

GET MOVING . . . GET STARTED ON YOUR WIN.

GENERATE YOUR OWN LUCK

Stop your "bad luck" talk right now. To a winner, the synonym for luck is hard work. "Breaks" come through perseverance, focusing on the project at hand and staying with it until the job is done.

Complaining won't change your luck, it will just keep you too preoccupied to find the time to succeed. If you want to be in "the right place at the right time," look for an arena in which you can strive and devote great effort. Luck isn't an accident. Put in more hours a week at your job . . . and discover the invitation that summons Lady Luck.

LIVING HER FANTASY

Diane Von Furstenberg is an exciting winner whose around-the-clock energy blends dynamically with her business acumen and exotic good looks. She has created a remarkably successful career. She is competitive, aggressive and decisive . . . as well as extremely feminine, caring and sensitive.

Born in Brussels and educated in Spain, England and Switzerland, Von Furstenberg came to the United States in the 1960s after her marriage to Fiat heir Prince Egon Von Furstenberg. In 1969, they were the darlings of the New York jet set, the city's new "fun couple." Then the marriage floundered.

Von Furstenberg was only twenty-three when, with a $30,000 loan from her father, she set up her own dress designing business. After separating from the prince, she built her organization into a fashion empire that today does $200 million in annual sales.

She went on to found her own cosmetics firm and has licensing arrangements with other companies to produce shoes, handbags, scarves and other products under her name. She accomplished all of this within five years.

Now divorced, Von Furstenberg owns a luxurious sixteen-room Park Avenue apartment and a fifty-three-acre farm in Connecticut, a gift she bought herself for her twenty-seventh birthday.

She is a mother as well as a businessperson, fulfilling the dream of many contemporary women to *have it all.* "When you want to, you can," she says. "I have found you really don't have to give up other things."

At twenty-nine, Von Furstenberg was on the cover of *Newsweek.* The story inside described her 8 A.M.-to-midnight work schedule. About her long hours, she says, "Sometimes I think, my God, I'm so exhausted! Why do I keep doing all this? But it's very exciting and I am in control of my life. I envy no one."

How does this great business and fashion force define winning? "When you think of life as a journey, winning is arriving at an oasis —taking a break, looking around, enjoying and breathing, sleeping and then going on again. I think *winning is living*—to be able to enjoy all of it—the good and the bad events."

Von Furstenberg says she is propelled by a desire to keep growing. "When I make an effort in a direction, it brings me to the next level of something. It's a road that opens up and starts a new life. *I don't always know where I'm going.* Things, circumstances and disasters happen. And the road opens even more. I always believe in keeping flexible, letting the opportunity for other things and other people merge into my road."

Hard work remains the bottom line. "There are some people who don't even try. They feel they cannot become successful. They are the ones who will never make it. You can only be what your fantasy wants you to be."

"I don't think things happen to you in spite of you. I think you have to *help* yourself—at least visualize what you want, project it —and dream. Otherwise it won't happen."

The payoff? "I always wanted to be this woman in her thirties, zipping in and out of cars, zipping around and being very independent. Well, I *am.*

"One thing about me I will tell you for sure is that I *do live my fantasy.* I do."

MAKING YOUR DREAMS COME TRUE

I am in the business of helping people make their dreams come true. I live this way, I believe in it and I teach it. My patients become highly successful at work and in their relationships with family and friends. In the process they have so much more FUN that they find work actually becomes easy. They have markedly increased energy and can do much more!

You can make winning part of *your* life. You can turn the fantasies you had yesterday into realities today. But you can't do it by hoping or wishing. Rather, you need to get to work in order to make your dreams come true. Remember Thomas Edison's words:

Genius is one percent inspiration and ninety-nine percent perspiration.

Successful people know how to put in overtime when it is necessary. They even work on weekends if the pressure is on to meet a deadline. They don't look at the clock. Rather, they just keep at it until the job is done . . . and done well. Winners take pride in all they can accomplish during their action-packed days.

British prime minister Margaret Thatcher has this kind of energy.* A "self-made woman," she rarely takes a vacation and sel-

---

* Both Margaret Thatcher and Dr. Kassorla were chosen by the University of Southern California's Pan Hellenic Council as being among "the ten most influential women of 1980 who share one thing in common: All are trend-setters whose activities present women with new options."

dom needs more than five hours of sleep a night. The long march
from her humble beginnings to becoming the first woman prime
minister in European history is a triumph of her fierce determination and pride. Says author Paul Johnson, a left-wing convert to the
Thatcher faith, "She's got the qualities Britain needs as a nation:
old-fashioned Christian morality, hard work and guts. She's got a
bit of the bulldog breed in her."*

MULTI-MILLION-DOLLAR CLOUT

A hard-working and successful American businessperson who
knows how to pack her days with productive effort is Mary Wells
Lawrence, chairman of the board of Wells, Rich, Greene Advertising Agency. By virtue of the impact her marketing strategies have
had on consumer purchasing, Lawrence wields enormous influence.

She started Wells, Rich, Greene, which now bills $250 million
annually, in a New York hotel room, with her mother answering
phones and no one taking a lunch break. Sixteen years later, she
still doesn't go out for lunch.

"I run my life the way a lot of people run their businesses; I have
to," Lawrence once told a *Vogue* reporter. "I don't literally draw
charts and graphs, but it's how I think. Everything is written
down, planned in advance. I plan the year, I plan the month, I plan
the week, I plan the day—I plan for the emergencies that are
always lying in wait for me. There are too many requests for my
time to leave anything to chance—client requests, potential-client
requests, employee requests, requests for me to speak, requests for
me to participate in some project, or a request from my family."

Lawrence has successfully combined the responsibility of heading her thriving advertising agency with those of being a homemaker. "When I'm home, with my family, I'm not wishing I were
somewhere else or doing something else or having something else.
When I'm with them, I am really with them. And since I have
never been able to be with them all of the time, it's the biggest
treat when I am."**

Like most winners, Lawrence has an appointment book
crammed with commitments. Up at 6:30 . . . and going until

* Angus Deming, Anthony Collings, Tony Clifton and Allan J. Mayer, "Britain's
'Iron Lady,'" *Newsweek* (May 14, 1979), p. 51.
** Edith Loew Gross, "The All-Out, Attractive Style of Mary Wells Lawrence,"
Vogue (February 1978), pp. 200, 206, 243.

8:00 P.M. . . . she has dressed, read the papers and prepared notes for the first meeting of her day by 7:30. Then one of her key assistants arrives. After their conference, Lawrence heads either to her office or to the airport for one of her frequent trips to visit clients, who are located all over the country. When traveling by plane, Lawrence either studies business materials or works on solutions to clients' problems. By her own account, she is "incredibly organized" and incredibly happy.

ARE YOU A NINE-TO-FIVER?

If you are interested in working only a nine-to-five day, you will probably remain "average" in your job, because *smaller* labors yield *smaller* results. If you want to explore changing, at the beginning you can think about doing a bit "more." You don't need to be concerned about putting forth the maximum effort of fully packed days of work and excitement that stars like Mary Lawrence do. But for a start, you could consider increasing your work time 10 or 15 percent. This could noticeably improve your effectiveness and productivity. The favorable by-product of working harder is that your pride, pleasure and self-esteem will be enhanced . . . which is a step in the direction of turning work into FUN.

EXERCISE 4: MAKE THE MOST OF YOUR TIME

You can learn to be a winner by observing how successful people do it. Their behaviors can become your guidelines as you begin to make more productive use of your time. In the days ahead, start putting these key principles to work in your own life:

Step One: Manage Your Time Better

If you don't have one, buy an appointment book, and start planning your schedule more carefully. Become a note taker. Write down the things you plan to do later; don't try to rely on your memory. Keep a pad and pencil in your pocket and your car so you can jot down ideas and errands to remember when you are out. At home, keep a pad and pencil accessible in every room and another at your bedside.

Step Two: Use Every Minute Efficiently

Pack your day with productive tasks, phone calls and interactions with others that will have rewarding results for you. Be more cautious with how you spend your time. Consult that appointment book, and fit in every activity you can that might *pay off*. Fill each open slot, as you use each minute of your day, *helping you*.

Step Three: Don't Be Afraid to Do More Than One Thing at a Time

Arrange for business meetings at mealtimes, for example. Make phone calls when you're having your hair cut or nails done; listen to cassettes that will teach you new skills or offer inspiration while you are driving; use radio earphones to catch up on the news while you are jogging; watch documentaries and special events you can tape in advance on TV to become better informed as you do your aerobic exercises.

Step Four: Plan Ahead

Don't leave things to "just happen" at the last minute . . . or they *will* "just happen" . . . and badly. Prepare in advance for that sales presentation, exam, speech or whatever important events are coming up. You need to fit in time to plan for tomorrow, even though an important thrust of your work effort will be focused on accomplishing today's tasks.

Being a loser in life is NO FUN! You deserve to be happier, have a more exciting life . . . and be more successful.

START CREATING YOUR OWN LUCK
. . . YOU CAN DO IT NOW!

WINNER SCORECARD #4

Do you know how to overcome obstacles and create your own breaks? It will help you to compare your approach to life with the standards below.

LOSERS	WINNERS
1. Losers expend minimal effort, marking time as they grow older, waiting for their big break to "just happen."	**1.** Winners move forward in any way they can. They find the arena that interests them and via hard work they create their own breaks and opportunities.

2. Losers think they can start out with a top position because they have some talent. They are unwilling to get the training and experience needed to prepare them for the positions they long for. They are terrified to take the first small steps that eventually lead to success.

2. Winners get going. They start in the smallest way by becoming educated or trained. Then they will take any job that will eventually give them the experience they need. Because they work more and procrastinate less, they prosper. They know that talent is 99 percent perspiration.

3. Losers talk too much about the past and future. They use rationalizations to postpone productive action. "If only," "I used to be," "I could have been" are their insteads for *not* going for it today.

3. Winners get to work *right now*. They have little time for agonizing about yesterday or speculating about tomorrow. They're too busy living their exciting, "packed" schedules today.

4. Losers are interested in working only a nine-to-five day. They feel their employers are taking advantage of them if they are asked to stay late or do extra tasks occasionally.

4. Winners regularly put in overtime. An average day might be ten or more hours. When there is pressure to meet a deadline, they could be busy seven days that week. Even during normal workdays, they don't look at the clock until the job is done.

5. Losers fail to plan adequately. They waste precious time waiting for "Lady Luck" to smile down upon them. They believe that success results from a series of fortuitous accidents.

5. Winners organize their time and pack every available minute with activities. They don't believe that luck is responsible for success. They know that trying, training and experience will lead them to winning.

CHAPTER 5

Give It Everything You Have

If one advances confidently in the direction of his dreams,
and endeavors to live the life which he has imagined, he will
meet with a success unexpected in common hours.
— HENRY DAVID THOREAU

When I was in high school, I read fascinating biographies of history's great winners. These stories were supposed to inspire me, but the achievements of the giants of the past seemed so unattainable that I became discouraged. *I* could never lead legions across the desert or rule vast empires or discover new worlds. Instead of being inspired, I felt small and insignificant.

Would I need to match a Madame Curie, Joan of Arc or Florence Nightingale to become a winner? Was unusual physical stamina, or special emotional and intellectual capacities, required to be an outstanding achiever? Because I was so afraid to hear the answers, I stopped asking the questions and focused on what it was that I *might be able to accomplish.* I decided I would give every challenge that confronted me everything I had. All that I had to offer was my best.

And this is the bottom line in winning: Don't compare yourself negatively with the giants or anyone else . . . rather, use them as models. Then get on with whatever it is that *you can* accomplish with your life . . . and *give it everything you have.*

WINNING AGAINST THE ODDS

Many of us have been misled by myths that suggest only the rich can win, only the athletic can become superstars or only the beautiful can get what they want. This is simply not true.

Both history books and contemporary media tell of people who became winners despite tremendous physical handicaps. In spite of:

- a nervous system disorder that severely limits his speech and confines him to a wheelchair, Stephen Hawking has done work in theoretical physics that stands as one of the most important contributions to understanding the universe in our time. According to his colleagues, "he is to Einstein what Einstein was to Newton."
- blindness and deafness, Helen Keller learned to read and write and became a brilliant author. She attended Radcliffe, where she was graduated *cum laude* in 1904. She traveled, wrote and lectured, spreading the message that every blind child should have the opportunity for education and every blind grownup the chance for training and employment.
- deformities and dwarfism, Toulouse-Lautrec created exceptional paintings that made him one of the great talents of the Impressionist Era. Despite his small physical size, he is regarded as a giant today; his works are still as vital as they were in the Montmartre of the 1890s.

These people had formidable obstacles to overcome, and yet they made it. One could argue that, justifiably, they could have spent their precious creative time complaining about their unfortunate handicaps. Then they would have accomplished nothing, except getting older . . . and duller.

A SPECIAL BREED

Are winners a special breed? You bet! But their breed is distinguished by action, not by birthright. They are the producers, the forward movers of society who know that it is work that turns the key to success.

THEY *WANT* TO MAKE IT HAPPEN
AND THEY KEEP TRYING.

Winners may not be the brightest people in the crowd, but they are eager and tenacious. To win, it is *not* necessary to have a high

I.Q.; natural endowment is *not what counts*. Nor is it true that a person who has great talent will become a winner, because inherent ability *doesn't guarantee success*. We have all heard about the genius "whiz kids" who never lived up to their potential, the brilliant college graduates who have gotten buried in the corporate political system and never advanced and the high school valedictorian who was voted "Most Likely to Succeed" and was never heard of again.

But you can't help but hear about winners, because they make certain that you do! They take advantage of every opportunity that they can, rise above the crowd and manage to be seen, heard and known.

Did you ever see a twig growing up in the middle of an asphalt driveway and think, "How could that little thing push its way up through this tough surface and survive against these odds?" Winners are like this. They learn to develop a quality of "pushing through" when the going is tough. They make it . . . by working and trying harder, inch by inch.

I want to tell you about one exceptional man I treated who rose above the crowd, earned a Ph.D. and became the top man in his field in the entire country. Yet when he was a high school student, his counselor assured him he would fail if he went on to college.

"YOU'LL NEVER MAKE IT, HARRY"

Harry was the first of ten children born to an immigrant family in Brooklyn. His father was a janitor on the midnight train to Manhattan, and his family was so poor that often there was little to eat.

Harry wanted to change things, to see to it that there would always be plenty of everything for his family. And he knew how to do it. He had a plan: He would go to college and become a professional.

Throughout high school, Harry had to study late every night because schoolwork wasn't easy for him. He stuffed every moment he could with homework. Then he had to help his mother with housework and do odd jobs that brought in extra money. Harry smiled a lot as he worked. "Being cheerful helped me because sometimes I'd get so scared, I was worried I couldn't do it all. But when I felt myself smiling, I'd think things weren't so bad after all. Then I wasn't so frightened anymore."

Ever since he was a teenager, Harry's friends called him a

workaholic. "I had no choice," Harry explained to me. "I had to keep busy or I never could have gotten everything done. I *had* to be productive from the minute I woke up until I went to sleep."

He was determined to make it through college, no matter what. But his hopes were shaken when he received the results from his college entrance exams. The school counselor told Harry his S.A.T. scores were "borderline" and suggested that he give up his plans for college and enter trade school.

As Harry left her office, the counselor's last words rang in his ears: "You'll never make it, Harry; with your test scores the competition in college will be too tough for you."

BUT HARRY WOULDN'T LISTEN.

He was determined to get a college education, in spite of the counselor's warnings.

Harry told me it was extremely difficult for him to absorb the scholarly concepts and theories at college because he was a very slow reader. His reading skills were so poor that in order to comprehend the material, he needed to reread every chapter five times, underlining as he went. "I was never sure what I was reading, but I just kept doing it over and over," he told me. "I prayed a lot, and I was always shaking whenever I took an exam. But the information that I thought I hadn't understood seemed to come through, because I had gone over it so many times.

"When my teachers suggested that a paper would require five to six hours of preparation, I knew in advance that it was going to take me *thirty!* The minute I got an assignment I'd go straight to the library. I always ate lunch with a book in front of me. Everything took me longer, because I'm so plodding and careful to do it right. I'm the kind of guy who wears both suspenders *and* a belt.

"I remember feeling inadequate when I talked to other students after exams and they told me they had studied only a few hours, when I knew it had taken me weeks to prepare. I never understood how they did it. But I *did* know that if *I* wanted to make it, I just had to put in the extra time."

Those were rough years for Harry. He didn't have enough money to hire a tutor, and often he felt overwhelmed. He was a high-anxiety test taker and always worried he was flunking out. But he was grateful to be there . . . a college student, at last! And he passed all his courses because he never stopped studying, never stopped trying.

Harry not only made it, but he even managed to finish graduate school and earn a Ph.D. in health sciences. He eventually became a leading nutritional authority and now heads a chain of more than two thousand health food stores in the United States and Canada. Harry developed that "stick-to-it-iveness" that made him a winner.

HARRY *WANTED* TO MAKE IT,
AND HE FOUND THE WAY . . . HE KEPT TRYING.

In spite of being frightened, overwhelmed with too much to do and told, "you'll never make it" . . . he did!

* * *

When I talk to patients who have been successful in their work, regardless of how divergent their tasks may be in industry, films or finance, I am often struck by the similarities in their backgrounds. Most of them had enormous problems to cope with, some at very young ages. They had to learn how to hang in and struggle with their difficulties, frustrations and disappointments. Due to necessity, they were forced to learn the techniques that moved them toward their wins.

You don't need to have desperate circumstances to acquire winning skills. As an adult, if you really want to, you can absorb the philosophy and exercises I'm telling you about now. YOU CAN DO IT comfortably . . . and at your own pace.

NO PLACE TO FALL

A well-known media personality who learned how to turn a disadvantage into an advantage was the late Jessica Savitch. When I first met Jessica Savitch and we talked about her participation in my book, I told her that her exceptional vitality and warmth were infectious for me. I was thoroughly delighted with our times together and pleased that her dynamic words and personality would be included in the book. I was particularly saddened by the news of her death, and shocked to hear that the excitement and brilliance of Jessica Savitch will no longer be with us. I'm very pleased, however, that her thoughts in this interview can now be helpful to others.

Famous as the principal reporter and writer for the Saturday edition of *NBC Nightly News,* Jessica was also seen on the weekday *News Updates* on NBC-TV and did commentaries for NBC radio. Dubbed "NBC's Golden Girl" by *Newsweek* for her brilliant performance as anchor for the 1980 presidential conventions, Savitch was an attractive strawberry blonde who looked more like a fashion model than a reporter. She was the recipient of an Emmy Award for her documentary, "The Spies Among Us," and in a 1982 poll was voted one of television's most appealing anchors.

Traveling the long road from a CBS "gofer" (the lowly person in an office who "goes for" coffee or whatever else is needed) to national prominence, Savitch had to struggle through many frustrating situations. This was how she confronted new challenges: "When I've had to do something difficult, I've gone ahead because I couldn't go backward. So whenever I'm discouraged—and I've been discouraged—I have thought, 'There is no choice. I must keep trying.' When I was discouraged, I had nowhere else to go. I chose this particular career, and I was right out there. If I stumbled, there was nobody to catch me. I couldn't go home to my family and say, 'Take care of me'; I couldn't go to a husband and say 'Support me,' so I persisted.

"Bob Dylan had a line: 'You never stumble when you have no place to fall.' I find that most successful people have that in their lives—backward is not an option for them.

"I remember hearing something I liked from a character in a Broadway play: 'He had all the disadvantages necessary for success —no choice!' When you have nowhere to stumble or nowhere to fall, no one to catch you and no place to go—you tend to go ahead."

I want you to learn from Jessica's words: Don't give yourself "a place to fall," don't make it so easy for you to quit. Allow yourself the advantage of "no choice" except winning.

My guess is that you have a dream, and I want to help you move toward it. There *will* be roadblocks along the way . . . there usually are. But every roadblock can be a signal for you to become more self-assured as you get busy solving problems and finding solutions. Don't give yourself any other choice but to win. Adopt this slogan. Attach it to your bathroom mirror, above your kitchen sink, on your desk, put it in your car. Read it several times every day.

OBSTACLES DON'T MEAN IT'S TIME
TO QUIT . . .
THEY MEAN IT'S TIME TO GET TO WORK
AND START WINNING.

WINNER SCORECARD #5

Are you convinced you could be a success if only you had the personal gifts or family background of some of the winners of your acquaintance? Such thinking will never carry you closer to your dreams! To be a winner, you need to learn how to do all you can with the attributes you *do* have.

LOSERS	WINNERS
1. Losers compare themselves to great winners and believe that they are helpless and inadequate. This makes them feel useless . . . so they decide they can't possibly do anything significant and quit.	**1.** Winners work at accomplishing what they can. They meet the challenges that confront them and give it everything they have. They don't compare themselves negatively with the famous giants, but rather they use them as models . . . so they, too, can learn to win!
2. Losers believe only the rich can win, only the talented or athletic can become superstars and only the beautiful can get what they want.	**2.** Winners believe it is possible to succeed despite tremendous physical handicaps. They make it even with formidable obstacles to overcome. They are distinguished by action, and they know it is work that turns the key to success.
3. Losers bemoan real and imagined handicaps, wasting precious energy and time that could be put to productive use. What they accomplish is getting older and duller.	**3.** Winners overcome even the most severe learning difficulties through getting at it early, working long hours, repeated efforts and persistence. They do the necessary tasks over and over until they are successful.

4. When losers are advised that they'll "never make it," they tend to give up and stop trying. They believe winners are born with a special breed of unique attributes.

4. Even when told they *don't* have what it takes, winners never stop hoping and trying. The skills they develop while striving to master the tasks that are particularly difficult for them become yet another winning asset.

5. When losers face problems that are frustrating and difficult to cope with . . . they become discouraged and stop trying. Thus, they can never discover solutions and must rely on others to show them the way.

5. When winners get discouraged, they believe they can't go backward because there is no place to fall. They see no choice but to make it. There is nobody to catch them, so they persist and go ahead.

CHAPTER 6

Compete Only with Yourself

Not in rewards, but in the strength to strive, the blessing lies.
—JOHN TOWNSEND TROWBRIDGE

To some people, it may seem overly simplistic to separate people into just two categories: winners and losers. But this kind of uncomplicated analysis can provide a powerful tool for identifying the traits that will eventually help you in getting closer to personal success. In the last chapter, I discussed how winners distinguished themselves by doing their best with whatever they had, whether it was a physical handicap, inadequate reading techniques or overwhelming fears. In this chapter, we'll look at some of the steps you can practice in acquiring key traits that set winners apart from losers. These are skills that you will be able to learn and incorporate into your own life.

When I first began putting together my theories on winning, I had a thesis that people who were successful had highly similar behavior patterns. I believed that there was a common denominator among them, identifiable ways of doing things that caused them to win, which could be replicated by others. My goal was to reduce these patterns into uncomplicated terms that could be easily learned and understood.

Like a scientist creating a vaccine that could be synthesized from various substances and injected into the veins . . . I was looking for a body of rules and information that could also be synthesized, reduced to a psychological recipe for succeeding . . . and injected into the mind.

After conducting many intensive interviews, as well as treating hundreds of patients who are established winners already, I'm now convinced that losers and winners are DEVELOPED, not born. Successful people tend to talk, think and act so similarly, often it is easy to identify the dynamics of their behavior patterns. Some of them have many characteristics in common . . . winning skills that they use which almost mirror-image each other. I believe that these winning behaviors can be scrutinized and explained . . . and then taught and translated to every individual lifestyle . . . and most certainly to yours.

Most people have behavior patterns that include *both* loser and winner characteristics. You probably have both, too. In our work together you will learn to expand your existing winner repertoires and develop new ones . . . while reducing your loser behaviors.

You can start by taking these steps toward your winning behaviors.

STEP ONE: STRETCH YOUR CAPABILITIES

Winners have a strong drive toward accomplishment, they value achievement and strive toward it. Utilizing every fiber of their potential, whatever it is . . . great or small . . . they stretch to the limit of their capabilities. Winners concentrate on doing even the smallest job that faces them as well as possible. WINNERS TAX THEIR SPIRITS TO THE LIMIT.

A persuasive spokesman, who can show you how he stretched himself to the very limits of his abilities, is Edward Bennett Williams, one of the most celebrated trial lawyers of our time.

Williams was born May 31, 1920, in Hartford, Connecticut. His family was poor, but he went to College of the Holy Cross on an academic scholarship and studied law at Georgetown University, where his record was outstanding. He went on to defend a host of clients famous, infamous or both. Among them: former Treasury Secretary John Connally, mobster Frank Costello, former CIA director Richard Helms, Senator Joseph R. McCarthy, Representative Adam Clayton Powell, Jr., Teamster bosses Jimmy Hoffa and Dave Beck, LBJ protégé Bobby Baker, the Fords of Detroit, Gulf & Western Industries, fugitive financier Robert Vesco and would-be assassin John W. Hinckley, Jr.

A 1983 article in *The New York Times Magazine* identified Williams as "a man of law, sport and politics . . . a pillar of the Washington establishment,"* moving comfortably among presidents, legislators and journalists.

Williams has extensive achievements in so many areas that I was particularly interested in his interview. I was eager to hear what Williams had to say on winning: "When I extend my body and my mind and my imagination and my creativity and my spirit to its utmost, I am content. Regardless of the jury's decision, I know I have won by my own standards."

Williams believes that success lies within everyone's reach. "I define the terms 'success' or 'victory' as using your capacities— physical, mental, spiritual, emotional—to their ultimate, whatever you may be doing. If you do that . . . then you can be fulfilled . . . I think you are a success."

Edward Bennett Williams is an outstanding example of a winner who puts forth earnest effort and celebrates accomplishment. The desire to achieve, to stretch capabilities, to be all that one can be, distinguishes winners in many different fields.

The voices of other winners are like a single chorus, adding similar harmonies with their words:

> I want to win, and I always have, since those days back in high school. I want to succeed, to get into as many things as I can, and accomplish them all—in films, in any sport I attempt, in social work, in my activity for the government promoting this country, in the American Film Institute, as president of the Screen Actors Guild, or on any of the other numerous committees of which I'm a member.
>
> I bite off more than I can chew; I overextend; I take on more projects than I can possibly accomplish.
>
> —CHARLTON HESTON

> I like to play. I don't have to; I never did. Nobody makes you play. You make you play. I think it's mostly, for me, a striving for perfection.
>
> —BILLIE JEAN KING

> The only thing worthwhile in life is to do everything you can to make things better. Sure, people should laugh and celebrate. But what is there to celebrate if you're not achieving things?
>
> —JANE FONDA

---

* Phil Gailey, "Behind the Scene with Ed Williams," *The New York Times Magazine* (April 17, 1983), pp. 55–56, 60*ff.*

STEP TWO: COMPETE ONLY WITH YOURSELF

To many people, the word "competitive" carries a negative meaning. It may imply dishonest behavior, the withholding of critical information, taking advantage of another person's innocence and trust or using competition in some unfair way. Unsavory labels such as "pushy," "crass," "vulgar" or "scheming" are sometimes associated with being "competitive." We have all heard clichés such as "he would kill to get to the top."

At the same time, healthy competition is part of the American ethos. Everybody loves a winner . . . in sports, in politics, in business, in the arts. Since the days of the pioneers, America has been shaped by the efforts of individuals who strove to make their mark, to improve their lot, to succeed.

Studies done by Dr. Ernest Vanderweghe and his associate Dr. Laurence Morehouse of the Human Performance Laboratory at the University of California at Los Angeles confirm the importance of competition and winning. They concluded that "winning —at a game, a sport, at anything—has a profound positive effect on a person's self-esteem and well-being."*

Their research shows that winning not only influences the quality of a person's life in the present, but transforms his future attitudes as well. Winning, they found, builds self-confidence and produces high morale. It is a prize in itself, bringing rewards of recognition and approval. They also noted that the discipline and effort required in childhood competition are preparation for the real competitive issues and arenas of later life. In addition, an attitude of striving can spill over into other areas and increase interest in achieving more and overcoming one's own limits.

"Winning," according to Dr. Morehouse, "means being at your best. . . . There's no fun unless there is an opportunity that allows you to show your skill, get credit for your performance, or develop your abilities as a mature strategist. Man appears to have a need to win, a need to test his capacity."**

The notion of being competitive needs an updated, more humanitarian definition, which includes an increased emphasis on idealistic values. Competition has nothing to do with steamrolling over someone else or taking advantage of another. In fact, engag-

* Paula Rice Jackson, "Winning Is Everything," *House & Garden* (June 1979), p. 150.
** Ibid., p. 192.

ing in competition can be an enriching experience in which each person does his best, competes primarily with himself and feels a sense of social responsibility and caring for others.

WINNERS LEARN THAT THERE IS PLENTY OF ROOM AT THE TOP.

When most of us are frightened, overwhelmed or overworked, we tend to forget our own self-worth and personal accomplishments. We begin to feel jealous about our co-workers and neighbors. The child buried deep inside of us forgets that we, too, have value and winning qualities. Instead of accepting our own goodness and excellence, we exalt others. We judge ourselves too harshly and compare our behaviors negatively with others. Our excessive self-criticism leads to our feeling inadequate and diminishes our self-worth.

When you can be more positive and approving of yourself, you will have a stronger self-image. Then your philosophy of winning will expand to include more real concern for people. Your own approval will add to your self-confidence and give you the ego stability and personal resources to be more caring to others. Then you can include in your definition for winning: giving it everything you have, being competitive and having warm feelings for the humanity of the person beside you, while still stretching yourself to the limit and striving to do your best.

A winner works at finding a kind word for the competition because he knows there is room for him to excel and for the next person to be an achiever as well. Because he competes primarily with himself, a winner avoids being hostile or unfriendly or belittling others in an attempt to build himself up.

The pettiness and bitterness that characterizes many work and social situations . . . the effort to "get" the other guy . . . is too painful a lifestyle. Even worse, it is the kind of negative, nonproductive activity that will keep you so busy, you will have *no time left for winning*.

When you are willing to see your past errors and acknowledge them to yourself WITHOUT being punitive . . . you can change. And even more . . . by accepting your human frailties and being kind to yourself, you will feel like a giant!

Help yourself by thinking in terms of the long pull: Don't reach for a momentary victory that is achieved by using or misleading others; don't take credit for anyone else's efforts; don't try to make gains by backstabbing. Remember that you are a person of high self-esteem and don't compromise your values and personal pride for an ephemeral gain.

STEP THREE: REWARD AND MOTIVATE YOU

The patients whom I label "losers" when they first begin therapy often explain they are unmotivated because others don't appreciate their efforts and never bother to reward them for achievements.

"Why should I work overtime, or kill myself to make the project look good," they complain, "when no one else bothers to compliment me or seems to care?"

In helping them to change to winners, I urge them to practice rewarding themselves. "Put your own sense of joy into seeing that your job is well done. Reinforce yourself. Tell *you* how excellent *you are*, how impressed *you are* with your accomplishments, how excited *you are* with your achievements."

REWARD YOU . . . APPRECIATE YOU . . .
MOTIVATE YOU.

Malcolm S. Forbes, chairman and editor-in-chief of *Forbes* magazine, is a winner who does just this. He puts the fun and satisfaction into his work and also enjoys many of the material rewards of his success. He owns a chateau in Normandy, a lavish seventeenth-century mansion near London, a sultan's house in Tangiers, an island in Fiji, ranches in Wyoming and Montana and a 170,000-acre tract in Colorado. He has been decorated by the French government and holds sixteen honorary degrees.

Forbes is known not only for his publishing achievements, but as an internationally acclaimed balloonist. He set six official world records in hot-air ballooning in October, 1973, when he became the first person to fly coast-to-coast across America in one hot-air balloon. At his home in Normandy, he has organized the world's first ballooning museum.

Ask Forbes what motivates him to be a winner and he'll tell you, "I don't know what specific attributes are motivating me, except joy in the job and great satisfaction when something is done right. When an article is outstanding, we all share the enthusiasm.

"There are unbounded rewards that aren't measurable when you succeed. It isn't just the monetary reward; it's the satisfaction of being able to say, 'By God, that's a good issue. That's a good piece. Now, there's a good cover.' "

Joy in doing a job well relates to experiencing joy in the job itself. Says Forbes, "Your adrenaline has to run. Whatever business you are in, if you don't feel exhilarated by achieving your objectives and excelling in what you're doing, then you never will do very much well.

"You can do a lot of things competently. But you have to have a sense of being turned on by the thought of making something go well. It's doing something better than it has ever been done before, or creating a new refinement in what you're making or a better service than the other guy. This is how you build a business. I'm the first one at my desk each morning. It's not a job for me because I love what I'm doing."

STEP FOUR: PRESENT A PROUD IMAGE

A winner presents a dignified presence to the world. His manner lets people know "I am a good person. I deserve to be respected."

If respect isn't forthcoming, the winner corrects the situation. For example, if someone were to say, even in jest, "Boy, it was sure dumb of you to forget to bring those papers to the meeting!" a winner would cordially but firmly interrupt and correct him: "No, it wasn't dumb. But I certainly did forget them this time."

Often when people are hurt or insulted, they are afraid to respond. Instead, they sputter, blush, usually say something foolish and probably end up carrying a grudge. Days later they are still reviewing the humiliating incident to themselves and feeling very inadequate. Learning to handle disparaging remarks from others in an easy and friendly way is a valuable tool that will increase your winning skills.

Suppose a dinner guest of yours says, "My goodness, this soup is so salty. I thought you're supposed to be a gourmet cook!" With a warm and sincere smile you could respond, "Well, people *have* encouraged me and said I'm a gourmet cook. But once in a while, my hand is a little too heavy with a seasoning. What do you think about the soufflé? Everyone is saying that's great." You've smoothly moved to something more positive, and you have maintained an amicable, comfortable atmosphere.

Or you may be at a party and a neighbor greets you with "My goodness, you're skinny as a rail! Don't you ever eat?" Your pleasant, smiling response might be, "Oh, I really *enjoy* being thin. And I need to work at it every meal! I watch everything I eat, and half the time I'm starving, but I just love the way I look. I'm so glad that you noticed."

The point is: You don't have to buy someone else's reality of life. If you feel good thin . . . stay thin. They can prefer plump—and their preferences are fine, *but so are yours*. They can have their opinions and *you can have yours*.

THE WARMER YOUR ANSWER IS TO THEIR CRITICISM THE MORE DIGNIFIED YOU WILL BECOME.

Don't let anybody get away with calling you stupid or wrong or terrible. But remember your formula for answering them includes being your warmest, friendliest self, and presenting your point of view in a short, undefensive delivery. It is important to be able to *listen* to someone else's extremely different view and believe that *you are perfectly fine* . . . and *so are they*.

A winner refuses to allow negative or degrading remarks about himself to pass; but neither does he *volunteer* self-deprecating comments. A winner would *not* walk into a room muttering, "Oh, I was such an idiot. I missed my freeway stop and went the wrong way." That would present a negative first impression.

If someone were to say to a winner, "My goodness! You got lost again?" he'd have some fun and respond with something like "Oh sure, I've gotten lost all over the world." Winners don't present their faults and failings; they share their enthusiasm and energy.

A winner walks into a room anticipating that good things will happen. He extends his hand and says hello to everyone present. His remarks about others would be positive and uplifting. After inquiring about them he might mention a recent accomplishment, something adorable his toddler had said or share an exciting new idea or project he's working on. Winners are honest about the facts and proud to present their achievements.

STEP FIVE: SEEK HELP WHEN YOU NEED IT

Winners are skilled at getting help. They use the resources that are available to them in their community. They take counsel from doctors, lawyers, accountants, teachers and advisors . . . they are willing to learn from experts.

Why bother "going it alone" when you can solve your problems more efficiently, and with less trial and error, by taking your questions to the people who already have training and experience in

72 GO FOR IT!

the area you're concerned with? To be a more effective problem solver, you need to acquire the skill of getting help.

Whatever your dreams, you may encounter frustrating road-blocks en route that could prevent you from making them come true. In order to help you learn to become more of a winner, I want to familiarize you with the tools that can eliminate some of the obstacles in your life. The following exercise is intended to help you use the resources available to you that will be an aid in solving your problems and advancing you toward your dreams.

EXERCISE 5: BECOME A BETTER PROBLEM SOLVER

For this exercise, select a particular problem or goal. I suggest you choose an item from the "I Might Not Mind Being" list you created in Exercise #1 (page 10).

For practice now, however, let's say that you think you might like to go back to college, take lessons or get some other kind of training. Right from the beginning, avoid your verbal downers. That might discourage you. Don't lower your motivation with negative messages that begin like these:

—"I don't have the intelligence or the experience to . . ."
—"There is so much ground to cover, I'm afraid I'll . . ."
—"I just know I'll fail if I try . . ."
—"I'll never make it; why should I risk looking like a . . ."
—"I'm getting too old to learn new tricks, I'll never . . ."

STOP THE SABOTEUR IN YOU.
The good problem solver gives himself messages like these:

—"I'll get any kind of experience for a start, so I can get there faster."
—"There is so much ground to cover. I'll get some help right away."
—"Failure is *not* trying."
—"Talking to someone who has already done this and failed will give me valuable clues on where 'not to go.' "
—"I'll find people who have already succeeded and get some good pointers from them on how to proceed."
—"I'm getting older each day, anyway, so I might as well give this my best shot and see if I can win."

FOCUS ON GETTING HELP.

Sit down with a pen and paper and jot down the names of everyone you can think of who might be able to give you advice about going back to school or solving whatever your problem embodies. Then start calling or visiting with them. Take a pencil and paper with you, so you can write down their suggestions.

If the people you contact don't have the information you need, don't stop there. Ask them if they can refer you to other sources.

Don't worry about apparently unproductive steps like calling the wrong person for help or going to the wrong place.

KEEP WORKING AT IT.

Reassure yourself that you are trying, and that in itself is a win. If you reach a blind alley, be nice to yourself. These "misses" demonstrate that you are actively involved in the process, and problem solving has many steps that include trying . . . failing . . . trying some more . . . making mistakes . . . and eventually succeeding.

Stay with it: Make more phone calls, speak to more people, ask more questions. All the time, you will be inching closer to your answers and a rewarding direction to follow.

TALK WITH FRIENDS.

You can get useful leads by talking with friends who have already gone to school, taken the lessons or found a solution to the situation in which you're interested. Ask if they can advise you about the fastest and most reliable way to reach your goal. Perhaps they can make recommendations, or send you to teachers or other students who are involved in what you want to do.

GET PROFESSIONAL ADVICE.

There are people in your city who make a living at counseling. They know more than you do about your best course of action, because they work full-time at finding the best routes and assisting people in their area of specialization. Seek out reliable professional guidance. Check your telephone book. Talk to businesspeople, accountants, tutors, college administrators, educators or people who are prominent and successful in your field of interest. They have channels of information and are familiar with procedures that may not be accessible to the general public.

USE EVERY RESOURCE.

Other experts in the community can also help. Inquire at local institutions, corporations, universities and ask to speak to the heads of departments in areas of your interest; they will know various specialists from the community who are in the field.

Use all available resources . . . be they consultants, designers, therapists, artisans, city administrators, tax counselors, architects . . . anyone who can be valuable to you. Most of the well-established business, technical or professional groups will have local or state offices, licensing agencies, unions, ethics committees or information centers that may be able to assist you.

MAKE SEVERAL LISTS.

One list can be of the people you speak to and the contacts you make; another could be the organizations you write to or call. For your third list you can think through the steps you need to take to arrive at a successful conclusion, and write them down in what seems to be the appropriate order. You will probably be rewriting this list many times . . . reordering and expanding the steps.

Your lists will serve as reference points and guidelines that you can follow and refer to as necessary. Systematically investigate each lead your resources suggest. One by one, try to put each step into action. Praise yourself for every effort you make, regardless of the results, because you deserve credit for everything that you attempt to do. Praise yourself for efforts that *don't work out,* as well as those that do.

Work at stretching your capabilities to the fullest. Give up the comparisons and the jealousies. Compete only with yourself. Reward and motivate the person who needs your kindness most . . . *you.* Present a proud image and use the help and advice of experts. Then you will be moving closer to *your* win and GOING FOR IT!

WINNER SCORECARD #6

In this chapter, we've looked at some of the character traits that set winners apart from losers. You can help yourself daily by rereading the exercises and winner scorecards in this chapter, and those that are given throughout the book. When you review them regularly they will become part of your repertoire and thinking. Try to memorize these points and move yourself closer to a consistent winning style.

LOSERS	WINNERS
1. Losers put forth very little effort. They tap into only a fraction of their potential.	**1.** Winners use every bit of their capabilities. They do their best in whatever situation they find themselves.

2. Losers feel that competition embodies aversive behaviors like being "pushy" and overly aggressive, crass, vulgar and manipulative.

2. Winners believe that engaging in competition can be an enriching experience in which each person does his best, competes mostly with himself and feels a sense of social responsibility and caring for others.

3. Losers feel inadequate and think that by beating others down they will build themselves up. They engage in petty, energy-wasting efforts to "get" the other guy.

3. Winners know there is plenty of room at the top. They focus on improving their own excellence, rather than hurting another person's progress.

4. Losers' notions of competition suggest that they must win no matter what the cost. It is acceptable to be dishonest, withhold critical information, take advantage of another person's naiveté and trust or use people in some other unfair way for personal gain.

4. Winners are concerned with the long pull. They have a sense of high self-esteem and won't compromise their values to get ahead.

5. When people say something critical about them, losers rarely respond with anything favorable in their own behalf. Even worse, they present a negative first impression by volunteering derogatory statements about themselves.

5. Winners present a proud, dignified presence that lets people know "I am a good person. I deserve to be respected." They cordially but quickly correct negative or degrading remarks that are made about them.

6. Losers think it's a virtue to be a "do-it-yourselfer" and go it alone.

6. Winners know that seeking help from others who have more knowledge and experience makes problem solving much easier.

PART TWO

Winners Are Positive

CHAPTER 7

Discover the Beauty
Around You

I wandered lonely as a cloud
That floats on high o'er vales and hills
When all at once I saw a crowd,
A host, of golden daffodils . . .
I gazed—and gazed—but little thought
What wealth the show to me had brought . . .
And then my heart with pleasure fills,
And dances with the daffodils.
—WILLIAM WORDSWORTH

For many years, people have been sharing their problems with me on radio and television talk shows. Whether the calls come from Australia, Great Britain or the United States, I am always surprised to realize how few people there are who can experience pleasure. It is rare to come in contact with someone, whether it is friends, patients or business contacts, who can "see the daffodils" on their hills.

CAN YOU SEE THE BEAUTY OF YOUR SURROUNDINGS?

Do you notice that colorful Bird of Paradise when it is bursting with life and ready to bloom? Or do you get bogged down thinking about the weeds that are nearby? Do you smile when you breathe in the sweet smell of the air after a rain, or are your eyes focusing on the mud puddles that remain? When you pass by a mirror and unexpectedly catch sight of your reflection, is your expression filled with joy or with pain?

Maintaining an upbeat, optimistic attitude is a core issue in winning. Often, the same event can be labeled "good" or "bad" . . . "happy" or "sad." The deciding factor usually relates to the individual's frame of reference, rather than what is actually happening.

Your perception of reality will color your thinking and behavior. You are the designer, the architect who is drafting the structure. YOU HAVE THE POWER TO BE A MAJOR INFLUENCE ON THE COURSE OF YOUR LIFE.

When you believe everything is going to be bad, you will probably *unconsciously create unhappy situations.* Once you have verbalized feelings of doom, you have a commitment to create something negative and give credibility to your prophecies.

On the other hand, when you channel your inner thoughts and spoken words into uplifting and encouraging ideas and observations, your thinking will be directed onto a positive course. Then your tongue will become more familiar with your optimism. You will be surprised to find how your actions will follow the same pathways. When you believe that today is going to be a great day and that tomorrow will be even greater, you will *set it up and see to it* that it happens. You will make your predictions come true.

The importance of a positive attitude was recorded centuries ago in the Bible:

> If thou canst believe, all things are possible to him that believeth.
>
> MARK 9:23

Unfortunately, few of us remember the good things that have happened in the past . . . or "believeth" they will occur in the future.

YOUR EMOTIONAL ROCKS

Losers weigh themselves down with what I call "emotional rocks." Like beasts of burden, they carry around heavy, unresolved problems and conflicts from the past. Losers discuss and repeat their worries daily. They drag them along like rattling chains throughout their lives.

The experience of joy and laughter is almost nonexistent for negative losers. They miss the fun and pleasure that is available to them in the present, because they are recalling their unhappy memories from yesterday and wallowing in the pain they accrue today.

Gloom and doom are the domains most familiar to losers. They fill their lives with negatives . . . they talk about them, count them and store them away to repeat in the future.

Losers continually refer to tragedies from the past:

—"Things have never been the same since Dad died."
—"I'll never forget how poor we were when I was a child."
—"I was so ashamed of the hand-me-downs and torn clothes I had to wear."
—"My mother used to yell and embarrass me whenever my friends came over."
—"The kids at school always made fun of how fat (thin, tall, short, etc.) I was."

Losers bemoan all the hard times in the present:

—"I'm always blamed for everything that goes wrong."
—"The trouble with this family is that no one ever thinks about me."
—"It's impossible to meet a good man in this city."
—"I don't have a thing to wear!"
—"You can't get ahead in times like these."

Losers predict calamities for the future:

—"With my luck, I just know those stocks will go down."
—"It's certain to rain tomorrow and ruin our trip. I can just feel it."
—"I'm sure I'll get lost and never be able to find this place again."
—"At the rate you're going, you're bound to get yourself into trouble."
—"Don't do that. I'm afraid it will be too strenuous for you, and you'll get hurt."

The depressing jargon of losers surrounds them the way a wall surrounds a jail. They contaminate the atmosphere with their suffocating gloom. Wherever losers go, they run up against their own self-imposed prisons and their own debilitating negative remarks.

How can losers possibly have any fun? They can't. And more important . . . *you can't if your* outlook on life is negative.

I have worked with many patients who can only think about the dark side of things when they first come into therapy. Regardless of the situation in which they find themselves, they systematically judge every failure . . . single out every mishap . . . and record every flaw. They can rarely smile or be happy. No matter what position they are in, it is wrong, or it is uncomfortable, or it is not what they want. If they are north, they long to be south, and when the day is sunny, they wish it would rain.

When they receive loving affection and caring from their mates, they insist on having more space. But when their mates say "no" to them or are busy . . . they complain about being neglected. Somehow, nothing is ever quite right!

THEY ARE NEVER SATISFIED . . . NEVER CONTENT.

How do people get that way?

YOUR NEGATIVE TAPES

During our formative years our parents become our first school, our prototypes . . . our teachers. The emotional "tapes" that they play again and again become our models. If they constantly play negative programs, we develop deeply ingrained negative patterns. This early training prevents us from enjoying ourselves as adults. Often, we can appreciate the rewards available to us only when we lose them.

If you are sitting around focusing on what you are missing, or what is wrong, you are letting that negative tape of yours reel on and on. This will keep you forever boring and miserable.

Being with negative people can be catching . . . they not only make themselves unhappy, but they often "bring down" the people around them. Positive people will "bring you up," because their attitude is also catching. When you are with them you'll FEEL BETTER and have more FUN.

MRS. MISERABLE AND MR. ENTHUSIASTIC

When I was in Britain, I treated a married couple I used to call "Mrs. Miserable" and "Mr. Enthusiastic." During their therapy sessions, I was struck by the contrasts in their points of view. Even their observations of events they had attended *together* were so different that it was difficult to believe they were talking about the same occasions.

When they went to a party, for example, their descriptions of the evening were remarkably different in quality and feeling.

Mrs. Miserable would offer a detailed report on the "terrible" party they had attended, complaining about the food, the crowds, that her host had ignored her and of the boredom of the evening. It would quickly become apparent that she had had an awful time.

Her husband, Mr. Enthusiastic, would come in for his private session and proceed to give me a lively account of the same party. His spirited gesturing and happy observations conveyed the very opposite of what his wife had described.

"I had a bloody good time," he told me with obvious pleasure. "It was wonderful! Smashing! And there were so many interesting people. The food was marvelous; Clive was a perfect host."

Could this have been the same party? Clearly, the polarity in this couple's basic attitudes created a dramatic contrast in their feelings about the same social situation. When one person focuses on criticizing, complaining and looking for the negatives and finds them . . . and the other person expects to have a good time and does . . . they truly *are* attending different parties and living in separate worlds.

Who would you like to be with, Mr. Enthusiastic or Mrs. Miserable? And how do you see yourself? Do you feel miserable and resentful much of the time? Or can you enjoy the opportunities for pleasure, growth and fun that are available in your life?

Constantly expressing negative thoughts can quite literally drive people away. This destructive habit was a problem for one patient, who was worried about her inability to get a second date.

"THEY NEVER ASK ME OUT A SECOND TIME"

Emmy was thirty-two when she came to see me. She was "dying to get married" and worried because she was getting older and there was "still no man in sight."

Emmy continually met new men through her work, and they asked her for dates. The problem was that none of them called her a second time.

I asked Emmy to describe what had happened during her most recent date. As she related the details, it quickly became clear why she rarely received a second call. Emmy's negative remarks and criticisms had flowed freely from the minute she answered the doorbell until her date drove her home.

Opening the front door, one of her first remarks had been, "Oh, you shouldn't have worn that sport shirt. It's going to be a more formal affair. I hope you won't be the only one without a tie!" Then, as she and her date walked to his car, she instructed: "Don't forget to put all the windows up. If the wind blows on me, my hair will look terrible."

As Emmy's date opened the car door, she had cried, "Oh, I'm afraid I'll get my new dress dirty! There's such an *awful* mess on that seat! Why don't you take a minute and clean it up?"

Finally, I interrupted. "Emmy, I wouldn't take you out a second time, either!" I said. "Who wants to hear all those put-downs? Even before his car left the curb, you became his critical mother and buried him with your humiliating comments. It's no fun to be told what's wrong with you all evening!"

Emmy and I went over more positive phrases she might say when she greeted her dates: "You look so good in that suit," or "That's a flattering color on you," or "I like that aftershave you're wearing."

I also encouraged Emmy to offer favorable and honest comments as she and her date drove along (i.e., positive remarks about the car, the plans for the evening, what a good time she was having, etc.).

If you are saying to yourself now, "Dr. Kassorla, this sounds too phony to me—too saccharine," I could understand. But I wasn't a bit concerned about Emmy's being *too sweet*. She needed to reach for the other extreme just to land somewhere in the middle.

Emmy had another problem that was closely related to her negative delivery: She didn't know how to smile. She had a peculiar way of covering her front teeth whenever she tried. I showed her how to expose both her upper and lower teeth, much as a horse does when he makes a "neighing" sound. When I demonstrated this for Emmy and did my imitation of a horse smiling, Emmy thought it was so funny she burst into giggles.

The minute she started laughing I said, "Good, I like to see you so amused. It would be wonderful if you could be like this on a date. Think of that image of the horse smiling and showing all his teeth. When you imitate the horse, you'll have fun, too. Try to be more playful."

Emmy hadn't even realized that she frowned that much. She explained that she was so worried about what her date was thinking that it was difficult for her to feel adequate . . . let alone smile!

"He's worried about what *you are thinking!*" I reassured her.

"You might as well share your frightened feelings with him. He will identify with what you're saying, and then you both can be more relaxed."

I like to give patients homework to practice during the week, so Emmy and I went over her horse-smiling exercise several times in my office before she left. Whenever she did her neighing routine, she laughed and remarked how silly and childlike she felt.

"Good," I said. "Most of the time you are like a scowling old lady. Acting like a child for a change will be a welcome relief!"

I also instructed Emmy to give a smile to every mirror and window she passed. I wanted her to discover how approachable and attractive she was when she had a warm look on her face.

After a couple of weeks, Emmy returned to my office. "I'm smiling so much now, my jaw hurts," she said. "But I have noticed the strangest thing—people are smiling back! It always surprises me when someone seems pleased when they look at me. Now I remind myself, 'It's because I'm the one who started the smiling first!'"

Emmy's new behaviors had freshened the air. And guess what happened when she used the warm positives and friendly skills she had learned with the men she dated? They started calling her back!

* * *

IT'S TIME TO PUT *YOUR* SMILE ON.

When *you* first begin to use more positive messages, your family and friends may be somewhat suspicious. But keep it up. Try to find pleasant and optimistic things to observe and talk about. Eventually everyone will believe you. They will realize that this is your new style and you are very sincere.

DEIRDRE HAD A POSITIVE MOTHER

Losers tend to believe that circumstances must be ideal before they can be positive. They insist anything less wouldn't be honest.
NONSENSE!

A winner searches for the good aspects in every situation. And he finds them . . . even when there may be major elements of painful disappointments or tragedies involved, as well. This was the attitude of Deirdre's mother.

Deirdre was one of the few patients I have treated who had the benefit of being raised by a parent who was both extremely positive and an excellent problem solver. To be trained under the supportive tutelage of a parent with these winning qualities is a great advantage.

Deirdre was twenty-nine when she came into therapy seeking help in dealing with her mother's sudden death in a car accident.

In describing her past, she told me she had been just six years old when her father, a young man, died of a heart attack. Her mother, who was only twenty-seven at the time, had been devastated. With two small children to raise and no money, she had been rendered nearly helpless by what seemed a cruel blow dealt by a capricious fate. But she had managed to pick herself up and summon the courage to go on.

Deirdre told me that for years after her father's death, her family had been so poor that just having enough food was a concern. Rather than agonize about their poverty, however, her mother had found a way to earn money. She typed legal briefs at home for a neighbor who couldn't afford a full-time secretary. Deirdre had also discovered a way to contribute. At the age of eight, she was at work teaching the neighborhood preschoolers their ABC's and earning quarters from their grateful parents.

Deirdre looked proud when she told me she admired her mother's positive attitude: "I appreciated her spunk and her 'never-say-die' outlook. If five crises faced her, she'd say, 'Aren't we lucky there aren't six!' When we couldn't afford a car, I remember her remarking, 'Isn't it great that we live close to public transportation?' When there was no money to buy me a Halloween costume, she created one from bits and pieces of old garments around the house. She made it all seem like fun. When I ran for office at school and lost, she said, 'Good! Now we have time to plan a better campaign so you will definitely win the next election!'

"Whenever I was negative, complained or had trouble at school," Deirdre recalled, "she would help by reminding me of similar situations in which I had felt discouraged, but had kept going and ended up with outstanding results. She always encouraged me by pointing out my strengths. It was very much the same whether my mother was dealing with my problems, my brother's or her own."

After years of hearing her mother's positive attitude, Deirdre had incorporated the same values into her own way of living. Whenever challenges arose, she tackled them with the positive point of view she had learned . . . and she succeeded! When she was still small, she loved to draw and wanted to take art lessons, but there wasn't enough money. Instead of bemoaning her hardships, she practiced drawing on her own. At ten, without any formal training, she decided to enter a national art contest that she saw advertised in the Sunday comic section of the newspaper. One of her friends cautioned that it was useless to bother. "There will be thousands of kids trying out for that. You haven't got a chance! Why stick your neck out and make a fool of yourself?" But Deirdre didn't listen to these negatives. "Unless I *do* stick my neck out and try, I'll *never* have a chance!"

Ten weeks later there was a letter in the mail announcing that she was one of the winners. The prize was a year's scholarship to the art school of her choice.

Deirdre's powerful skills for winning continued to serve her as she grew older. She finished law school at the age of twenty-two, and at twenty-five she was a junior partner in one of her city's leading legal firms. When problems confronted Deirdre . . . whether they were serious tragedies or the usual frustrations and disappointments that we all struggle with every day . . . she acted with hope and confidence. She used her powerful childhood tools and worked them out, by focusing on the positives.

While treating Deirdre and giving her emotional support during her mourning period, I was impressed with the durability of her emotional fabric. She was sturdier than most of the people I see, and though she grieved deeply over her mother's death, her ability to cope was exceptional.

* * *

TURNING THINGS AROUND

Many of us, at some point in our lives, are faced with tragedies or trying circumstances that are painful and distressing. But stating and repeatedly restating whatever it was that hurt or was troubling us, whenever someone will listen, isn't healthy. Besides, reexperiencing events that were once difficult or irritating doesn't help you now. So stop your grumbling and start doing something! Instead of spending valuable time relisting your grievances . . . BE MORE EFFECTIVE.

Make a Herculean effort to dig out all of your positives when you go through painful times. Work at finding creative solutions and problem solving.

Use your creativity and imagination to do this . . . not your negative tongue. Discover how powerful you can feel when you turn things around and improve the quality of your life.

YOUR EMOTIONAL VACUUM CLEANER

Now I want to give you another tool to help you move closer to your goal of becoming a winner. It is an "emotional vacuum cleaner" that will enable you to sweep away all those negatives from your eyes and mind.

The first step in using this tool is your willingness to *hear yourself* when you talk.

LISTEN TO YOURSELF.

Do *you* usually talk about all of the disagreeable aspects of your environment? Do many of your words end in "n't," like can*'t*, won*'t*, don*'t*, shouldn*'t*, wouldn*'t?* Do your most-used adjectives focus on these negative modifiers: *awful, terrible, selfish, wrong, boring, impossible, inconsiderate?* Do you assault others with an endless string of *Why don't yous* and *How come you haven'ts* and *You nevers?*

IF YOU CAN HEAR YOURSELF . . . YOU CAN CHANGE.

But before you can change, you need to become aware of what it is that you are doing that harms you. Once you honestly look at your behaviors and hear those negatives pouring out of your mouth, you will be able to put your vacuum to work and sweep them away. In this way you will make more space to house good things and have the emotional room for your more positive thoughts and messages.

You may be saying now, "I guess I do use a lot of negative words. I've never looked at it that way before. I wonder if my friends think I am a Mr. or Ms. Miserable? If I am, is there still time for me to change?"

Absolutely! And your emotional vacuum cleaner will help you. Actually try to visualize this image:

See a tiny, toylike vacuum cleaner sweeping across your forehead, picking up all the debris: tragedies from the past, hard times in the present, calamities in the future . . . your "n't" words and your "couldn'ts, wouldn'ts, shouldn'ts."

Whenever you hear yourself using these negative words, STOP! Put that vacuum to work and make those damaging and depressing "mind fillers" vanish!

REPLACING YOUR NEGATIVE IMAGES

Unhappy thoughts come into our heads at the strangest times, and it is important to learn not only how to get rid of them with your emotional vacuum cleaner, but how to fill up the space they leave empty with healthy, positive ideas and feelings.

Let's imagine that you are taking a shower. You have just finished your aerobics class, and the freshness of the warm water feels soothing on your skin.

As you savor these good feelings, thoughts about the fight you had with your neighbor last month creep back into your awareness. Suddenly unpleasant memories flood your head.

But you're in the shower . . . having a good experience . . . and you can't possibly solve this problem with your neighbor at that second. You can't speak to him and try to work it out while you're covered with soap! You can deal more effectively with the neighbor problem *after* the shower, when you can *actively and creatively* problem-solve.

Look at what you're doing: You are unconsciously using the problem with your neighbor to rob yourself of the joy of your bathing ritual.

DON'T STEAL AWAY YOUR OWN HAPPY TIMES!

Get out your vacuum cleaner and sweep away all thoughts of your neighbor. There is nothing you can do about that quarrel now, but you *can* enjoy your shower. You deserve these good feelings, and it is *your responsibility not to destroy them*.

After you have wiped your head clean of your painful image, you can make a choice of what positive images to replace them with. My choice is flowers. I envision them, because flowers are one of the favorite visual pleasures of my home and work environment. Your positive replacement image can be anything *you* enjoy visualizing and thinking about.

One of my patients likes to envision a baseball game. She takes out her emotional vacuum cleaner, sweeps away her disheartening mental pictures, then substitutes the image of her favorite ballplayer sliding into home plate. This invariably lifts her spirits, gets her smile going and enables her to move on to happier thoughts.

Try this exercise, and once you get good at practicing it, you will feel much happier as you transplant pleasant visions into your head.

If, after a few minutes, the haunting negative memories return . . . get busy and repeat the vacuuming and replace the good images.

No matter how many times you find it necessary to sweep with your vacuum, do it. As long as your unconscious wants to drown you in unhappy thoughts, you must consciously get to work and push them out.

KEEP REPLACING NEGATIVE THOUGHTS WITH POSITIVE ONES.

Your depressing thoughts may intrude more frequently during peaceful times, when you are trying to relax and enjoy a rest. Many patients report that at bedtime, when there are no competing noises or other stimuli, they begin to feel anxious or depressed and their downers start flooding in.

Whenever negative thoughts or problems come into your head, do something about them. You are the only person who has control of your mind. Do it with your emotional vacuum cleaner and make space for the happy times and wins that are coming!

LEARN TO BE AN IMMACULATE MENTAL HOUSEKEEPER.

EXERCISE 6: PLAYING SHERLOCK HOLMES

This exercise is designed to guide you to be on guard as you speak. It will help you recognize when you are observing life as being the half-empty, instead of the half-full, cup.

Step One: Discover . . . Don't Defend

As you try to change your behavior, develop a special attitude. Adopt the joy of discovery that Sherlock Holmes was famous for. Seeing and hearing how negative you are, and *not* hiding this reality from yourself or others, or trying to defend why you are right is the exciting detective work you need to do to help yourself change. SEEING will help you replace your negatives and CHANGE.

Step Two: Reward Your Slips

As you become more aware that you are talking like a loser, it is essential for you to be very warm and kind to yourself.

REMEMBER THAT CHANGE OCCURS WHEN YOU ARE POSITIVE TO YOU.

When you hear yourself delivering a "downer" like one of your "if onlys," "n'ts" or other verbal garbage, be *pleased* that you were able to hear it. *Don't criticize or punish yourself when you slip* . . . for that, too, would be negative. Instead, pat yourself on the back for your willingness to acknowledge you are delivering an unhealthy communication.

The nicer you are to yourself, the faster you will change. So be undefensive and friendly and give yourself a pat whenever you can see that you're going back and slipping in those negative messages.

For example, if someone asks whether you enjoyed your meal at a new restaurant, you might hear yourself respond with a double negative, saying "It was<u>n't</u> too *bad* a dinner." Once the "n't" and "bad" are out of your mouth, you can't pull them back in. But you *can* smile to yourself. Be pleased and grateful that you heard the negative words, and rephrase the sentence in your new positive and healthy way.

It might sound something like this: "I'm so glad you asked. I had a *wonderful* dinner. I hope you'll be able to go there one day and taste some of their delicious specialties."

Step Three: Behaviors Follow Words

This step will take a good deal of practice, before you will become aware of how the process of making changes works. But you will notice that gradually, as your mouth becomes more positive, your actions will slowly begin to catch up with the new regime . . . and follow suit.

Be patient and keep finding the positive aspects of your problems, even when you feel discouraged and are losing hope. Winners hang in, keep trying, and good things happen. Once you make the commitment to yourself to search for the positives, your healthier behaviors will model after your positive words. As you develop love and respect for yourself . . . you *will* change.

A SECRET DESIRE

I had the exciting opportunity to meet an incredibly positive woman and great mental housekeeper. The memory of her infectious smile still warms me. Her name is Paula Kent Meehan, the chairman of the board of Redken Products.

When I first met Paula at the door of the beautiful mansion she bought from Elvis Presley, she greeted me with that memorable smile. Her high energy, enthusiasm and exceptionally positive attitude were as contagious as her warmth.

A dynamic and optimistic woman of action, Paula has her own personal formula for making her secret desires come true.

She began Redken with her beautician, Jheri Redding, whom she later bought out. Paula has since developed the hair-care products business, which was founded with just $3,000 in savings, into a huge national organization that earned over $86 million last year.

Meehan's first job was pumping gas. After that came stints as a secretary, a receptionist, an airline stewardess, typist and actress on 77 *Sunset Strip*. But all along she had a secret desire . . . to be in the cosmetics business.

Meehan believes everyone has a secret desire. "It is the inner voice telling you what you can do. I think an awful lot of people feel that their secret desire is too good for them, too fanciful. They are worried that they can't do it.

"Your secret desire is a message that you should follow and apply yourself to. And then you can be *sure* that you are doing what you like."

Because Paula is doing what she *wants* to do, she is happy putting in long days at work. "Now and again, I'll grumble to my husband, who is president of our company, 'Why don't we go out more—why don't we do this or that?' If I really wanted to, you know, I would. You find time for what you want to do. And work is what I enjoy.

"When you're doing what you love, you throw yourself into it," says Meehan. "I can't imagine how someone could be successful if they were doing something they didn't like. My advice would be 'Quit it, quick, and go find something you do like!' "

Meehan's faith in the power of a *positive outlook* extends to every aspect of her life. "I believe in autosuggestion. I use it on myself, knowing that if I tell myself something, that is what I am going to be. So I not only think I'm lucky, but I instinctively feel it."

Meehan was fortunate enough to have a very positive parental model. "I know I am positive, but my mother is the most positive person I know. Nothing bad has ever happened to her in her whole life, because she manages to find the good in everything.

"My mother is eighty, and she just got married again last year. She's the first one on the dance floor and the last one off. She really has positive energy! I hope I am like her."

* * *

SEARCH FOR YOUR POSITIVES

There are wonderful things all around for you to discover. If you want to be a winner, go out and find them for yourself. Right now!

There is an old fable about a man who was seeking the bluebird of happiness. He traveled the world, searching everywhere. But when he at long last found it, it was right outside his own front door.

Be a winner who seeks out beauty. Fill your head with the roses that are already close by in your life.

Search out all the wonders out there. Stay with it until you find something positive that you can put into your head.

EXERCISE 7: COUNT YOUR POSITIVES

Let your mind become a healthy computer recording all of your positives. This is a winner's skill.

EVERYONE HAS POSITIVES.

You will find yours when you stop longing for what you *don't* have and start appreciating what you *do* have.

I have made a list that you can study for homework. If it isn't totally accurate for your circumstances, use it as a place to begin.

As you practice my words, you will be able to substitute even more positive descriptions that accurately and realistically fit your life.

Stand before a mirror as you read the following list: Find your infectious smile and talk aloud to yourself.

SPEAK SINCERELY AND WARMLY.

—"I'm a good person."
—"I'm a caring person."
—"I really like people."
—"I'm a thoughtful woman/man."
—"I value myself."
—"I appreciate my healthy body."
—"I'm very caring."
—"I'm an individual . . . an original human being."
—"I'm concerned about others."
—"I'm a loving mother (father, grandmother, grandfather, aunt, uncle, brother, sister)."

Find other simple things to add. You won't need important discoveries to help you to feel good about yourself. They can be little things that you do or say much of the time. *Practice this exercise every day.*

EXPAND ON YOUR LIST WITH PRAISE ABOUT YOUR ATTRIBUTES.
CONTINUE ADDING YOUR POSITIVES.

—"People know they can trust me."
—"I have courage."
—"I'm a loyal friend."
—"I like to help people."
—"I'm a good cook."
—"I'm reliable."
—"I keep my house comfortable."
—"I volunteer service to my community."
—"I'm a religious person."
—"I smile at strangers."
—"I'm good company."
—"I enjoy making others happy."

List even the smallest facts about yourself that you may believe are inconsequential. I want to *shatter* your negative speaking patterns and to get your head started in thinking more positively about yourself.

Abraham Lincoln said that people are just about as happy as they make up their minds to be. You can decide what goes on in your head. You have control over your thoughts.

USE YOUR CONTROL.

Whenever a negative thought does pop into your head, get that vacuum working and clean it out.

You have been talking about and regurgitating all those negatives for years. And has it helped? No! All it has done is to breed *more* negatives, which have led to *more* disheartening thoughts, following by *more* glum worries.

Stop your old tapes. You can't win by breeding negatives. When they do surface, sweep them away. Then you can get busy deciding to be happy . . . and choosing to feel wonderful. Talk about joyous moments: stimulating plans for the future, rewarding memories from the past and positives you are experiencing now. Then your actions and feelings will follow your positive words.

MAKE YOUR LIFE RICHER AND MORE
FULFILLING!
BE A WINNER WHO THINKS POSITIVELY.

WINNER SCORECARD #7

What about you? Are you the eternal critic? Are you unrelenting with your negatives and complaints?

If you are ready to throw away your negative ideas and start feeling happy, keep these winner traits in mind. They will help you move closer to your goals.

LOSERS	WINNERS
1. Losers notice and count every flaw in their surroundings. They are so bogged down with judgments and negatives that they have great difficulty letting themselves experience pleasure.	**1.** Winners delight in the beauty and natural wonders around them. They enjoy little things: the flower ready to burst into bloom, the sweet smell of the air after a rain.
2. Losers believe everything is going to be bad, and unconsciously, they're motivated to create unhappy situations that will make their predictions come true.	**2.** An upbeat, optimistic attitude is one of the key characteristics of winners. They channel their thoughts and words into uplifting and encouraging ideas and observations.

LOSERS	WINNERS
3. Losers weigh themselves down with "emotional rocks." They carry around unresolved problems and conflicts from the past, fill their discussions with old tragedies and current hardships and predict future calamities.	**3.** Winners experience the good things that are happening in the present. The past is a library of information to learn from and the future a happy, inviting land of unlimited promise.
4. For losers, nothing is ever quite right. When they finally get what they want, they don't want it anymore; and when they lose it, they must have it back. Their negative tapes reel on and on, making misery and boredom a major theme in their lives.	**4.** Winners focus on what they *have* that is pleasant and rewarding and find creative ways to go about getting whatever else it is that they want.
5. Losers grow accustomed to experiencing only the negatives in their lives, even when they are safe and secure and everything is going well. They feel miserable and resentful too much of the time.	**5.** Winners quickly problem-solve and minimize the negative aspects of situations, and seek out the positives. They work at finding the opportunities for growth and learning in their environments.
6. Losers let negative remarks and criticisms flow freely. They bury others with put-downs, directions and humiliating comments.	**6.** The winners' smile mirrors what they give and receive from others. They make favorable comments about the activities they experience and speak enthusiastically about the times they share with others.
7. Losers are often traumatized and immobilized by seemingly insurmountable problems. They sink into despair and are unable to function.	**7.** Even during trying circumstances or tragedies, winners dig out the positives and summon the courage to take the next step and make things better.

8. When losers are troubled or annoyed, they devote their energies to blaming, gossiping and complaining.

8. When winners are irritated or unhappy, they get busy turning the situation around. They realize that having a good time is *their* responsibility.

9. Losers use many words ending in "n't," like ca*n't,* do*n't,* wo*n't,* should*n't* and would*n't.* Among their most-practiced adjectives are *awful, boring, terrible* and *selfish.* They assault others with an endless string of *Why don't yous?* and *How come you haven'ts?*

9. Winners use their "emotional vacuum cleaners" to sweep away their unhappy thoughts and pessimistic feelings. They search out the positives, even in adverse situations, and stuff their heads with words or phrases that include *wonderful, good, warm, important, I love, exciting, great!*

CHAPTER 8

The Power of Honest Positives

The applause of a single human being is of great consequence.

—SAMUEL JOHNSON

I have treated a wide range of people on six continents. Among my most troubled patients were a mute child living in squalor on a sampan in the Far East and an autistic teenager in Rome who scratched out one of her eyes during a tantrum. Among my normal, emotionally stable clients, there have been individuals ranging from royalty to the unemployed who have trusted me with their most precious secrets.

If someone were to ask, "Dr. Kassorla, what is your most valuable tool for helping people?" I would answer without hesitation, "There is a kind of magic in one technique I use. It has enabled me to help mute people speak, depressed people smile and couples in miserable marriages strengthen their bonds. Whether I'm treating schizophrenics or normal people, it is the most effective tool I know. I call it 'the power of honest positives.' "

If you are wondering how to get some, I won't need to *give* you this power, because you already have it. It is the ability to be honestly reinforcing, honestly positive and honestly uplifting to yourself and others. And finding out how to apply this power can be easy to learn.

WHAT IS AN HONEST POSITIVE?

"Honest positives" are complimentary, rewarding and reinforcing words or phrases you say to other people that you *sincerely believe to be true.* By delivering honest positives "on the spot," you can offer important feedback and direction to someone when he says or does something you approve of or value.

Receiving reinforcement feels good. Receiving honest positives feels especially good. But remember: The most important part of your verbal reward is that it is *genuine.* If it isn't, the other person will sense that your words don't ring true. The value of the honest positive will be lost if people suspect that you are being manipulative or using them for personal gain.

When you use *honest* positives, everyone will detect an aura of sincerity about you, an honest "smell." You will be believed and trusted. Moreover, the person who receives your positives will feel appreciated, and his self-esteem, which is essential to winning, will grow.

Whether you are raising children, dealing with your mate or family or interacting with people at work, your communications will be enhanced by the use of honest positives.

To use honest positives effectively, be sure you eliminate any hint of criticism from your words. Suppose you have repeatedly asked your husband to take out the trash, but he usually forgets to do it. Then one day when you drive home you see that the refuse container is on the curb. A common response in this situation might be to go into the house and say, "Honey, I'm glad you took the trash out. *And it's about time*—I've been begging you to do it for about four months!"

If you respond in this manner, your husband may be very annoyed because too often when we give an honest positive, we also take something away. If I hand you a dollar, and then take the dollar back, you may get angry when you look in your hand and see the dollar is gone. If you compliment your husband with an honest positive which starts out with "Honey, I'm glad," then take it away by saying "I've been begging you for months," he will be resentful. He heard the honest positive, but it doesn't feel good, because he also received a hidden putdown.

You want your honest positive to be pure, complimentary and reinforcing. Don't include the slightest reprimand about what *wasn't* done. When something good is happening, don't rehash old complaints. Instead, make your response *current:* Talk about the healthy behaviors that *are happening today* with warmth and kindness.

A healthy, honest positive would sound like this: "Honey, I noticed that you took the trash out. That is really helpful. Thank you." The key is to acknowledge and encourage healthy behaviors. Rather than look back and discuss what annoyed you yesterday, it is far more effective to focus on rewarding the behaviors you like today.

VERBAL REWARDS CAN MOTIVATE BEHAVIOR.

Even when a reward is registered at an unconscious level and cannot be explained rationally, it can still have the power to be reinforcing.

HIDDEN POSITIVES

Many years ago, a researcher by the name of W. S. Verplanck conducted a study which I vaguely recall. One of my professors in experimental psychology discussed it when explaining the effects of operant conditioning. The study showed how powerful rewards can be, even when they enter awareness at an unconscious level.

Verplanck used college students as his subjects. For the purpose of this project, his goal was to demonstrate that what people said could be modified according to the reinforcements that were delivered or withheld.

After making an initial measurement of how often the students discussed political subjects, the experimenters spoke individually to each of them. Whenever something political was said, the experimenter would consciously look very interested . . . he'd move forward in his chair, talk enthusiastically and give the student his full attention.

However, when the student spoke about other things, the experimenter, without being overtly rude, would "tune out" in some way, such as withdrawing his attention by looking out the window, studying his fingernails or staring into space. If the student returned to a political topic, the experimenter would reinforce the behavior and focus his full attention again, and show great interest.

By the end of this study, all of the students had significantly increased their rate of talking about political issues. When questioned about their conversations with the experimenter, they made very general kinds of responses such as "Oh, he was nice; we had a pleasant chat." None of them had recognized the experimenter's methodical attempt to use positive words and attention to manipulate the conversation, yet all of them had been greatly influenced by it.*

USING POWERFUL PSYCHOLOGICAL TOOLS

In my own experimental studies with schizophrenics, I have had dramatic success in changing their bizarre psychotic behaviors into more appropriate patterns by using powerful psychological tools . . . my honest positives. The results have been so remarkable that an untrained observer might have wondered if I were administering a potent new drug. But my "drug" was often little more than presenting warm, caring words. Whenever there was the slightest sign of a healthy behavior, I gave my full *attention* and *praise* . . . my reinforcements to reward them. When their behaviors were psychotic, I ignored them by turning my head away. My formula was simple:

Healthy behaviors earned praise (or positives).
Sick behaviors earned being ignored (or negatives).

The impact of this formula is well illustrated by my work with a patient I treated at Springfield Hospital, in Britain, an institution for the mentally ill. His name was Charlie Blake.** He had been called the "sickest man in Britain."

CHARLIE WAS "MR. ZERO"

Charlie did virtually nothing all day except sit in one chair. He rarely looked up or moved, and he hadn't spoken an intelligible word in *thirty years*. One of the orderlies on the ward called Charlie "Mr. Zero." Using success/failure terms, he could have been labeled "Britain's most *unsuccessful* man." He certainly wasn't concerned with blocking, competing, trying or going for it

* W. S. Verplanck, "The Control of the Content of Conversation: Reinforcement of Statements of Opinion," *Journal of Abnormal Social Psychology,* 51 (1955), pp. 668–76.
** In 1967, Mr. Blake's sister gave me permission to use her brother's name and my experimental work with him as the material for a BBC documentary. The program was then entered into an international competition by the BBC and won the Italia Prize in 1968, for "excellence" in TV/radio documentaries.

in *any* area of life. Charlie was an unfortunate and pathetic example of a gross extreme in failure . . . he was a total loser.*

My goal was to reward the slightest sign of his trying . . . any movement he made around his face or mouth. I looked for a twitch of his nose or even a grunt or a burp so I could start the process of encouraging healthy behaviors with my positives.

I knew from the therapy I did with autistic children that change would be a struggle because it occurs slowly, in small steps . . . day by day . . . positive by positive.

When I worked with mute children, I had reinforced any mumbling or other sounds they made until I got healthier verbal behaviors to reward. Eventually I was able to shape normal speech.

THE CRUELEST PUNISHMENT

When Charlie was mute or bizarre in any way, I would turn my head away for ten seconds. I want to emphasize that this was the most negative or cruel punishment I ever gave Charlie . . . *ignoring* him. I never shouted or got angry, and I certainly never hit him or was unkind.

By the end of the thirty-first day of the experiment, Charlie was talking, reading newspapers and magazines aloud and answering my questions correctly more than 90 percent of the time. Powerful positives such as "Good, Mr. Blake," or "I like that sound you're making," were part of my *simple* armament of *powerful magical tools.*

THE POWER OF HONEST POSITIVES
REALLY IS MAGIC!

I have learned in my years as a therapist that large doses of genuine feelings of warmth and honest, positive reinforcement are uplifting. They create an atmosphere so rich in approval and acceptance that even a man who has been emotionally dead for thirty years can be motivated to listen, learn, work and change.

Just think what *you could accomplish* if you started putting positive reinforcements to work in *your* life! Whatever you want to happen: motivate your child to study, your spouse to be more affectionate, your boss to give you a raise, your parents and friends to appreciate you more . . . use your *honest, honest* positives to

* Irene C. Kassorla, "The Modification of Verbal Behaviour by Operant Conditioning in Chronic Schizophrenia: an Experimental Single-Case Study," Unpublished Doctoral Thesis, Senate House Library, University of London, 1968.

achieve it. Remember that "something beats nothing." Hunt down that "something" and reward it.

GIVE YOURSELF A KISS

Now that you're starting to look at the power that lies in using honest positives, I don't want you to overlook a wonderful person in your life who *needs your reinforcement and acceptance* in order to blossom and thrive.

THAT PERSON IS YOU.

Not only are honest positives miraculous tools for encouraging the behavior you desire in *other* people, but you can also use their power to help yourself in *your own* efforts to grow.

REINFORCEMENT BUILDS . . . PUNISHMENT
DESTROYS.

Remember that formula when you begin your self-criticism. Change occurs in a warm bath of approval, with *you being nice to you.* If you want to develop new behaviors or skills as quickly as possible, be very *self-reinforcing.* Some words I use to express this attitude comprise one of the most significant phrases in my work. I hope you will adopt this slogan:

GIVE YOURSELF A KISS.

It is particularly important to remember to kiss yourself when you fail or make a mistake. This is precisely the time for you to respect your past efforts and to believe that *trying deserves to be rewarded.* If you are going to be cruel to you, you will sabotage *your* own performance and progress.

Remember, negatives don't work . . . except to destroy motivation . . . positives do. Give them to yourself, and generously. And give yourself a kiss for the accomplishments you <u>are</u> able to achieve *before you make the error.* Here is an example you may be able to identify with:

> Give yourself a kiss when you pick up that first cigarette after you have already stopped smoking. Almost without realizing it, you accepted one from a friend. You were feeling badly because of a problem at work that was difficult to resolve. Before you knew what was happening, the lit cigarette was in your mouth, and you inhaled it to the very last drag.
>
> STOP REPRIMANDING YOURSELF.
> Remember that you were able to quit smoking once . . . it will be easier the second time. Give yourself a kiss for just *wanting* to stop

and for the long period of time that you didn't smoke . . . and as soon as you can, get back to abstaining. You did it before, and you will do it again.

When you know you have failed, it is tough to give yourself encouragement. BUT DO IT! Being negative is self-destructive, because it will kill your future motivation and inhibit your ability to change.

Suppose you want to start exercising. You are determined to become fit. You plan that tomorrow you are going to get up early and begin toning those flabby muscles.

When your alarm clock rings the next morning, however, you decide that you simply *must* sleep another ten minutes. Ten minutes later, you make the very same decision once again. And so on, until finally you barely have enough time to dash into the shower and rush to work.

Even if this pattern goes on for two weeks . . . don't become discouraged. For setting the alarm clock early the night before and trying to exercise . . .

GIVE YOURSELF A KISS.

Be patient and say, "Soon I will be able to get out there and jog." And you will, if you are *kind* to you. Making changes is difficult, but they will occur more quickly if you ignore your inappropriate behaviors, as I did Mr. Blake's, and stop scolding yourself so much. Remember:

REINFORCEMENT MAKES BEHAVIORS GROW, SO FOCUS ON YOUR HEALTHY, POSITIVE BEHAVIORS.

When you are trying something new, if at first you can do it only one out of every twenty trials, that's good! Reinforce yourself for the one time in twenty that you were successful. Then, keep going. If you encourage yourself, your success rate will increase and the incentive to keep trying and the motivation to learn new things will grow.

WELCOMING A BEATING

We all work at getting approval and recognition from the people who are important to us. They, in turn, need *our* attention and approval, too, and will work to get it as we do.

It is disarming to realize that most of us reinforce the very things in others that irritate us by giving those behaviors our attention.

Criticism and complaints are forms of attention, as are smiles and praise. They *all* have the power to influence behavior. While people claim they only want warmth and affection, when healthy positives are *not* forthcoming they will seek whatever attention they can find, even if it takes the form of physical punishment.

A study that I heard about as an undergraduate impresses me to this day. The scientists conducting the experiment were evaluating the effects of an absence of stimulation and human interaction on a group of normal men. The subjects of the study were totally isolated, lying down, in coffinlike chambers, and periodically were questioned about the content of their thoughts and desires. At first, all of them reported they felt comfortable. Some admitted they were quite content to be paid to rest and sleep; others shared enjoyable fantasies about happy events, food or sex.

But as the hours rolled by, complaints about physical discomfort, loneliness and isolation grew. Finally, toward the close of the study, each subject reported that his fantasies centered around hoping for stimulation of *any* kind. Many of them went so far as to say they would welcome being pushed or beaten, because they were so desperate for some kind of physical contact and attention.

Many parents who come into therapy complaining about their "naughty" children have said that they believe their youngsters are often "just asking for a spanking." It would be interesting to find out how frequently these parents hug and touch their children affectionately. If it is rare, being hit may be the only vehicle the child has to engage his parents in physical contact.

People will do what they can to gain the notice and recognition they are seeking . . . whatever the traffic will bear. If an abundance of reinforcement is offered for being talented, brilliant and dynamic, fine! That's what they'll work to become. But if the only way they can earn care and interest from their "significant others" is by being delinquent, bizarre or inappropriate . . . that is surely how they will behave.

WHO ARE YOU REINFORCING IN YOUR LIFE, AND FOR WHAT?

Too many of us live with people day after day, unconsciously giving most of our attention to the very behaviors that we *hate the most*. Parents tend to ignore or neglect their children when they are behaving nicely, and pay attention to their "squeakiest and naughtiest wheel." We are unaware that it is our *own* methods of giving positives or negatives that are actually responsible for *increasing* the very things that we are complaining about! Totally naive about our participation in creating our own unhappiness, we resent what we think has been inflicted upon us rather than accepting that we had a role in keeping the pain going.

The fat woman who grumbles that her husband is always bringing home ice cream doesn't know that the only time she smiles at him is when he has sweets in his hand for her. She is reinforcing him, unwittingly, for helping to keep her fat.

The husband who is annoyed that his wife is frigid because she has sex with him only infrequently has no idea that he rarely looks interested or tries to embrace her unless she is saying "No." He doesn't realize his embraces are very reinforcing . . . and to get him to hug her she needs to say "No."

WATCH OUT FOR THE SABOTEUR

Are you feeling guilty now, thinking to yourself, "OK, Kassorla, you've convinced me. I do it all backward! I beat my kids up verbally for hours at a time when they do their delinquent numbers, and I'm on the phone with my friends . . . ignoring them, when they're good. I guess that's the negative reinforcement you've been talking about. So now *I'm* the guilty saboteur! I admit it. I must have kept their awful behaviors going regularly with all the attention my nagging and lecturing gave them. I was only trying to help and teach them what's *right*. I never dreamed it would increase their mistakes!"

I *BELIEVE* YOU . . . SO STOP FEELING GUILTY.

Most of us tend to reverse the communications that would be healthy in our interpersonal relationships with the goal of doing what's *right* and *helpful*.

OUR INTENTIONS ARE GREAT . . . OUR
ACTIONS AREN'T!

Few of us deliver our positives *on the spot* when someone has pleased us or done something we like. We usually have convincing reasons: "I don't need to say anything. They *already know* how much I love and appreciate them. I don't have to *overdo* it."

NONSENSE! They *don't* know. TELL THEM. By withholding your rewards, the behaviors you adore may never surface again. Keep healthy behaviors alive and thriving with your positives. YOU CAN'T OVERDO IT.

When you discover *you are the saboteur* who has been setting up your problems, give yourself a kiss. Whenever you realize that you have handled a communication badly, failed a task or made a

mistake . . . this is precisely the time for you to respect yourself
for your efforts and trying. Believe in your own sincerity and
goodness. You *learned* to sabotage yourself, even though the entire
process was unconscious. Now you can *consciously learn to stop.*
Scolding yourself will serve as attention that will keep *your* unhealthy behaviors flourishing.

BE YOUR OWN KIND PARENT

In order to change now, you need a parent to help you. That
person must be nonjudgmental and very accepting. There is only
one person in the world qualified to take over that position.
THAT PERSON IS YOU.
You are perfect for the job. Enlist yourself.

Practice your winning skills with me now. Be your own kind
parent as you imagine that this is your problem: Let's suppose that
you've promised yourself to stop swearing. Although you've been
trying for about a year, you don't seem to be able to quit. Every
time you slip and use profanity, you become furious and mutter
abusively, "I feel so ridiculous. I can't believe I'm still so foul-
mouthed, after I've already said I'm *definitely* going to stop! I feel
like a darn fool because I haven't kept my word and quit this
stupid habit!"
STOP BEING SO MEAN TO YOU!
It is precisely this kind of cruel language that could keep you
swearing forever. Instead, bring in your kind parent . . . you
. . . for positives about your wise decision to stop. Changing well-
established speech patterns is difficult and takes time.

For hearing yourself use those four-letter words, and for wanting to work on controlling their frequency, *give yourself a kiss.* Say
to yourself enthusiastically, "I'm going to stop using profanity as
soon as I can. Now, let me see how I can change that sentence and
restate what I've just said the way I'd prefer."

Don't waste your efforts with reprimands. Instead, concentrate
on rephrasing the sentence . . . say it again without the obscen-
ities . . . practice whether you are with someone else or alone.

This procedure of rewording your speech after you've made the
error can be seen with top-seeded tennis players. Often after they
have made a losing shot, they will recreate the moment and swing
correctly at the nonexistent ball.

When you can stop an old habit, your friends and family will
eventually notice. They'll probably secretly admire your ability to

change, but they may not openly compliment you. While their thoughts about you may well be very positive, they may not have that kind of supportive verbal skill.

So it is very important that *you* make the effort to reinforce *yourself.* Praise yourself out loud. When you hear yourself use profanity, correct it. Then put a smile on your face, give yourself a kiss and say something like "Good for me! I'm so glad I caught that swear word. I'm going to stop . . . because I'm sure working on it!"

Beating yourself into the ground for making errors won't result in change; being positive will.

> I have an everyday religion that works for me: Love yourself first and everything else falls into line. You really have to love yourself to get anything done in this world.
>
> —LUCILLE BALL

Using my philosophy of how to change, you can substitute overeating, overdrinking . . . or whatever old pattern you want to get rid of . . . or modify. Just remember to reinforce yourself with kisses when you become aware and can SEE yourself in action. You have to SEE the duck to shoot it, and you have to SEE the behavior to change it.

When you are kinder to you, others will pick up this pattern, too. After a while, they will imitate your behavior and offer reinforcements to you themselves. By reprogramming yourself to be more tender with you, before you know it, your old habits will vanish from your repertoire altogether.

EXPERIENCE MORE CONFIDENCE.

As you receive your own kisses, your feelings of love and self-respect will grow. Within this emotional framework of appreciating your own efforts and treating yourself as a dignified person, you will unconsciously learn to be more loving and respectful to others, as well.

Here is some homework for you to practice as part of your healthy reprogramming procedures. Repeat these formulas every day:

REINFORCE YOURSELF FOR EVEN YOUR
SMALLEST EFFORTS.
USE AN ABUNDANCE OF POSITIVES.
GIVE POSITIVES TO YOURSELF AND OTHERS.
HONEST POSITIVES=SUCCESS=WINNING!

WINNER SCORECARD #8

In this chapter, we have explored principles you can use to influence the behavior of others positively or to help yourself grow and change. The following points will sharpen your understanding of how to set off this "storehouse" of personal power.

LOSERS	WINNERS
1. Losers ignore the positive behaviors of others and pounce on them for the things they find irritating. The changes they are seeking seldom occur, because they tend to punish signs of healthy behavior when they surface, by ignoring them.	**1.** Winners deliver honest positives "on the spot" when someone says or does something they value. They reinforce others for the slightest show of effort in the direction they want. They understand that progress proceeds In tiny increments and increases slowly, positive by positive.
2. Losers attach a hidden put-down to their rare compliments by reminding others of every mistake they've ever made in the past. Their remarks result in the recipient feeling cheated and becoming angry and immobilized.	**2.** Winners motivate others by delivering positives that are honest and rewarding, without negative additives. They talk about what is happening in the present, reinforcing *today's appropriate* behaviors with warmth and kindness.
3. Losers berate themselves when they're slow to learn or change. They discourage themselves and kill their own motivation with negatives like "I'm making a fool of myself!" or "I really look stupid taking so long to do that!"	**3.** Winners make learning and changing easier by giving themselves positive reinforcements each step of the way. They deliver praise to themselves for trying and accomplishing even the smallest thing they do that takes them in the general direction of their goals.

LOSERS	WINNERS

4. Losers reinforce the very behaviors in others they dislike the most by giving them negative attention, which *increases* these behaviors! They do this by scolding, nagging, complaining or physical punishment.

4. Winners tend to ignore the behaviors they don't like. They tell others briefly and warmly what they want and focus on offering enthusiastic encouragement and help for the slightest evidence of *positive* behaviors.

5. Losers have difficulty changing because they get discouraged counting up all their failures. Their style is to focus on errors, instead of their strengths. They are afraid to take a chance and try, because there is so much self-punishment for mistakes.

5. When winners make a mistake, they reinforce themselves for *trying* and being willing to *see* what went wrong. Acknowledging themselves for things that were accomplished before their error, rather than focusing on mistakes, they immerse themselves in a warm bath of their own positives for efforts expended.

CHAPTER 9

Are You a Motivation Killer?

If you hear a song that thrills you,
  Sung by any child of song,
Praise it. Do not let the singer
  Wait deserved praises long.
Why should one who thrills your heart
Lack the joy you may impart?
  —DANIEL WEBSTER HOYT

What is a motivation killer and how do you know one when you see one? Are you one of these killers?

Are motivation killers aware of their behaviors? Do they wake up in the morning planning to make emotional mincemeat of their children, spouses, families, or employees?

Of course not!

Motivation killers are well-meaning people. Like you and me, they have no idea that they are insulting or hurting others. In fact, their conscious goal is probably to do the reverse.

As they see it, they are just trying to communicate and get the job done. They may even believe they are *helping* or encouraging the person whose ego they are mangling. They have no idea this is occurring, or that they are snuffing out the very behaviors in others they are seeking.

I call motivation killers "perennial losers," because they are so blind to the consequences of their actions . . . and they can't get the help they need from others.

If you want to be a winner, you can't "go it alone." On your way to achieving your goals, whether personal or professional, you will need to enlist the help of other people.

In the last chapter, I introduced you to a powerful tool, positive reinforcement. When used generously and honestly, it can help to motivate the behaviors you desire in other people. In these pages, we'll look at another aspect of how motivation works. You will begin to understand the ways in which you may be unwittingly *undermining* the willingness of other people to offer you assistance or do as you ask. Once you SEE this, you can start eliminating your motivation-killing behaviors from your own repertoire.

DOING IT IN REVERSE

In trying to get others to do what they want, many people use harsh negatives, continual nagging and punishments. Much of the time, such intense negativism produces precisely the opposite of the results they desire. Still, with loving hearts and the best of intentions, people all over the world continue to employ ineffective and punishing techniques in their attempts to influence and motivate others.

As I have already described, in my work with psychotics, the most severe punishment I ever delivered was ignoring them when they behaved inappropriately.

I want to stress here that *any* kind of punishment can be very destructive unless it is given in very small doses, surrounded by huge amounts of positive reinforcements.

When I was a student at UCLA, a scientist from the Rand Corporation observed my work with autistic children. He carefully counted exactly how many times I gave positive reinforcement (smiles, praise, food or affection) to a mute autistic child, and how many times I delivered negative reinforcement (the punishment of turning my head away and ignoring the child). The count came to at least 150 positives to only five negatives in a one-hour session . . . and each one learned how to speak.

I've done a lot of work with teenage delinquents, and it's my observation . . . which has also been noted by many other therapists . . . that their parents tend to be extremely negative toward them. If you were to watch the way they interact, you would probably find that they reverse my ratio and deliver perhaps 150 *negatives* to five or fewer positives. Faced with constant criticism and complaining, these youngsters soon start to feel that they "just can't win." The destructive results are revealed in the high incidence of delinquency that exists in children whose parents are emotionally (and/or physically) critical and punitive.

DESTROYING INDIVIDUAL INCENTIVE

Using negatives . . . on yourself or others . . . won't get you the behaviors you're looking for. What it will get you is a multitude of new problems, which could include depression, rebellion and delinquency.

When complaints and criticism mount too high, they can push the receiver into a depression that will lower his activity level. Negatives can be so debilitating that they absorb most of an individual's vitality and incentive to keep trying, to work and to enter into life. When motivation is low, the person's unconscious reasoning may sound like this: "It doesn't pay for me to make a move and get punished. Whatever I do or say is wrong . . . it's always too much or too little . . . it seems I can never please anyone. It just makes more sense for me to sit here and do nothing. The less I do, the less reason they will have to punish me."

A severe, controlling, overly punitive environment can also result in physical problems such as asthma, colitis, ulcers, headaches, backaches, acne, hemorrhoids, viruses and excessive fatigue. In therapy, even the common cold is a symptom whose genesis can often be traced to hidden anger caused by people at work or in your family. This can be seen in parent-child interactions when rigorous emotional restraints, negatives, guilt and harsh discipline are used as motivators. Finally, the frightened child's body cries out a message of pain . . . hoping the punishments will stop.

Too many families ignore old sayings like "You can catch more flies with honey. . . ." Instead, they drench each other, and themselves, in emotional vinegar.

WHAT ABOUT YOU?
DO YOU CRITICIZE, NAG AND COMPLAIN?

And do you sometimes feel unsupported or unloved because a spouse, child or friend is reluctant to give you help when you ask for it? If your answer is "yes," it may be useful to examine how you handle your requests when you want something done.

If what you ask for isn't taken care of immediately, do you keep criticizing, nagging and complaining? You may believe this will get you the help you are seeking. Nonsense . . . the opposite will occur!

YOU WILL *KILL* MOTIVATION!

Haranguing and needling each other is a familiar way of communicating for many families, even though this is *counterproductive* and usually ends up in fighting, not cooperation. Negatives and punishment rarely move anyone into action . . . or get the desired results.

Nothing exists from whose nature some effect does not follow.

—SPINOZA

When you are negative, other people will be less likely to come forward to assist you. If you want to encourage others to help you, remember to use honest positives as your fuel. Here's an example:

If you ask someone for help, and he grudgingly gives you a quick ten minutes when what you are looking for is *three hours* of assistance, reinforce him for the ten minutes that he *does* give you. Use warm, sincere positives like "I really appreciate your help." If you can do this, it is likely that he will leave with good feelings about you and himself. This will encourage him to help you again. The next time, you'll probably get a bit more . . . perhaps only fifteen minutes . . . but *more.* If you continue with your reinforcements, the fifteen minutes will multiply and eventually you'll have the three hours you were originally looking for. And as a bonus, there will be a happy worker at your side.

When you punish and complain, what you will get is too little help and too much rebellion and sabotage. Use positives; they can be powerful motivators, shaping the responses you want and stimulating healthy behaviors to grow.

NEGATIVES DON'T WORK.
POSITIVES DO.

We all do a lot of motivation killing. Because it is an unconscious process, we are rarely aware of the deadly effect our words can have on people.

It is clear to us when *other* people's remarks are killer messages. When they are directed at us, we can feel it . . . in our stomachs. The emotional experience of being the target of harsh negative words is much like a physical blow.

But when *we are the ones* who unwittingly deliver the destructive messages, it's difficult for us to understand why we continue to meet with so much resistance and failure to perform. We don't realize that it is our cutting criticism and castigating judgments that crush the fragile egos of those around us.

Most parents want to raise their children properly, and to advise and guide them as they grow up. It's a difficult task they face, attempting to transform their mewling and puking infant into their dream of a Harvard business school graduate. Their objective is to carry out the difficult task of socializing their child as efficiently as possible. Because they are so eager to do a good job, along the way they usually use *too much punishment* and *too many negatives.* Instead of achieving the hoped-for results, these techniques only serve to convince their impressionable youngster that he is inadequate, worthless and ugly.

Most people understand from their own experience that giving and receiving positive communications is a powerful and extremely uplifting interaction. Yet they move into the loser's corner by using negatives to punish themselves and those they love the most. With demeaning glances, annoyed sighs, ugly, harsh words and even physical punishment they attempt to get their spouses and children to change and do what they want.

TREATED LIKE A DOG

Parents seldom realize that verbal and physical punishments can have long-term damaging effects on a child's motivation in future life. Over the years, I have used hypnosis with some of my patients, and many of them have recounted traumatic childhood incidents. Some of their memories have been almost too painful for me to hear.

While under hypnosis, one of my patients, Stuart, sobbed as he recalled parts of his pathetic early history:

"As soon as my mom would get home from work, she would start hitting me or yelling with that horrible expression on her face. I never really understood what I had done wrong. I just knew that my body was shaking and my heart was thumping right out of my chest. Whenever she beat me, I was afraid that one day she'd go out of her mind completely and kill me.

"Once, when I was only five years old, she beat me because I accidentally spilled hot soup all over my pants. I can still hear her screaming at me because I had wasted food. She didn't even care that I burned myself. She said I was so stupid that I deserved to be treated like a dog, and made me sleep outside on the doorstep all night. I was so scared. I remember crying and feeling like I really *was* a dog."

More than twenty years later, Stuart was harming himself the way his mother had told him he *deserved* to be treated. He seldom worked, so he couldn't support himself; at twenty-nine, he was still living with his parents and extremely dependent upon them. When he did earn a little money, he compulsively gambled it away. He had few friends because, like his parental models, he was too caustic. He harmed himself even more by destroying his health with a combination of alcoholism and obesity. Stuart was still being treated like a dog, but now *he* was the one who was delivering the punishment and brutality.

Painful daily interactions during our earliest years can become so deeply embedded in our unconscious minds that without our awareness, they are incorporated into our adult behaviors. When he was still very small, Stuart's parents had convinced him, with their complaints and extreme emotional and physical cruelty, that he was "no good." According to them, almost every move he made was wrong. Immobilizing himself and *not doing anything* brought Stuart the least amount of punishment.

Now that Stuart was grown, his parents called him "worthless," and his closest friend said he was a "lazy bum." He told me that he dreaded getting up in the morning because his bed was his one "safe haven." It was only when he was sleeping that no one would humiliate or demean him.

Stuart's case history illustrates motivation killing in the extreme. He never heard a kind or supportive word as a child . . . or as an adult. With this constant negative feedback and assurances of how useless he was, his parents had convinced him that he was worthless. Finally, Stuart believed there was nowhere for him to go . . . except down.

THE KILLER BOSS

Are *you* a motivation killer?

Whether you are raising children or dealing with friends or business associates, you need to listen for the verbal abuse that you may unconsciously be delivering. You can't be a winner in life . . . whether you are at home or in the business arena . . . if you are killing the motivation of others. The love and caring concern of your family is essential to your emotional well-being; and the loyalty, cooperation and help of your colleagues and employees will enhance your economic growth. Destroying these behaviors in others will leave you alone and struggling . . . forced to "go it alone." This is how Bud, the motivation-killing boss, behaved with Lana, a very dependable and effective employee.

Lana was a highly ambitious employee at an educational consulting firm in San Francisco. She was cheerful and hard-working. She always did her best because she was eager to advance, and she enjoyed receiving the approval her efforts brought her.

Lana usually jumped out of bed in the morning before the alarm went off. She loved her job so much that she couldn't wait to get to the office. She would arrive early and often stayed overtime without being paid extra. Even on weekends, she was frequently at her desk planning new projects for her department.

The picture changed dramatically, soon after Bud took over as department head and became Lana's new boss. She started coming in late almost every morning and began taking two-hour lunches. Each afternoon, Lana would dash out of the office at exactly five o'clock as though the building were on fire.

This profound change in Lana's behavior occurred because Bud had unwittingly killed her motivation to work.

His destructive approach was vividly apparent when Lana was assigned to visit one of the firm's clients, a government agency in Washington, D.C. Six months earlier, this client had cut back on half of its contracts. Lana was given the difficult task of reestablishing rapport with the agency's very hostile management.

On her trip East, Lana was very effective. She was not only able to save the old business the agency had previously cancelled, but she stimulated so much *new* interest that they tripled their contracts for the coming season! Lana felt she had created a miracle!

She was so proud of her accomplishments that on her first morning back home she reverted to her old style and rushed into work early.

The minute she arrived, she burst into Bud's office wearing an enormous smile. "I did it!" she exclaimed. "Wait until you hear the *wonderful* news!"

Bud looked up from his paperwork, frowning. "What's all the excitement? You startled me by dashing into my office without knocking."

"I have orders for almost *three times as much business* as we had before!" Lana was bubbling with enthusiasm. "Isn't that sensational?"

Bud responded angrily, "Those darn fools in Washington *should* be reordering from us. They're just proving that their judgment was stupid when they cancelled in the first place."

Lana felt as though her boss had struck her with a sledge-hammer. She was stunned by his insensitivity and his inability to acknowledge her obvious victory. Although she was feeling discouraged, she tried to hide her feelings and went on, "They were so *thrilled* with me! They were pleased that I knew so much about the needs of their operation. They even took me out to dinner. Imagine! I was so happy, I could hardly believe it was all happening!"

Bud still seemed unimpressed. "You're going to be impossible to work with now," he said. "You'll need to go out and buy a bigger hat. Anyway, my dear, you only did precisely what you were hired to do—increase business."

Lana left her boss's office on the verge of tears. At lunch with a friend later, she lamented, "I don't understand that man. He doesn't appreciate anything! I can't believe he wasn't excited! I saved an important account from completely going under!"

Bud *was* a real motivation killer.

He had been given an ideal opportunity to reward Lana's excellent selling achievements with some well-deserved reinforcement . . . a kind word, a smile, a pat on the back, the gift of a day off. She had certainly earned it. Instead, because he was so unaware of her feelings and so unskilled at delivering positives, he had destroyed every ounce of Lana's motivation and loyalty to the company.

Three weeks later, Lana abruptly resigned. Because of Bud's motivation killing and inability to give credit and appreciation, his company lost an ambitious, talented employee.

SQUELCHING THE HELPER

Marriage partners frequently destroy each other's motivation, too. While both husband and wife may be complaining that they are neither appreciated nor understood, they are usually unaware of their *own* participation in reducing the other's incentive to be warm and supportive to them.

One of my patients, Nancy, was often irritated with her husband. "My lazy old man will never pitch in with the household problems," she would complain. "And he never gives me a hand with our four daughters."

I always felt very sympathetic with Nancy's list of grievances, until I met her husband, Mark. Once he came into therapy, it became clear to me why he rarely helped her. I first observed the painful and unproductive way they interacted when there was a problem with their oldest daughter, Kelly, who came home from school one afternoon with a note from the nurse. It said her vision had been tested and seemed to be blurred. The nurse recommended that she have her eyes checked right away.

Concerned about Kelly, Nancy wanted to get her to a specialist the very next day. But she was so swamped at home that she asked Mark to help her find a good ophthalmologist. He said he would be happy to do it.

When he got home from work that night, he looked pleased. "I found out that my union will pay 50 percent of the eye doctor's bill!"

Nancy looked up from the sink and shouted angrily, "I didn't ask you to find out about financing! I asked you to find a reputable specialist! Why are you talking about your union? I'm not interested in that now!"

Nancy's response was what a loser who *didn't want help* would say. When winners want to motivate someone to help, they look for the smallest response to reinforce. Using winning skills, Nancy would have rewarded Mark's eagerness and interest with, "Great! I'm glad to hear that. That will be useful when we find the right doctor. At least it's a relief to know we'll only have to come up with 50 percent of the charges."

Mark's comment that he had found a way to pay for half of the doctor's bill was a step in the right direction . . . it moved the couple closer to their goal of taking care of Kelly's eyes. But Nancy was a motivation killer and didn't know how to encourage Mark.

SOMETHING BEATS NOTHING

Looking at the behavior patterns of people who know how to enlist others' help, it is easy to see great differences. At every opportunity they reinforce *anything* that even *approaches* what they are seeking.

Remember the positives that I gave Charlie Blake at first for his burping and grunting? Those noises were a long way from talking, but they *were* in the "general vicinity" of speech . . . sounds were coming out of his mouth. He hadn't spoken in thirty years, so I was grateful to hear *anything* from his voicebox. I believed that if I reinforced these noises he would be motivated to keep working.

This could *move him in the right direction toward speech* . . . and it did!

In your life, if you will reinforce other people's responses whenever they come <u>close</u> to what you want, you will be motivating them into action. Gradually their responses will move closer to your target. With your continued support, they will finally hit the bull's eye, and you'll get exactly what you originally wanted.

Moving toward your goal this way is analogous to climbing a mountain. A goal can be attained by taking many tiny, but necessary, steps along the way. Progress sometimes comes in increments so small as to be almost unnoticeable . . . pebble by pebble . . . step by step.

Let's say you want to get to the top of a mile-high mountain. If someone can help you climb a few hundred feet up at some point of the incline . . . that's good . . . it will be helpful. Grab their assistance and reward it. Remember, *something beats nothing,* and any kind of support will move you closer to the summit.

Here's a graph of what climbing to your goal would look like:

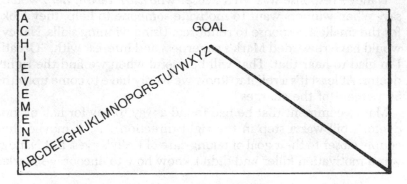

Figure 3: Climbing to your goal by accomplishing tasks A through Z.

In Nancy and Mark's case, Nancy wanted to take care of their daughter's eye problem (symbolized by the letter "Z" at the top of the mountain). En route to this goal were several other steps, represented by each of the letters of the alphabet. For example, Step "A" could have been getting a referral for a competent eye specialist; Step "B" could have been checking the doctor's credentials and background; Step "C" could have been calling to make an appointment; and Step "M" could have been paying the bill. Numerous steps followed on the way to "Z," at which point all of the steps leading up to the top of the mountain . . . all of the problem solving that had to be done . . . was completed.

Nancy didn't realize that the order in which she received help was not important. When you need to deal with and complete twenty-six steps to finish a job, receiving help with step "R" or "T" is just as valuable as getting help with "B" or "E." Completing each step eliminates one of your twenty-six problems and moves you closer to the top.

When losers ask for help, they reinforce only what in their view is the "perfect" solution. Criticizing anything that falls short of their precise request, they punish the helper unless the answer they hear is exactly on target . . . as they see it. When someone who is helping receives too many negatives or suffers by being viciously attacked for his efforts, he is reluctant to volunteer to be supportive again.

Mark was so hurt and discouraged by Nancy's barrage of insults that he didn't even tell her that he had a recommendation for a well-known eye specialist as well. Instead, he stormed out of the room, shouting, "You beat down everything I do. I hate trying to help you. It always leads to a fight. Do it yourself, baby! I'm sick of trying my best and always ending up the bad guy."

By punishing Mark's initial efforts, Nancy had squelched his motivation altogether. Her critical comments insured that she would get no further assistance from Mark.

STIFLING THE SPEAKER

In many marriages, the partners unconsciously trample on each other's spirits so completely that one or both of them becomes depressed or immobilized. In other relationships, being too negative can reduce the frequency of a particular behavior . . . or kill it almost completely. This was the case with Judy and Alex.

Judy was unaware that she was a motivation killer who had virtually silenced her husband, Alex. They were both in their early thirties and had been married for six years. For the first three, they were very much in love and had enjoyed wonderful times together. After that, Alex became increasingly discontent and was considering divorce.

Before therapy, Alex had no idea that he had fallen in love with someone very similar to his mother, who talked constantly. Though he didn't realize it when they first married, Judy always dominated the conversation, whether they were alone or with friends.

Alex complained that he could "never get a word in edgewise. "Whenever I do attempt to join in the conversation, Judy makes it difficult for me to speak," he said. "She raises her voice and drowns out my words with her steamrolling conversational style."

Alex claimed that Judy also killed his motivation to talk by interrupting him . . . correcting what he said . . . and improving on his stories or jokes. If he ever suggested that the best direction was "south," Judy assured him that "north" was the only way to go. If he mentioned "up" as a route to explore, his resident motivation killer contradicted him quickly with "down." A typical verbal exchange in their home sounded like this:

ALEX: Pete is looking for a new car, and I advised him to buy a station wagon like ours.

JUDY: A station wagon! A small gas-saving car would be a lot more practical for their limited budget.

ALEX: Pete said his parents were going to give him around $4,000 to help him finance the station wagon.

JUDY: No, honey, you're way off. Pete said it was going to be $3,000.

Then Judy would pat Alex affectionately, smile and say, "Can't you get anything right?"

No wonder Alex kept silent!

He found Judy's attitude toward him not only hurtful, but confusing. When he sat quietly, she complained, "Why don't you speak up more? You're so dead! Sometimes I wonder whether you're here or not!"

If company had come over for the evening, Judy's going-to-bed conversations would include, "Why were you so wooden in front of our friends?" But when he did voice his thoughts at a social gathering, she stopped him and cut him off with a correction or comment like, "You're wrong, honey, it was . . ."

Judy *adored* Alex and didn't realize that she admonished him after almost every word he spoke. She wasn't aware that she found fault with whatever he discussed or that she made it difficult for him to complete a thought without interference from her. She didn't understand that, worst of all, she made a fool of him in public by acting like a mother who was forever scolding her small child.

Being corrected by your mate at home is painful enough, but

when it happens in front of others, it can also be very embarrassing. If you love and trust your spouse, you tend to believe that what he or she says is probably wiser and more accurate than the ideas you have to offer. So when your mate contradicts you, you wonder if what you said was foolish or worthless. Feeling unsure, the motivation is to stop, retreat and become mute.

Alex often abdicated and let Judy have the floor because he was afraid to start a fight or challenge her. By remaining quiet, he prevented Judy from hurting him with her carping critiques. But the penalty was high: Alex failed to develop into a mature, involved person who could participate in adult conversations.

* * *

These case histories illustrate various ways people can unconsciously kill the motivations of the important people in their lives. You may be able to learn from these examples by paying attention to what you say and striving to eliminate the nagging, complaining and criticism from your *own* exchanges with others. When you can understand how negatives kill motivation, you will be successful in getting more of what you want.

In addition, however, *it is just as important* to learn how to respond effectively when *you* are the *target* of a motivation killer. With the winning skills you're learning about, you can start to limit the killer messages you receive and turn the interaction toward a more positive and productive outcome. In each of the cases that I've just described, if the person who was on the receiving end of the killer messages had handled the situation differently, he or she could have come out a winner.

GETTING ALONG WITH A "BELLIGERENT BUD"

Let's go back to the story of Lana who tripled her company's business and was rewarded with frowns and angry words by her boss, Bud. Have you ever had an experience like Lana's? Do you live with or work for a motivation killer like Bud? Do you feel that your contributions are unappreciated and you are discounted as a person?

If you face such a problem at work, it may be too difficult for you to just get up and leave. Unless you can seek other employment, as

Lana did, you will need to learn how to get along with your own "belligerent Bud."

Here's how Lana could have done it. No matter how excited she felt, it *was* disrespectful of her to rush into Bud's office without knocking on the door the morning she returned from Washington. It may have frightened him when Lana came bursting in. And when Bud said he was startled, Lana ignored his comment and kept talking about herself. She might have entirely avoided Bud's negative attitude, or at least softened it, had she acknowledged his complaint with a warm response. She could have said, "You're right, Bud. I *did* almost break down your door. That was inconsiderate of me. But I was so happy, I forgot my manners."

In most personal interactions, you need to be thoughtful of other people and include them in your discussions. When you talk only about yourself, and aren't interested in them, you may provoke feelings of inadequacy and hostility. Lana's entire delivery was "I . . . I . . . I," which probably made Bud feel slighted and unimportant.

Often a motivation killer may act as he does because he feels left out, overlooked or ignored. As a new employee in the huge firm, Bud may have been experiencing many self-doubts and anxieties about his ability to step into a managerial position and do a good job. If Lana had been more aware of his concerns, she wouldn't have been so insensitive, and could have included him more in the conversation.

Once she realized that Bud was annoyed with her, she could have cleared the air by delivering some honest positives: "Thanks to your trust in me (honest positive #1), and your willingness to place such an important account in my hands (honest positive #2), I was able to get almost three times as much business as we had before! The advice you gave us at the last sales meeting about handling sluggish accounts really worked (honest positive #3)!"

When Bud persisted in his killer talk, by telling Lana she would need to buy a bigger hat, she could still have reversed the mood by using even more warm, honest positives: "Well, if you keep giving us all that great advice in our sales seminars, I hope I'll be bringing in more business! Then I *will* have to go out and buy that bigger hat!"

By including Bud in her victory and adding her honest positives about him, Lana could have turned her motivation-killing boss into a supportive friend. That would have been a *giant win!*

A SOOTHING RESPONSE

Let's look at the situation between Nancy and Mark, the married couple who were worried about their daughter's vision problem. Nancy, by being overly critical of Mark, had put herself in the foolish position of having to handle all the problems alone.

But Mark had acted like a loser, too! He didn't have the winning skills to communicate more effectively with Nancy. Shouting back at her and walking out solved nothing. Both of them acted like losers spending their energies seething with anger and blaming the other . . . rather than joining forces to help their daughter.

I want to replay the scene now, so you can see how Mark *might* have dealt with Nancy's "killer comments." Let's go back to that night when he came home from work with the information that his union would pay half of the doctor's bill.

Immediately after Nancy blew up and criticized him, Mark might have realized she was overreacting because she was frightened. The night before, he and Nancy had stayed up talking until very late. Then in the morning Nancy explained she had been too worried to sleep. She had expressed her apprehension that her daughter's problem might be a brain tumor or some other serious condition.

In my group therapy sessions, sometimes patients will suddenly explode with anger as they are speaking . . . with what seems to be very little cause. Their behavior appears to be highly inappropriate. The basis for their overreaction is often an unexpressed fear that has built up over time. Nancy's outburst was probably just such a fear reaction. If Mark had remembered that she hadn't slept and was probably worried about a tumor, he could have soothed her with a more gentle response, like "Honey, you sound frightened, and I am, too. But Kelly may only have a minor problem. Perhaps she just needs glasses. Whatever happens, the money from the union will be a big help. Besides, I was able to get a specialist's name, too."

By answering in this way, they both could have ended up winners, working together on effectively finding solutions to their problems. And Nancy would have felt happy and supported, with a competent doctor's name in hand, and money available to pay the bills.

STOPPING THE STEAMROLLER

Let's take another look now and see how Alex and Judy could have used more winning skills and been more effective in dealing with their problems. You will remember that Alex felt that Judy had rendered him virtually silent by her interruptions and corrections.

Judy didn't realize that she was unconsciously reinforcing her husband's passivity . . . that it was *her* criticism that helped to keep him frozen and withdrawn.

But what about Alex? He was a loser when he didn't assume the responsibility to take care of himself and speak up. He *wasn't* a child, and Judy *wasn't* his mother. It wasn't fair to blame the entire problem on her.

Alex could have used some *positive* winning skills. For example, he could have initiated discussions with Judy when they were alone at home telling her that he believed she loved him, as he did her . . . and that she would never knowingly insult or embarrass him. He could have added that he knew how *good* her intentions were, but her corrections and comments were difficult to receive. Often, he was so afraid of being judged, that he wouldn't speak. He could have asked Judy to cooperate with him on the problem: He would work on speaking up more . . . and she could work on not interrupting or correcting. Whenever she did, Alex could warmly limit her with "I'm not finished yet, love." This could act as a reminder to help her from taking over.

Alex could have been more of a winner in many of their interactions: In the conversation about the car, for example, Alex didn't have to accept Judy's comments as gospel. He might have acknowledged her remarks without anger, and with a pleasant attitude and still asserted his own opinions. He could have said, "Honey, I certainly think you're right about a gas saver, but with Pete's two dogs and three children, he needs more space. A small station wagon would both save gas and give him plenty of room."

When Judy patted Alex and asked, "Can't you get anything right?" she wasn't aware that she was condescending and insulting. Alex needed to let her know. In an easy, conversational tone his reply might have been, "Judy, I think you're trying to be helpful by correcting an error I made with a number. I don't mind that, honey, but I feel inadequate when you suggest that I *never* get anything right. I don't think you meant your comment to mean that or to be so strong . . . did you, honey?"

When you are speaking up for yourself, it is important to be warm and good-humored with the other person, because he or she usually has no idea he has been insensitive and wounded you. Typically the other person is just trying to earn *your* approval by sounding bright and helpful. Knowing this, each time Judy interrupted, Alex could have smiled and touched her arm softly as he stopped her, then picked up where he had left off and gone on.

Alex had to learn in therapy that it was his *job* to "get his word in edgewise." He needed to take action. Calling Judy a "steamroller" didn't solve his problems or make him more verbal.

In our work together, he practiced developing several *action* skills: speaking up and presenting his ideas, however divergent from Judy's; gently reminding her when she was intruding on his conversations; and being more aware of how little he spoke.

Before coming into therapy, Alex wanted a divorce. He had been so unhappy about being what he called a "second-class citizen" in his marriage that he had discussed a trial separation. Counseling was a final effort toward reconciliation. Once he understood that *he shared 50 percent of the responsibility* for the problems in the marriage and that it was up to *him* to make himself a first-class citizen, he stopped blaming Judy and started working on talking more.

That's what winners do in their marriages: They accept 50 percent of the responsibility for interactions that are unrewarding or painful and 50 percent of the credit for the joyous moments, as well.

BLAMING IS A LOSER'S GAME

Do you find that too often in your daily conversations you fight and argue, making the other person feel guilty and defensive? Have you noticed that in your verbal messages with the important others in your life that you get bogged down with issues of "right and wrong" or "blame and guilt"?

Blaming is a particular form of negativity that can be very destructive in reducing motivation. Getting bogged down in arguments about who's at fault is a loser trait and a motivation killer.

Sometimes a member of your family or an employee may neglect to do what you have requested. Let's imagine that such a problem has developed between you and your secretary, Lil.

Returning from a business trip, you ask Lil to type a letter to the president of a company, someone you met on the plane. When several weeks pass and he doesn't reply, you become impatient and a bit concerned.

You ask Lil when she sent the letter. Looking surprised and annoyed, she responds, "You didn't tell me to write to anyone! You were just worried about getting those new orders out in time, remember? You *didn't say a word* about a letter to a man who was on the plane!"

At this point, if you're functioning like a loser, you start arguing with Lil, determined to give her every small detail that proves you are RIGHT and she is WRONG. "Are you kidding?" you demand. "I put it in my memo to you the minute I got back. Don't you remember . . . I mentioned it to you when we were standing at the water cooler? Anyway, I have proof! One of the other secretaries was standing there right beside us!"

THIS WOULD MAKE YOU RIGHT!

You begin acting like a district attorney and arguing that you have a substantial case for the prosecution: recorded notes, evidence, the precise scene of the crime and witnesses. As you are playing D.A., your secretary is thinking how much she hates you and how soon she can quit!

What will you accomplish by proving that Lil is wrong and you are right? It will only cause her to become preoccupied with resentment. When this happens she will be too busy with angry feelings to have time to be motivated to help you. Then you will never get your letter out!

WHO DONE IT?

Losers become entangled in endless arguments and debates about "who done it?" They waste their energies playing master sleuths and following up every clue that sustains their position in a disagreement.

THIS TAKES TOO MUCH TIME.

And it neither corrects the problem nor finishes the job!

If you get caught up in "who done it?" or the various blaming arguments, other people's eagerness to help you will diminish. When people feel that they have to start putting energy into self-protection or counterattacks . . . work ceases. Negative feelings snowball; one ugly emotion builds on another. All that gets produced under such aversive conditions are wounded egos, anxiety and distress.

Winners adopt an alternative that is healthier, more creative and more advantageous in terms of solving problems. Rather than wasting time discussing the details of what *"you* did wrong yesterday," they cooperate with the members of their team in getting the job done *today*.

It is precisely when you are in the eye of the conflict that you need to assume the responsibility. At the moment when Lil responded, "You didn't tell me," you could have moved her out of the defensive position in which she had to justify every step of her behavior. Then she would have been able to get the job of typing the letter done.

A winner would stop the controversy by saying in a friendly tone, "I'm concerned I didn't handle this well, Lil, or make myself clear. I did want to ask you to do this letter for me. Apparently my message was confusing." Then, as a winner, you could go right to the task and outline in detail what you want her to do *now*.

PROVING AND ARGUING WHO'S RIGHT
TAKES TIME!

When you want to stimulate action and enthusiasm, it's important to promote harmony and positive feelings. When you can develop a setting filled with caring and camaraderie, you will generate loyalty and dependability among your co-workers or family members. In such an atmosphere, motivation and creativity flourish.

PEOPLE WILL WANT TO PITCH IN AND HELP.

When good feelings are high and resentments are low, it is easier to get the job done. To maintain personal harmony, winners pick up the emotional tab when there are disagreements. Petty emotional jousting is just too costly . . . and probably 50 percent of the time you *did* make the error!

THE EMOTIONAL "CHICKEN OR THE EGG"

Many of my patients enter therapy because they want to improve their marriages. In fact, some people have called me "The Marriage Saver," a label which I value.

In most cases, in a couple's therapy when there is a conflict, I find that each partner feels he or she is right and innocent. Each believes the other is the source of all their grievances and sorrows.

STOP YOUR BLAMING!

I have worked with thousands of couples, and whenever there are problems, I invariably discover that *each one* of the partners is responsible for creating 50 percent of the mess. I never find one "good guy" and one "bad guy."

This is probably true in your life, too. If you are convinced that your spouse or someone else important to you is continually hurting your feelings or is repeatedly doing something that you hate . . . IT'S NO ACCIDENT! Believe it or not, somehow you are actively involved in helping to set up the pain in every one of these interactions.

You could spend years talking about which came first . . . the emotional version of the chicken or the egg. You could argue about whether it was you who wounded him first or he who slighted you initially.

What's the difference? In a few years, after the tears subside, the lawyers are paid and the children's splattered egos repaired . . . you may not even remember who was responsible for the breakup of your relationship.

But I don't want you to think about an "ex" or your present mate right now. I am interested in helping *you* to become aware of your half of the responsibility in *all* of your interactions so that you can improve your life and become a winner.

SO STOP FOCUSING ON THE ACCUSATIONS AND COMPLAINTS!

What is critical is that you learn more about yourself and about how your *own* behavior damages you and sets up the conflicts in your life. It would be a great step in your personal growth to become more aware of how *you* participate in creating your own unhappiness.

You are probably a very good and sincere person with fine intentions. That isn't in question here. Blaming is the way good people who are emotionally blind spend their time.

When you can acknowledge your share in the difficulties and work on eliminating the roadblocks to your happiness, then you will be moving toward success.

EXERCISE 8: STOP THE BLAMING

Perhaps you had an argument with someone you care about. Before you realized what was happening, what started out as a casual discussion burgeoned into a serious verbal battle. You each left the scene furious with the other, certain of *your innocence* and disgusted with the other's *outrageous behavior.*

As a winner you would take 50 percent of the responsibility for everything that happened in your interactions with others . . . both the exchanges that went well and those that didn't. To start repairing the relationship, you would avoid "loser" phrases like:

—"The fight was all *your fault.*"
—"*You started* all the trouble."
—"*You're the one* who's to blame."
—"I was right about that and deep down *you know you're wrong.*"

Thinking or talking like this may make you feel better, but it will also keep you a chronic loser. You are preoccupied with losing skills whenever you're blaming . . . you're not solving problems . . . and there's little chance for your relationships to improve.

The minute you hear yourself blaming or accusing someone else, recognize that it is destructive talk that will prevent you from using winning skills that could help you. So stop! Just this one gesture can push you closer to a win.

Try something new. Think and talk like a winner:

—"What did *I* do to set up that fight?"
—"How did *I* provoke the anger?"
—"How was *I* annoying, disappointing or frustrating?"
—"Where am *I* blind and denying *my* participation?"

No one comes out a winner in a fight . . . *everyone* loses. Spend your energies on repair, not blaming. Go and speak directly to the person with whom you had the argument. Remember, first, to be *honestly positive* about them in every way you can. People tend to respond less defensively when you acknowledge their efforts and kindnesses in the past. When they know you *do* appreciate and approve of them, they will be able to relax, open their ears and hear what it is you want to say.

Talk to them face to face. Come up with something vulnerable like "I'm not sure how I set up my share of our problem. I know I must have contributed to our conflict. Please tell me what it is. I'd like to understand what happened from *your* point of view . . . how *I* was insensitive. I think you are a good person and I would like to get to a happier place with you."

The other person will be less likely to attack you if you are very generous and sincere with your *honest* positives:

"I have known you for many years (months, days), and I know what a *wonderful* person you are . . . *caring, honest* and *fair.* Somehow, I have made a mistake or an error in judgment, and offended you. I'm not certain how, but I want to correct that now. I hope you'll tell me because I *value* our friendship (or relationship)."

Once the other person does start sharing his feelings with you, *he* will probably begin *his* "loser" blaming techniques. Try to just listen. There is important information in his complaints.

DO NOT DEFEND YOURSELF.

DO NOT ARGUE.

DO NOT EXPLAIN WHAT YOUR

INTENTIONS WERE.

Keep listening so that you can grasp his point of view. It won't be the same as yours, but it will be real for that individual. His differences offer useful feedback for you to consider, as a learning experience rather than a source of conflict. Also remember, when hearing the other person's side of an argument, that you are a wonderful person, too, who wants to recreate a mutually friendly atmosphere for both of you.

If you want to get along with someone else, it will be helpful for you to learn how your own style of motivation killing is translated and received.

Losers become hostile when they hear criticism. Winners are grateful for insights into their "negative-loser" behaviors so they have an opportunity to change.

*   *   *

This last exercise was designed to help you see *your* part in difficult interactions, so that you can learn to communicate more successfully and reduce your interpersonal conflicts. The exercise that will follow can guide you in expressing your feelings of anger and resentment toward others, without destroying relationships. It may also help the person who is the motivation killer in *your* life to take 50 percent of *his* responsibility in your conflictual interactions, and stop the blaming, nagging, criticism and complaints that *he* is directing at you.

BUT WHAT ABOUT YOU?

DO YOU HAVE A BARRAGE OF PURE ANGER?

How do you deal with motivation killers? Do they arouse feelings of rage in you when you have a disagreement with them? Are you the person on the receiving end of their messages who represses his emotions and withholds his wrath? And sometime later, when you have suffered repeated attacks, do you retaliate with an *avalanche* of uncontrolled anger that finally breaks through?

Let us say that this is your style. When you unleash a barrage of pure anger at someone who is important to you, it may devastate him. Because the motivation killer you are angry with is generally well intentioned, he may be shocked and confused by your unexpected outburst. Being unaware of how he has wounded *your* feelings, he will assume *you* are assaulting him unjustly and that *you* are the motivation killer! A long time might pass before the damage to the relationship could be repaired.

Now, while it is extremely important for you to get out your feelings, the "how to" do this separates the winners from the losers. A winner remembers:

> IT IS TOO PAINFUL FOR ANYONE TO RECEIVE
> JUST STRAIGHT ANGER.

No one is "old enough," emotionally, to tolerate an enormous jolt of fury, even when he deserves it! When you want to express your hostility with the motivation killer in your life, it is important that the person be emotionally receptive. When you frighten someone unexpectedly by dumping your anger, he will be too upset to listen. If you want him to change, soften your delivery with frequent reminders of how much you care. This is a tough order to follow! When you finally *do* get up the courage to "pay back" the motivation killer in your life, you may say to yourself, "Who can think up positives for someone who is insulting me and is a negative idiot?" Because your goal is to get them to stop their killer messages, respect you and communicate better . . . here is a new method that you could learn.

EXERCISE 9: THE POSITIVE SWIM

A good way to temper your expression of anger when you really want to "tell someone off" is to add honest positives . . . and to imagine yourself swimming. Think for a moment how you propel yourself through the water . . . reaching out first with one arm and then the other. Your stroking motions continue in a rhythmic beat: left arm . . . right arm . . . left arm . . . right arm.

As a swimmer, it would be foolish for you to struggle along using only one arm when you have two with which to transport yourself through the water. Similarly, it is foolish for you to flounder in an uncomfortable, negative interaction that is accelerating and getting worse. Why use only half of your communication skills? Why not take advantage of all of the potential power you have in both of your emotional arms when you are talking to someone?

I want to help you apply this image psychologically. Visualize that your left arm represents your anger and your right arm represents your positive feelings about the person with whom you are having a disagreement. Start first with your honest positives, and use a voice that is easy and friendly. If the person were your spouse, you might say words like these:

RIGHT HAND (POSITIVES):
"Sweets, you know you're so important to me. I really love and need you."

LEFT HAND (NEGATIVES):
"Because your approval means so much to me, I'm afraid to express my anger to you."

RIGHT HAND (POSITIVES):
"I love talking to you. I'd rather be with you than anyone else in the world."

LEFT HAND (ANGER):
"And I was angry with you last night when you humiliated me in front of our friends, but I was terrified to tell you."

RIGHT HAND (POSITIVES):
"Your praise means so much to me that I cherish your words when you say I do something well."

LEFT HAND (ANGER):
"But when you repeated over and over to our friends that I'm sloppy and *always* leave the house in a mess, that wasn't true, and it really hurt me."

RIGHT HAND (POSITIVES):
"You have such great taste, and I enjoy all the expensive possessions we can afford because you work so hard."

LEFT HAND (ANGER):
"But when you joked about my being careless and not appreciating them, I was really embarrassed and upset."

RIGHT HAND (POSITIVES):
"You are so generous, and I love all of the beauty that you have brought into our lives."

LEFT HAND (ANGER):
"But in front of our friends, singling out the times when I am in a

hurry and don't clean up makes me sound like I'm *always* a slob
. . . and that *isn't* true."

RIGHT HAND (POSITIVES):

"I enjoy complimenting you, because you really deserve it. *And
I do, too.* I want *you* to compliment me in front of our friends,
honey."

If your spouse is a motivation killer, he will have no way of
knowing it, if you don't tell him. But do it lovingly, within the
framework of the positive swim. Remember all of your acknowledgments to him. Otherwise *you* might become the motivation
killer.

Be careful to see that the ratio of positives to negatives is very
high. When you follow the "positive swim" exercise model, there
will be no loss of affection or closeness between you and the person
you care about. Then your negative feelings can be quickly com-
municated and dispensed with.

If you want to become more of a winner, you will need to be able
to enlist help from your mate, your friends . . . from everyone;
you will need to remember that the people beside you have a
fragile, childlike ego. And you must handle them gently.

Begin to notice the number of positives and the number of
punishments that you are delivering daily. Try to catch yourself
when you are saying negative things like this:

—"Why can't you ever . . ."
—"You call that mess the right way to do this?"
—"At the rate you're going, you won't be able to . . ."
—"How come it's taking you so long?"
—"Unless you can do better, I can't respect your . . ."
—"I'm afraid you're bungling the job."
—"You're never going to finish it the way you're fooling
around!"

Remember that these are the kind of insulting messages that
losers give. They stamp out rapport, self-esteem and motivation.
They inhibit good feelings and they prevent the flow of help.

Stop killing the contributions of others. Even the smallest bit of
assistance can be useful. If you can reward and accept it, you will
have something to build on that will increase in quantity and
quality.

If you want people to love, support, care about and/or help you,
start carefully monitoring your language. When you hear yourself

issuing those killer messages, give yourself a kiss for admitting it
. . . THEN STOP! Watch to see that your output of positives is
PLENTIFUL. Once it is, the motivation of the people around you
will surely grow to match it.

MOTIVATION INCREASES WHEN YOU DELIVER
HONEST POSITIVES GENEROUSLY.

WINNER SCORECARD #9

Can you enlist the help of other people when you need it? Do you
know how to make them feel so good when they are close to you that
they're eager to pitch in the next time you need them? Or are you
stuck "going it alone" because no one is willing to lend you a hand?

If you've been delivering motivation-killing messages to the people
around you, it's not too late to change. Check the following tips.

LOSERS	WINNERS
1. Losers deliver few, if any, positives. They try to get others to do what they want by making them feel guilty with their demeaning glances, annoyed sighs, harsh words and even physical punishment. In the process, they create a myriad of new problems for themselves as their negative interactions can cause depression, rebellion and delinquency. They remain losers because they can't get the assistance they need from others.	**1.** Winners get the assistance they want and need. They reward helpful behaviors with approval and appreciation. They deliver generous amounts of positives like smiles, praise and affection. They keep the positives high and deliver few negatives.

2. When there is a misunderstanding, losers start arguing to prove that they are right and the other person is wrong. They become entangled in questions of "Who done it?" and waste their energies being master sleuths, following up every clue that sustains their position. In this way, they destroy the willingness of others to help them.

2. Winners work at maintaining an atmosphere of caring and camaraderie. They defuse conflicts by assuming the burden of responsibility in controversies. This quickly moves the other person out of his defensive posture and onto the job at hand.

3. Losers blame the other person for all the difficulties in the relationship. They believe they are totally innocent of creating conflicts. Their script says, "I'm not at fault. You're the one to blame."

3. Winners accept half the responsibility for unhappy situations in their relationships. Their script reads, "What did I do to set up the pain in this interaction? How did I create anger in the other person?"

4. When losers hear criticism, they become hostile and argumentative. They are unable to benefit from feedback. Instead, they defend against it or argue it away.

4. When winners catch themselves blaming or accusing someone else, they speak directly to the other person, by offering honest positives and saying, "Tell me *your* point of view." Then they listen, without arguing or defending.

5. Losers kill the motivation of people who try to help them by withholding reinforcement until the "perfect" solution is arrived at. They reject and even viciously attack any assistance that falls short of precisely what they requested.

5. Winners use positive reinforcement to stimulate the smallest healthy behaviors and help them to grow into larger ones. They conscientiously reward any offering of information, cooperation or help that even approaches the general vicinity of their objective, hoping that the next time they will get something closer to their goal.

LOSERS

6. Losers kill motivation by focusing on their own problems to the exclusion of anyone else's. They make others feel unimportant, left out or ignored.

7. Losers are unable to respond to, or stop the motivation killers in their lives effectively. They try to discourage the onslaught of negatives with self-destructive guilt, blaming, sarcasm, anger, silence or complete withdrawal. Their reactions solve nothing; they are confusing and create more distance and pain in the relationship.

8. Losers go dead when a motivation killer interrupts and they can't complete a thought or sentence. They finally become almost mute, because they fear the other person will judge their remarks and embarrass them in public.

WINNERS

6. Winners acknowledge the contributions of others through the generous use of honest positives. They encourage increased participation and achievement by rewarding all efforts and accomplishments.

7. Winners realize that outbursts of anger or criticism are often based on fear. They understand that the other person may be troubled and calmly talk it over with him. They formulate warm, reassuring responses, correcting negative assertions directed at them, and remind others of their personal accomplishments and problem-solving skills.

8. Winners don't allow themselves to be silenced. Being both kind and firm, they assert their own thoughts and ideas. When someone tries to interrupt or correct them, they warmly limit the other person with a smile, saying, "I'm not finished yet," and continue talking.

9. When trying to deal with a motivation killer, losers often repress their feelings of anger for a long time, then unleash a torrent of rage. This devastates the recipient and may even mean the end of the relationship.

9. When winners are upset by a motivation-killing message, they speak up, being careful to temper their expression of anger with frequent statements of acknowledgment, praise and saying how much they care for the other person. In this way, they release their rage, stop the motivation killing *and* preserve their relationship with the other person.

PART THREE

Winners Are Real

CHAPTER 10

Your Hidden Power: Honesty

I want . . . to endeavor to speak truth in every instance; to give nobody expectations that are not likely to be answered, but aim at sincerity in every word and action—the most amiable excellence in a rational being.

—BENJAMIN FRANKLIN*

I want to give you still another positive tool that will help you become a winner. It is the power of being honest.

You may never have thought of honesty as either a power or a helpful tool, but it is. I believe that honesty is a symbol of strength. It demonstrates high self-esteem and inner feelings of security and dignity. Honesty is magnetic and will draw people to you. They may not be certain why they are attracted to you, but they will like you because honesty is so engaging.

YOU WILL BE TRUSTED

When you are an honest person, people learn to trust you. Whatever the situation, they will know that you won't cover up and make excuses or be defensive about your behavior. They will know you speak the truth.

In my therapy work, I have treated many corporate executives

* L. Jesse Lemisch, editor, *Benjamin Franklin: The Autobiography and Other Writings* (New York: New American Library, 1961), p. 185.

and leaders of industry. It is interesting to note how many winning characteristics they have in common. Invariably, one of those traits is being honest. This quality describes one of my patients, George, a successful, internationally respected real estate developer. I affectionately call him "my real estate mogul."

When recounting his early history to me, George talked about a house he had shown to a potential buyer in Lake Forest, Illinois, when he was just starting out. The owner of the property had confided to George that while most of the structure was in good condition, the roof was so old that it would have to be replaced that winter.

The first clients to whom George showed the house were a young couple who said they had an extremely limited budget. They were very frightened of getting in over their heads financially, so they were looking for a house that would need few repairs.

When they saw the Lake Forest house, they fell in love with it on the spot. They were excited and wanted to move in immediately when George explained a problem: The house needed an $8,000 new roof!

George knew that by disclosing the condition of the roof, he was taking a chance and might kill the deal.

And he was right! The couple withdrew their offer when they heard about the money needed for repairs. A week later, George learned that they had gone to another real estate agency and bought a similiar house for less money.

When his boss heard the sale had been lost to a competitor, he was furious. He called George into his office and demanded to know how he had "blown it."

He wasn't satisfied with George's explanation or his concern about the couple's financial problems. "They didn't ask you about the roof!" he shouted. "You had no responsibility to disclose it. It was stupid to volunteer that information! You had no business doing it. Now you've lost everything!"

He fired George.

Had George been a loser, he would have thought, "I was a fool to tell that couple the truth. Why should I worry about other people? They're not my problem. I'll never open my mouth and lose a commission that way again. I really was stupid!"

But George *wanted to be honest.* He had been brought up to tell the truth. His father had always said to him, "When you shake a person's hand, that's a contract. Your word has to stand for something. And if you want to stay in business you've got to give people a *fair deal.*" So George's first priority was his integrity . . . not money. While he had hoped to sell the house, it wasn't important enough for him to compromise his values. Even after he had lost his job, he still believed that his only available course had been to disclose all of the facts.

George borrowed money from a relative he had once helped, and moved to California. With the funds he started a small real estate agency. Over the years, he became known for giving people a fair deal and telling the truth. This cost him many sales, but people learned to trust him. Eventually he gained a reputation that paid off: His business expanded to offices all over the country and George prospered.

* * *

In your personal life or in your career, you may lose something you want because you're honest. But losing one reward has little meaning over the long haul. You need to establish your credibility and build a reputation for integrity. Your word must be respected. People must know that you are dependable and worthy of their trust.

NO CRYSTAL BALLS NEEDED

Honest people have an aura of safety and solidity about them that you can recognize right away. When you're interacting with an honest person, you won't need a crystal ball. You won't have to guess what they're thinking or what they want . . . they'll tell you.

I choose friends who are truthful and can share their feelings openly with me. Whether I'm making a new friend or hiring an employee, it's critical that he or she be straightforward. My days are packed with visits from patients, my talk-radio and TV programs, media appearances, lectures and writing my books. I move so fast that occasionally and unwittingly I can be insensitive to others. I need friends and associates who give me honest reactions as to how my behavior is affecting them. I want to know, because I care about them . . . so I need to hear their honest feedback.

Often I treat patients who deliberately withhold information that they believe might hurt others. They are afraid to get angry or express their perceptions or be direct. They worry that someone will reject or disapprove of them if they do. It is difficult to maintain friendships with people like this. It's too much work. It's far less costly emotionally to be with people who can share their reactions with you openly and directly. You feel less anxious because you always know where you stand.

Truthful friends say what they believe; they have judgments and opinions . . . they take a position. You don't need to wonder if they're angry, whether they're gossiping or being deceitful about you. They won't put you down behind your back. If they have any argument with you, they'll get to you directly and explain their feelings warmly. Because the communication is so honest and open, you have the opportunity to deal with problems and dispense with them quickly.

OVERCIRCUITING YOUR MEMORY

Is your memory good enough to keep track of all the lies you've told over the years? Most people have difficulty remembering and dealing with the real things that are happening in their lives.
WHAT ABOUT YOU?
When you lie, pretend and withhold, you will find yourself so preoccupied checking old entries from your memory bank that you will have little time left for fun and creativity in the present.
IT IS EASIER TO BE YOURSELF.
Have you ever met someone at a cocktail party whom you disliked almost instantly? Within minutes of meeting new people, sometimes you get an immediate impression . . . either you want to stay and discover more about them or you want to escape because you sense something "unreal." This could happen in reverse: If you are not careful, the people who meet *you* may feel this way and want to flee!

When you present yourself to someone for the first time, whether in a business or social situation, it is important to offer the *true essence* of who you are right away. Let the other person recognize your authenticity and straightforwardness. The ancient Greeks wrote about this philosophy:

Truth ever has most strength of what men say.

—SOPHOCLES

Being honest and sincere is one of the surest ways to encourage new acquaintances to like you and want to get to know you better. It is the "most strength" you can present.

I'm not suggesting that it would be courageous to bare your soul and talk endlessly about your problems . . . that could be overwhelming and distasteful to the other person. What I *am* suggesting is that you deal honestly with what you are experiencing, at that moment, with regard to yourself and the other person.

This advice should not be construed as a license to make negative judgments about others. If your new acquaintance has an oversized nose, I don't want you to call him "Cyrano." Being honest *doesn't mean* criticizing another person's appearance, hurting his feelings or being cruel or punishing in any other way.

The honesty I'm talking about is with *yourself*. The spotlight of honesty needs to be directed at *you*. I want you to hold your head high, put a smile on your face and be happy to present the person you really are . . . with your past failures, meanderings off target and misses in life. This is normal . . . this is real.

Being honest and true to yourself can be a difficult test in social situations. But wherever you are, in order to earn your own self-respect, you need to pass your own honesty test. Here's how to practice. Let's imagine you're in a friendly conversation at a cocktail party, when someone looks at you as though you are intellectually impoverished and says, "You mean you don't like classical music?!!"

If, in fact, you don't, it's important for you to look at the person with an easy, very pleasant attitude and say, "No, I really don't."

Acting even friendlier, you might add, "You seem to love and understand classical music. I'd really enjoy knowing about your favorite compositions."

Patients often confide that whenever they meet new people, they relate things about themselves that they think others will approve of. They size up strangers quickly, and with little information to go on, they decide what kind of personality their new acquaintance would admire. Misrepresenting who they are, and acting out a role they believe will be acceptable, they adopt a false image to gain acceptance.

Do you do this?

The probability of accurately guessing someone else's preferences and desires is very small. What if you're *completely* wrong and the other person actually enjoys someone whose personality is entirely different from what you'd imagined! Then you're stuck.

Why take a chance, when presenting the authentic you is the easiest, most comfortable and most likeable way for you to behave?

Now let's look at the other side of this. Let's suppose you *are* a mind-reader . . . the best in the world . . . and you *are able* to guess correctly. Because of your faultless ESP, you *do know* how to pretend to be the person your new friend will admire. You are setting up a house of cards that is likely to collapse later, when your friend gets to know you better. Then there will be so much disappointment that you're not the person you pretended to be . . . that you will lose the relationship anyway!

I REALLY WANT YOU TO LIKE ME

One of my patients, Sally, had a blind date with a young attorney who was the son of one of her mother's friends. Greg, a Harvard Law School graduate, had recently joined a well-respected firm. Sally was impressed with his education and was worried he wouldn't be interested in her because she hadn't gone to college.

When Greg arrived to pick her up, she took an immediate liking to him and became hopeful that a close relationship would develop.

Because of his academic background, Sally assumed that he would prefer an intellectual partner, so she tried to act what her mother called "snooty and off-handish." She told him how much she enjoyed grand opera (which she had never seen); she discussed how interested she was in Shakespeare and the classics (though in fact she read only movie magazines and cookbooks), and she talked about her frequent visits to museums (the last visit had been when she was four).

Because Sally tried so hard to impress Greg, she came across as stiff and phony. Greg felt so uncomfortable with her that he never called her back. Sally was crushed.

A few months later, a friend told her that Greg was going steady with a girl named Jennifer. The irony was that Jennifer hadn't gone to college, either. She sold clothing at a local boutique. People liked her and said she was "straightforward, enthusiastic and good company." Jennifer was a good cook, and Greg loved food. She was also interested in backpacking and mountain climbing, and Greg, a longtime member of the Sierra Club, shared her love of the wilderness. Jennifer and Greg hit it off instantly. Not an intellectual word passed between them. But Jennifer had presented her *real* self to Greg, not the person she *believed* he would like to be with.

* * *

It is far better to be honest and "lose" someone on your first meeting, before you become invested and really learn to care. Not everyone will like you, so don't waste your time lying and feeling inadequate. If you are going to feign who you are, eventually the other person will get to know you and find out anyway. Why invest so much time? By being honest you will discover after one or two dates if the relationship ever had a chance to work.

Benjamin Franklin, who was considered one of the wisest men of his age, said this about being genuine:

> The great secret of succeeding in Conversation, is . . . to hear much . . . never to pretend to wit.*

Stop your pretending and present the honest, real you.

EVEN THE EXPERTS DON'T KNOW

When I was a doctoral candidate at the University of London, I had the opportunity to closely observe "professional authenticity." It was observable at a conference I attended in Belgium. As I sat in a room filled with internationally respected behavioral scientists, I noticed that one of the phrases spoken very frequently was "I don't know" . . . or its more scholarly equivalent: "At this point in the research, we don't have sufficient evidence to draw any firm conclusions."

Wise people in every profession have the self-confidence to accept that no one "knows" everything. They frequently say they don't know and research the information they are lacking later. These winners suffer no ego loss by this admission. Not knowing is an incentive for them to investigate further and acquire more knowledge.

EVEN THE EXPERTS AREN'T GOOD AT EVERYTHING.

Many of my patients are world-famous talents and entrepreneurs. They are exceptional in their own fields, yet working with

* Ibid., p. 185.

them I often discover how unsophisticated they are in other aspects of living. They spend so much time polishing their particular talents and expertise that, frequently, they remain undeveloped in areas that are not work-related. They may even have difficulty answering simple questions that are outside their field.

Winners know that it is neither possible nor necessary to cover the entire waterfront of information. Rather, they focus their energies on becoming specialists. They know that a "jack of all trades" is a loser . . . a winner is master of *one*.

YOU CAN'T DO IT ALL, EITHER, AND YOU DON'T NEED TO BE GOOD AT EVERYTHING.

No one can be all things at all times to all people. Nor is it necessary. When you doubt yourself, remember that even experts have limitations and are usually skilled within a very narrow range.

This acceptance of your own limits and those of others laps over into many fields. As an employer, I know that I am not going to find someone who can do every job in my organization well. I have hired people who are very capable in one area but who may have few aptitudes in another. As long as they are honest about what they can and cannot do, they are valuable to me in the places where they do excel. When I am fortunate enough to have employees who are loyal and hard-working, and whose egos don't crumble when they make a mistake . . . I am satisfied. I can hire someone else to do the tasks that they don't handle well. If people are truthful about their limitations, we can work it out together. When they pretend to have skills that they don't, however, I know I can't trust or rely on them or keep them in my employ.

PEOPLE WILL UNDERSTAND

A few years ago, I was treating a very well known actor. He had the starring role in a major film, and when the reviews came out, without exception, every newspaper criticized his performance.

He became very distraught in his therapy session, reading me one crushing comment after another. "I'm so depressed," he cried like a child. "I'll never be able to hold up my head again. I'm afraid to go out on the street. I just know the reporters will start asking me questions, and what can I say: 'Yes, I have egg on my face'? 'Yes, I did a lousy job of acting. I didn't know what I was doing'? The press will ruin me! I admit I flopped, but how do I live through this nightmare?"

"You are *not* a lousy actor," I said, reminding him of his previous outstanding performances. "You are a *fine* actor. And in spite of that, you weren't at your best this time and the picture wasn't successful.

"But you're forgetting you were in trouble during the filming," I added. "Remember, you were going through a divorce and you and your 'ex' were always fighting? Then, one of your children was having serious problems at school and your other child was so upset about the separation she wouldn't speak to you for months?

"Your life was in chaos, and obviously, it affected your work." He looked up and was listening to me intently as I continued. "That's normal. You're a human being, and a very sensitive man. You were 'stressed out' . . . weighed down by too much sadness in your life. It's fair that such serious problems affected your work.

"Now you're doing fine. You're putting your life back together. But I don't want you to forget that *you are* a brilliant performer and *you have* an outstanding track record to prove it."

I explained to him that people can be more creative when they are honest. Hiding and lying would keep him preoccupied with avoidance . . . trying to remember his falsehoods . . . and covering them up with more lies. He'd be exhausted trying to keep track of it all. Besides, he wasn't the only good actor who ever bombed and made a poor film.

My patient decided to face the press. We worked out a plan where we rehearsed all the issues he had been too frightened to share before. I convinced him this was the way to find peace with himself. He would present himself very honestly to everyone . . . the public, his friends and his fans.

With his knees shaking, he walked into the press conference. He simply explained that he hadn't been able to handle all the family stresses during the separation with his wife and children. He had been too depressed to make a successful film. A few minutes into the conference he was able to laugh at himself and relate some of the funny incidents on location where he made some silly blunders.

The reporters were so impressed with this superstar's candor that they were very sympathetic. Because he dared to be honest and tell the truth . . . the public found him even more appealing! His popularity actually increased, both with the press and at the box office.

* * *

Some four hundred years ago, William Shakespeare set down a profound and enduring statement about honesty:

> To thine own self be true
> And it must follow, as the night the day
> Thou canst not then be false to any man.
>   —HAMLET, ACT I, SCENE III

It is easy to be honest when you want to share information about yourself that is praiseworthy. Your self-esteem expands and your self-criticism quiets down.

But trying to be truthful isn't so easy when a little voice inside of you is cautioning, "Don't be a dummy. Only an idiot would let anyone know how stupid and childish they are."

Actually, your little voice is wrong. People are very loving when you are honest and openly share yourself. You will be surprised to find they will take your lead and invite you into their private worlds, too.

Winners talk openly about their mistakes in an easy, straightforward manner. They offer comments like:

—"I think I acted too hastily."
—"I said something in anger that really wasn't prudent."
—"My judgment was poor in that situation."
—"I wasn't properly prepared . . . I made a mistake."
—"I am not sure what to do in this case."
—"I was wrong."

If you want to be a winner, tell the truth proudly and simply. Remember that you are a person . . . not a machine, an encyclopedia or a Bible. Sometimes you are going to make mistakes, be confused, say things that you'll regret later and make serious errors in judgment. That's what bright, normal people do who are involved in life.

Most of us have experienced humiliation and embarrassment because of our own foolish actions and lack of wisdom. It's a relief for every one of us to hear the next fellow is just as foolish as we are. Being honest and open and acknowledging you didn't handle something well will earn you admiration.

HONESTY IS YOUR HIDDEN POWER . . . USE IT!

It will attract people to you like a bright light that signals safety and dependability.

I believe in honesty . . . I trust honest people . . . I will follow an honest friend.

BE A WINNER.
TAP INTO YOUR OWN POWER.
EMBRACE YOUR HONEST, AUTHENTIC SELF.

WINNER SCORECARD #10

Do you know how to use your hidden power of honesty to attract others to you, even on the first meeting? Have you put this power to work for you to build your credibility with others and to make yourself a valued person? You already possess this life-enhancing quality. Make the most of it.

LOSERS	WINNERS
1. Losers hide the truth for the sake of some kind of immediate profit. Like small children, they are not concerned about the welfare of others and focus solely on their own gain.	**1.** Winners won't compromise their value systems and be dishonest. People learn to trust their integrity. They build a lasting reputation for being reliable and dependable.
2. Losers withhold information about their feelings, so you have to guess what is really on their minds and in their hearts. Associating with them is emotionally costly.	**2.** Winners will tell you what they are thinking and what they need. If they have any disagreements with you, they explain them directly, face to face and warmly. Because they deal openly, interpersonal problems can be quickly resolved.

LOSERS	WINNERS

3. Losers overcircuit their memories trying to keep track of all the lies, half truths and withheld information from the past. Consequently, they are too preoccupied as custodians of the lies to function well in the present.

3. Winners find honesty to be easier and less energy-consuming than lying and pretending. It frees them to deal effectively with the people and projects ongoing in their lives *now*.

4. People are uncomfortable with losers and want to get away from them, because they often perceive them as being dishonest and "unreal."

4. When winners present themselves to someone for the first time, they are authentic and offer the real essence of who they are. Because of their straightforwardness, others trust them and want to get better acquainted.

5. Losers misconstrue honesty as a license to be cruel, and make negative statements and judgments about others. They hurt people's feelings by being critical and insensitive, under the guise of being honest.

5. Winners show their honesty by sharing themselves, not by pointing out the mistakes and problems of others. They believe in their goodness, and value the feelings of others. They are comfortable about acknowledging their errors and failures.

6. Losers misrepresent who they are because they fear they won't be liked. They act out a role they believe will earn the other person's approval. But they are setting up a "house of cards" that will fall later, when their friend gets to know them better.

6. Winners present themselves as the person they truly are, not the person they believe others will admire. They know it is impossible to accurately guess what someone else will like. They trust that who they really are is worthwhile.

7. Losers pretend they grasp everything another person is saying, even when they are completely confused. They are afraid they will look ridiculous if they ask questions or indicate that they don't understand.

7. Winners seek help and do ask questions when they need information. They believe that being confused or needing answers is related to lack of exposure to facts, not lack of intelligence. They are willing to say "I don't know" and get all the assistance they can from others.

8. Losers believe they would be liked more if they possessed certain other characteristics. Because they feel inadequate and undesirable, in order to be accepted they pretend to have skills and knowledge that they don't possess.

8. Winners know their limits and appreciate their strengths. They acknowledge the areas in which they do not excel. A winner specializes; he hasn't the time to be a "jack of all trades."

9. Losers cover up their mistakes by making excuses and rationalizations. When questioned about their behavior, they become defensive and justify their actions by blaming and criticizing others.

9. Winners are the first to admit their mistakes. They take the responsibility and talk about them in an easy, straightforward manner. Their honesty demonstrates high self-esteem and self-respect.

10. Losers are afraid to admit when they have performed poorly. They run from criticism by lying, hiding and denial. They believe that a truly intelligent person would perform well even under conditions of great stress or sadness.

10. Winners admit it when they haven't been able to handle things well. They realize they are human and are affected by personal conflicts and adverse family conditions, too. Their candor earns them admiration and genuine appreciation.

CHAPTER 11

The Hidden Power of Vulnerability

Keep me from the wisdom that does not weep, and the philosophy that does not laugh, and the pride that does not bow its head before a child.

—KAHLIL GIBRAN*

Exercising the hidden power of honesty enables you to be more at ease with yourself, enhances your communications with other people and increases your own feelings of self-worth. Another hidden power is vulnerability, the willingness and ability to share your deeper feelings, whether to express your love or to acknowledge your fears and needs. Vulnerability flows directly from honesty and has many of the same capacities. Together, being honest and being vulnerable comprise a truly magnetic winning quality, being *authentic*.

Most of us are so terrified of being rejected that we don't take the chance and express our vulnerable feelings. Rarely do we make demands openly or talk candidly about our emotions. Our fear of being rejected prevents us from telling the people we love *just how much we care*.

But you can't be too extravagant in sharing with others how

* Anthony R. Ferris, editor and translator, *Spiritual Sayings of Kahlil Gibran* (New York: Citadel Press, 1962).

special they are to you. You can't be too generous with your praise or too lavish with your show of caring and love.

DON'T BE AFRAID

Many of the people I've worked with express concern about being too dependent on their partners for attention and love. They fear that being that dependent will make them appear desperate or ridiculous. This is nonsense.

It is healthy to be dependent on the people you adore. You need their care and concern. There is nothing desperate about telling your partner that he or she is the center of your world.

When you can be vulnerable and talk about your feelings, the people who are important to you will be more loving and loyal . . . more thoughtful about your needs and cautious about treading on your sensitive areas.

We are all afraid, however, that by revealing our vulnerability, our listeners won't value us. Silently questioning ourselves, our doubts sound like this: "Will they get bored with me if they know how much I love them . . . or turn on me? Are my secrets going to be used for ammunition to hurt me in the future?"

By showing our vulnerability to someone who does respond with ridicule or judgments, we might feel too assaulted or frightened to hazard exposing ourselves again. We're certain that "the other fellow" is wiser, happier and more fulfilled . . . "and doesn't need me." So we decide that there must be no disclosing of real feelings. We cannot risk being exposed or compared unfavorably. Presenting our true personalities seems just too dangerous.

THE LITTLE TWO-YEAR-OLD IN ALL OF US

I believe that deep inside our emotional selves, most adults are small children. There is a tender and vulnerable part in each of us that never really grows up . . . a little two-year-old buried in our unconscious minds. We may have bank vaults filled with gold, imposing physical beauty or jobs governing nations . . . but most of us still feel very small and helpless inside. We are afraid of disapproval and terrified of being abandoned and ending up alone.

In treating thousands of patients . . . rich and poor, successful and struggling . . . I have found that at times *everyone* feels like a frightened child lost in a maze. We all know what it is to stumble along, praying we won't appear too foolish and hoping we'll make the correct turns.

Our two-year-old thinking permeates all of our relationships. Within our childlike egos we worry that "If you knew all about me, you wouldn't like me. If you knew my darkest secrets, my foibles, my history . . . then you would think I am hateful or undesirable."

OPTING FOR SAFETY

For many people, just thinking about sharing honest information about their fears and feelings makes them so anxious they opt for safety and withhold their emotions. This makes healthy communication impossible and creates the distance in relationships that is so lonely and destructive. Unconsciously, because the fear of abandonment is omnipresent, we set ourselves up to be rejected and unloved.

The authentic nature of our real selves . . . the part we withhold when we opt for safety . . . actually constitutes the very richness that others would find inviting and appealing. We stifle and deaden the qualities that could make us lovable. This is a diagram of the unfortunate and painful cycle we create:

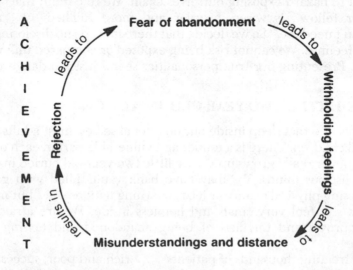

Figure 4: Fear of Abandonment.

After years of repeating these debilitating patterns, we feel *justified* in our terror of abandonment, because we have indeed experienced so much rejection. And we believe we are powerless to halt this cycle of emotional pain.

TOO AFRAID TO TELL YOU

Perhaps the *most* difficult and frightening time to express your vulnerability is when you're in love. This is equally true for married as well as single people who are going together and hoping to establish meaningful, long-term relationships.

Many of my unmarried patients complain that the people they are dating rarely articulate the true extent of their feelings.

Jennifer, who was in my Tuesday night group, had been seeing a man named Cliff for about a year. At every session, she would give us an update on the progress of their romance.

One evening Jennifer told us about an aspect of their affair that was troubling her. "We've been going together now for over a year and we really enjoy each other's company. Sex is great and so is everything else, but I feel awfully hurt about one thing. Cliff has *never once said* 'I love you' or even 'You really mean a lot to me.' "

The group listened patiently to Jennifer's laments before several of them spoke up:

—"What about you? Have you ever told Cliff that *you care about him?*"
—"How many times have you expressed *your* feelings of love?"
—"You two are exactly alike! You're *both* afraid to stick your necks out and take a risk."
—"Why should he spill his guts and be exposed if you won't? *You're both* withholding love!"

For a minute, Jennifer just stared at the group. Then she objected, "Well, I think *he* should make the first move. After all, I'm a woman. It's a *man's place* to speak up first."

One of the men in the group became annoyed. "You're full of it, Jennifer! That rubbish about 'a man's role' died off with *your* Women's Lib movement! Cliff is just as gun-shy as you are! He doesn't want to get burned, either."

Jennifer started crying. "I'm too scared to bring up love talk. What if I say I love him and he doesn't respond with the same thing . . . or repeats back that he loves me just because I said it first. That wouldn't mean anything to me. I don't want to *force him* to love me."

I interrupted. "Jennifer, where did you get the idea that you would be forcing him? You two slowpokes have been in love for over a year! Someone has to make the first move and start being vulnerable. You'll both be senile before you decide to say how you feel!

"I've treated patients whose relationships *broke up* because one of the partners believed he wasn't loved . . . and he left. You have been telling the group for months how much you love Cliff. *Tell him.*"

Jennifer kept shaking her head and wiping her tears. "I can't. I'm too afraid."

"Could you write it down and mail him a note?" I asked. "How about buying one of those funny romantic cards in a stationery store and at least *introducing* the word 'love'? If you're so afraid to speak, using the mail could be a first step. Then maybe a bit later you could put a note in his pocket saying 'I really think you are wonderful.' You can start slowly, giving him cues. If it's too hard for you to say 'I love you' right away, say something close to it. Get going! Being vulnerable will get you both closer."

The following week Jennifer got to the group room early and put candy on everyone's seat with a note: "I told Cliff how much I loved him. Save August 18th—you're invited to our wedding!"

* * *

Many of my therapy hours are spent in working with couples. Some of them have good relationships and start therapy seeking to learn how to communicate better and prevent future breakups. Still others seek therapy hoping to repair their unhappy lives and empty marriages. In observing the dynamics of all of their interactions, I often see how their terror of rejection prohibits the sharing of loving feelings and leads to what they fear the most: the destruction of the relationship.

A MAN IS A MAN

Men in our society have the most difficulty in communicating vulnerable feelings because they are shackled by archaic mythology and special fears. They believe that if they expose their weaknesses they won't be considered manly. This fear is reinforced from early childhood and sometimes throughout life. It prevents many men from expressing themselves when they feel inadequate, troubled or lonely.

As a therapist, I have had the unusual opportunity to hear the precious secrets, the tears, the embarrassments and private humiliations that my male and female patients have shared with me. Most of the men I treat admit to me at the onset of therapy, "I have never expressed any 'weak' feelings to anyone. A 'puke-y' word has never left my lips!"

When asked a question like "Are you afraid?" their pat response is "Me afraid? Of course not! I'm *never* afraid." Many of these men's feelings have been so deadened over the years that they can honestly answer this question with their "nevers."

Of course healthy men experience fear some of the time . . . everyone does. But not until therapy, where they have the opportunity to develop trust in me and the safety of our confidential relationship, can they reveal themselves and get in touch with their vulnerable emotions.

THERE'S NO TIME LEFT TO CRY

Many parents in this country are so concerned about making "sissies" out of their sons, some of them won't permit even an occasional moment of tenderness to pass. At a very young age male children are pushed toward becoming emotionally sterile, unfeeling men. Once a boy gets to be seven or eight years old, some parents begin punishing affectionate bodily contact or any signs of frailty, labeling these traits "forbidden and feminine." Historically, this damaging thesis has been supported by cultures and their creative arts and literature:

Frailty, thy name is woman!

—HAMLET, ACT I, SCENE II

A patient named Henry explained how difficult it was for him to measure up to all the so-called male standards. "It's tough to be a guy these days. There are so many 'shoulds' and 'musts' to measure up to. You need to be a combination of Superman and Jehovah. I feign invincibility so much that I've become used to it. There's no time left for any feelings . . . or to cry."

Henry was forty-five years old, a six-foot-five "jock" and a former all-city high school basketball star. He sounded very sad when

we discussed his problems with experiencing his fears or expressing them.

"In my family," Henry said, "men are never allowed to cry.

"I've never had a chance to feel *anything,*" he went on. "I have
been too busy pretending I'm 'macho.' I kept trying to do it 'right'
and discover what a man 'should be,' so my dad wouldn't yell at
me. I still feel like a little kid waiting for my old man to jump on me
with 'What's the matter with you? Boys are *always strong.* Quit
acting like a pansy. Only girls talk about being weak, or cry.' "

* * *

Occasionally a man escapes this unfortunate early conditioning.
When he does, there can be a stunning portrait of healthy male-
ness and an ease in sharing feelings. When a man is secure in his
masculinity, he sounds the way my friend baseball star Steve Gar-
vey did in a 1981 story:

"Do you ever cry?" the interviewer asked.

"Yeah. Yeah," Steve replied. "I've cried at movies, or over emotional events. I think you can be *more* of a man for crying in certain
situations because you're showing your true feelings. Machoism
can stop you from it, but shedding tears shows that you're human
and capable of loving."*

LEARN FROM OTHER CULTURES

The way most boys are raised . . . to become invulnerable,
wooden examples of what a man "should" be . . . is one of the
tragedies of our society.

When I lived in Europe as a student, I was able to observe the
"acceptable" masculine standards of behaviors in other cultures. It
was a relief for me to see men in the Mediterranean countries
embracing and kissing one another, and heartwarming to notice
their open affection and caring. They seemed to have no concern
about labels like "sissy," "effeminate" or "too emotional."

When I worked and lectured in the Far East, the Middle East
and South America, I saw similar patterns. Men were comfortable
with behaviors that we in the United States would call "feminine."
It was customary in these places for men to hug, kiss and caress

* *Playboy* (June 1981), p. 116.

each other. American men displaying these *same* kinds of affectionate gestures fear they might be misconstrued. When they do dare to hug each other, they feel compelled to instantly start slapping each other on the back. Whenever they get physically close, it must be made clear that nothing sensual is going on.

Why is it that in other cultures men are free to walk hand in hand, kiss and hug and be warm and loving with no fear of being thought "different" or perverse? Why are we in this country so full of anxiety about closeness and friendliness? Why should we miss so much joy?

STOP SUPPORTING THESE NONSENSICAL
MASCULINE RULES.
MEN CAN BE AFFECTIONATE, LOVING
AND VULNERABLE.

MEN, GET GOING

Men, you can start establishing new rules . . . your *own* model for what a man "should" be. Start by kissing and hugging your son, father and male friends.

When was the last time you told a close male friend or relative that you loved and cared about him? When was the last time you put your arm around him or held his hand in yours?

Why all this caution?

Stop thinking about what you've been taught and become a person who can risk . . . who can tolerate more happiness, affection and love. Limiting and constricting your honest feelings isn't healthy. By sharing your vulnerability openly and proudly to everyone, your pride and self-worth will grow.

While I have been focusing on men, it is also frightening for many women to acknowledge their vulnerability. While women are not burdened by the cultural mandate of "machismo or else!" they, too, are afraid to show fragile feelings, admit dependency or experience intimacy.

Male or female, however, the range of permissible affectionate gestures Americans may give one another is very circumscribed, because being affectionate is often judged warily. While women *are allowed* to hug and kiss each other, the amount of warmth and closeness that is tolerated is very limited. Holding each other closely, side by side, for a brief time, is allowed. But the time spent facing each other nose to nose with arms around each other must be *very* short. Kissing on the lips is out, though kissing quickly and lightly on the cheek is acceptable.

STOP PROMOTING THIS RITUALISTIC
NONSENSE!

It's time for women *and* men to give up thinking about what their roles "should" be and simply become their own kind of person. Don't miss out on the shared feelings and close contacts that are emotionally nutritious for your mental health.

NOURISHING WARMTH

A scientist named Harry F. Harlow experimented with rhesus monkeys and the effects contact during infancy had on later life. His studies suggested that the monkeys who lacked the nourishing experience of soft body contact during their formative years suffered greatly as adults. They had special problems, including sexual sterility. Also, some of them rocked rhythmically for hours in their cages in lonely isolation.*

Like those monkeys, too many people suffer being alone. They sit in their apartments, isolated in front of television sets or rocking their lives away in solitude. Even when with their families, the least threatening environment for closeness and vulnerability, they are uncommunicative.

Actually, it is often with the people we cherish with the full range of our deepest feelings that we are unable to get close to. We create distance, because breaking the barriers and relating as interdependent-dependent human beings is too strange and unfamiliar.

THE ALWAYS-PERFECT PERSON

Too often at home and at work, we increase our distance from others by offering an image of ourselves as perfect. Not an ounce of problems or weakness can be displayed . . . as we present only our perfection! We think this will help us win esteem, but the reverse occurs . . . we are avoided and disliked.

The juvenile delinquents I worked with when I interned for my doctorate at the University of London almost invariably talked about having "perfect" parents. They hated these parents who

* Harry F. Harlow, "The Development of Affectional Patterns in Infant Monkeys," *Determinates of Infant Behavior*, Vol. I, ed. by B. M. Foss, (London: Methuen; N.Y., Wiley).

insisted that they were *always* right and their children were *always* wrong.

A strong parallel can be seen between the relationship of the delinquent child to his parents and the relationship in marriages between one partner who acts like the righteous, scolding parent and the other who plays the part of the misbehaving juvenile.

Spouses who assume the role of the parent repeatedly emphasize that they are the responsible, prudent, correct and hard-working ones. They always are considerate and think of the other's needs first. They can't understand why the consideration and thoughtfulness they offer is not returned.

Nonsense! It is neither healthy nor possible to assume this foolish perfectionist's stance! Only a gullible child, spouse or lover would believe them. And who could live up to the stellar performance they feign? Certainly no mere human!

In marriages, as long as one partner continually maintains an aura of perfection, then the other may rationalize that the only role left is being irresponsible and rebellious. By mishandling money, making their partners jealous, being alcoholic, overweight, drugged . . . or whatever, they play out their delinquent posture.

The person who tries to convince himself and others that his behavior is perfect is striving to maintain an impossible image. Perfection is a loser's goal. And those who act as the perfectionist's supportive and naive audience, who are convinced by his "I'm right" and "you should," are even bigger losers. In a healthy relationship, the partners are peers who share the entire spectrum of their vulnerable selves, without anyone being the superior "perfect one."

WE ARE ALL FLAWED

Years ago, when I first spoke to Jack Lemmon over lunch, I remember being moved by his vulnerability and willingness to share so much of himself with a new friend. Speaking to him socially helped me to understand his greatness and the intangible qualities that make his film characterizations so memorable.

Since his first film in 1954, Jack Lemmon has made thirty-nine motion pictures and has been nominated for the Academy Award seven times. He won twice . . . an Oscar for Best Supporting Actor in 1955 for his portrayal of Ensign Pulver in *Mr. Roberts* and another for Best Actor in 1973 for his leading role in *Save the Tiger.*

Lemmon has the unique capacity to be credible as either a comedian or a romantic lead. I believe his ease in talking freely about his own vulnerability and fear of rejection . . . both as a performer and as a man . . . is part of his rare talent.

The beauty of his vulnerability can be heard in his words: "Ultimately, if you really do want to be an actor who can satisfy himself and his audience, you need to be vulnerable. To do this, it is imperative that you reach the emotional and intellectual level of ability where you can go out stark naked, emotionally, in front of an audience, and expose yourself. Without fear or with fear, but be willing to do it!

"Go for the moon. And if you miss the moon by a fraction of an inch, you will know that you are 250,000 miles closer than when you first started.

"But if you do hit it—it's lightning. It's total lightning. Brando can do that. He's done it many times. When he's bad, he can be very, very bad. But when he's good, nobody else is going to be able to give that performance."

Lemmon treasures the advice that the late Rosalind Russell once gave to a group of girls in an acting class. "She said, 'You have to be able to expose yourself totally—to stand in front of an audience nude . . . and turn around . . . very slowly.' That's the phrase that got me. It's a wonderful image. You really have to reach that plateau, where you're not bending every part to what you find you can do and playing it safe."

He believes that an actor must "stick to his guns" . . . be faithful to his principles and his own level of taste. "You're going to make a lot of mistakes doing it. You have to be ready for that, and just swallow it and go on. It's all peaks and valleys."

Lemmon describes himself as a late bloomer. "I know that I had many more misgivings about myself, and I don't know why. I had fears and frustrations, and I was just covering up. I was all *la face,* as Camus said—the face one presents but not the real person.

"I'm not sure how much I am now. But I know damn well that I'm on much better terms with myself as a human being. I'm not as worried about my shortcomings, whatever the hell they are! They're so myriad, I can't even count them—but I don't care as much."

People respect vulnerability and can empathize with it "because we all have it, and we're all frustrated," says Lemmon.

"These qualities can work for you when you're honest. Don't try to be macho when you're not macho. Don't try to be anything except what you truly are. Whatever your qualities are, let them fly. I think that there is an innate respect you will gain from others when you are vulnerable.

"The thing that pleases me most is that I think I'm respected. I care more about that than anything. I want that. That's my applause. I want to be respected on a high level, if possible, as an actor . . . and as a human being."

Lemmon notes that he's always played "flawed" characters. "I am fascinated by them. I am flawed . . . we're all flawed. It's just more interesting to see a multidimensional character than a superman or the guy in the white hat who doesn't seem to be flawed. I'm not attracted to those kinds of heroes, because they're not as vulnerable, and consequently not as colorful.

"I have always considered myself a character actor, not a leading man. And the roles that I usually play are character leads. Thank God—because they are richer parts."

* * *

You, too, can be a multidimensional character, a richer personality. Don't hide your flaws . . . they are the medals of honor you have earned being scarred on the battlefield of life.

Stop and think for a minute about all the people whom you enjoy and admire. They are neither superbeings nor flawless characters. They are authentic people who err, cry, ache, and despair . . . they are real and vulnerable human beings.

ALOOF, STIFF AND UNFRIENDLY

Every society encourages certain behavioral characteristics and punishes others. In the developmental process of a child, some of the characteristics of his personality are shaped by the rules set down by his culture. But the greatest influence on his life is made by the parents who raise him. Their habit patterns become his, as do their values, judgments and lifestyles. Yet, even the habit patterns a child despises in his parents, he unconsciously learns to imitate.

At the beginning of his therapy, Albert, a middle-aged patient I treated in Britain, was stiff, aloof and unfriendly. He explained to

me that he was an unhappy child who believed that he was unloved. While this certainly wasn't true, his parents' inability to
express their feelings of love for their son was misinterpreted by
Albert as hate.

After a year of working in therapy with Albert, he felt safe
enough to let me hypnotize him. I regressed him back to his
childhood. While he was in a deep trance, he shed many tears
about how lonely his early years had been.

Sobbing like a small child, he remembered feeling that neither
of his parents loved him because they sent him away to boarding
school when he was only five years old. He was particularly sad
when he recalled, "I know my father hated me, because he *never*
kissed or touched me. I felt like I was diseased . . . he was always
so aloof, stiff and unfriendly."

Under hypnosis, Albert underwent a dramatic personality
change. Feeling very relaxed and trusting, he allowed his fragile
and vulnerable feelings to emerge. He became a very lovable,
relaxed and appealing human being when he spoke. As I listened
to his poignant story and wiped the tears from his cheeks, I had
very tender feelings for him.

But there was an instant change when Albert came out of the
trance. He immediately became uncommunicative again . . .
the stiff, guarded and unfriendly man he had been when he first
walked into my office.

When I pointed this out to him and imitated his rigid posture
and the stiff movements of his hands and mouth, he appeared
genuinely shocked. "I have the chills," he said. "You looked just
like my father when you were showing me what I do. I can't
believe that I am behaving exactly the way he did. Surely you are
exaggerating! I know I could never be as severe and unloving as he
was."

"But you are," I interrupted. "You are just like your father! Look
how far from me you always sit. You're way across the room! I think
you are so frightened to be close to another human being that you
would sit on the next street if you could.

"And like your father, you never show affection. Usually when
my patients have been working with me for over a year, they're
comfortable giving me a kiss or a hug when we say hello or goodbye. Because we share so much, we become good friends. But
you're as aloof and unfriendly with me today as you were on your
very first visit.

"This doesn't mean that you hate me, or that your father hated you. He *didn't* hate you. Your father simply didn't know how to show affection with you or anyone else. He was just too frightened to share emotions . . . he didn't know how . . . so he couldn't let you know how much he cared.

"You *learned* how to be cold and distant by modeling after your parents. They taught you, just as their parents taught them. Every generation is innocent . . . and so are you, but it's time to change."

As part of his therapy, I asked Albert to move his chair one inch closer to me every weekly session. While it took several months, he proceeded haltingly, inch by inch, and eventually he was sitting directly in front of me. Soon after that, this staid Englishman began giving me hello and goodbye kisses. These behaviors generalized outside of therapy to the new friendships he was making.

In therapy, we proceed in small, easy steps, knowing that every little bit of progress has meaning; it draws us closer to our goals. This is what happened with Albert. As I continued to work with him, he was able to expose a little more of his fears, even when he *wasn't* under hypnosis. This slowly generalized to his work setting. He also reported he was able to practice his new behaviors socially. "You'd be pleased with me, you know." Albert smiled proudly. "I'm actually moderately friendly and a trifle vulnerable. In fact, some of the new acquaintances that I have met recently find me quite lovable!"

Albert *did learn* to be more vulnerable and expose himself as a warm, caring and sometimes even fearful human being.

* * *

PEOPLE ARE LOVABLE

Are you ready to be lovable? You can start right now. Take a chance. Begin by sharing more of your feelings. Become more open and people will share more of their vulnerable selves with you. This is how meaningful relationships develop.

As a therapist who "hears it all," I know that once people begin exposing their true selves, and you learn more about them . . . you can't help but care. Often, this caring turns into love. When you hear people's stories, see their tears and understand their failures, disappointments and frustrations . . . you get hooked!

Are you shaking your head "no" right now? Has it been your

practice to hold back everything in a covert way, using innuen-
does, sarcasm or jokes to hide your real feelings? Does your meaning trickle out and dance between your words? Do people have to
read your mind to guess what you really want, then hope that
they're meeting your needs correctly? If so, no one will really
know who you are. It will take too much guesswork to be with you
and figure it all out.

Start experimenting with your winning skills by offering others
the valuable information about yourself that is vulnerable. Then
everyone will find you more lovable.

Being vulnerable is infectious. Set the example, and others will
"catch it" and follow your lead. As *they expose themselves,* you will
become increasingly sensitive to the many facets of *their* personalities, too. It will be like wearing special three-dimensional glasses.
Once you put these glasses on, they will provide you with insight
into the humanity, goodness and innocence of others. This will
make you more considerate and loving and give you still another
hidden power to help you become a winner.

Successful people who practice the philosophy of combining
vulnerability with tolerance inspire great devotion because they
understand the fragility of others. In Margaret Truman's biography of her father, President Harry S Truman, she refers again and
again to his concern for other people:

> My father hated to use the buzzers on his desk to summon a man
> peremptorily. Nine times out of ten he preferred to go to the aide's
> office. When he did summon a man, he would usually greet him at the
> door of the Oval Room office . . .
>
> This constant consideration for others, the total lack of egotism with
> which Dad conducted the day-to-day affairs of the White House, was
> the real source of the enormous loyalty he generated in those around
> him.*

Vulnerability has a kind of beauty . . . so startling, so magical,
that it shines even in the night. In my view, being vulnerable will
put you among the tallest, the strongest and the wisest people.

> Tenderness and kindness are not signs of weakness and despair, but
> manifestations of strength and resolution . . . strength and tolerance
> are partners.**

---

* Margaret Truman, *Harry S Truman,* p. 3.
** Anthony R. Ferris, editor and translator, *Spiritual Sayings of Kahlil Gibran*
(New York: Citadel Press, 1962).

To win, you need to present yourself as you really are. When you do, those close to you will respond so warmly, you will enjoy more love and acceptance than you ever dreamed possible. When you let yourself be vulnerable, it's like looking in a mirror. Suddenly, the world reflects approval and understanding right back to you.

WINNER SCORECARD #11

Are you ready to take a risk and share your feelings of love and dependency, your fears and your self-doubts with the important people in your life? Winners take the chance . . . and reap respect and caring in return.

LOSERS	WINNERS
1. Losers are apprehensive about making a direct request, because in their minds hearing a "no" means they are unloved. They believe that if you truly *do* love them, you will *know* what they are thinking and give them what they need.	**1.** Winners talk about their fragile feelings and ask directly for what they want. Consequently, other people understand them more and become careful about treading on their sensitive areas . . . and are more thoughtful about their needs.
2. Losers rarely tell the people whom they love how much they care.	**2.** Winners are generous with their affection and lavish with their expressions of love and caring.
3. Because of their fear of abandonment, losers withhold their emotions, concealing the very qualities others would find appealing. In this way, they set themselves up to be unloved and abandoned. Then they feel justified with their fears about rejection.	**3.** Winners gain the love and acceptance of others by revealing the richness of their true emotions. Rather than opting for safety, they present their authentic selves, which draws people to them.

LOSERS

4. In a love relationship, losers rarely express their vulnerability or articulate the full extent of their feelings.

5. Losers are constrained in their expression of vulnerability and affection, as prescribed by cultural mores and sex roles. Male losers hide their feelings when they are troubled, lonely or afraid, and refrain from displaying affection toward other men.

6. Losers fear touching and physical closeness. They criticize their parents for the very behaviors that they themselves practice daily.

7. In a loser relationship one of the partners hides his problems and never exposes any sign of weakness. Hoping to win more esteem . . . the reverse happens and he is avoided and disliked.

WINNERS

4. In a love relationship, winners make the first move and risk being rejected or abandoned. They openly share their vulnerable feelings.

5. Winners, whether men or women, reexamine the behaviors and sex role models set down by society. They concentrate on being their own kind of person. Male winners reveal their vulnerability and can be verbally or physically affectionate with other men.

6. Winners enjoy the comfort and emotional nourishment that can be derived from sitting near a friend, hugging and holding a friend's hand. They enjoy the physical reassurance and feelings of safety and security that being close can give.

7. Winners strive to be open about who they are, revealing the many aspects of their personalities. They let others see their flaws and shortcomings, as well as their winner qualities.

8. Losers pretend to be all-knowing and put up a facade of perfection and invincibility. They emphasize that they are always responsible, sensible, prudent, hard-working. In so doing, those close to them may choose a delinquent role . . . anything to get away from the criticism and find a place of their own.

8. Winners work toward a peer relationship where the partners are neither "righteous" nor "wrong" . . . where both are human, make errors, share frailties . . . and are mutually respectful and loving.

9. Losers who believe their parents or marriage partners are perfect think the only role left for them is to be irresponsible and rebellious. By mishandling money, making their mates jealous, or by whatever strategies they can invent, they play out their delinquent postures.

9. Winners realize that perfection is a false image and is not only unobtainable, but unhealthy and undesirable.

10. Losers don't worry about other people's feelings. Because they are so troubled with what they view as their own inadequacies, they brusquely order their subordinates around and reprimand them severely when they make mistakes.

10. Winners use large amounts of kindness and consideration that offset any intimidating feelings others may have about their power and influence. By combining strength with sharing their weaknesses, they inspire devotion and loyalty from others.

PART FOUR

Winners Communicate

CHAPTER 12

Talk Your Way into Success

Speech is civilization itself. The word . . . preserves contact
. . . it is silence which isolates.

—THOMAS MANN

Your ability to communicate effectively with others could be one
of your most valuable assets. Developing and refining this behavior will make a tremendous difference to you in expanding the
quality of your interpersonal relationships and the magnitude of
your achievements.

You have the capacity to communicate like a winner. You can
learn to express yourself clearly, explain your ideas convincingly
and motivate others to believe in you. In order to help you do this,
we'll look at the various aspects of communication that are
preventing you from achieving the rewards you are seeking.

I think of myself as an expert in communication. As a therapist, I
have been able to teach people verbal skills that have enabled
them to double and triple their incomes at work and increase their
happiness at home. My success in helping so many couples preserve and improve their marriages has been largely due to their
working in therapy on *talking more openly* about problems and
feelings. This has made their relationships meaningful and
brought them closer together.

IT'S TIME FOR *YOU* TO DEVELOP
YOUR VERBAL EFFECTIVENESS.

The way you communicate is *learned*. And starting today, you
can begin learning something new . . . acquiring, in a step-by-
step fashion, the communication skills of a winner.

Words are tools. They can enhance your relationships, or they can destroy others. As you strive to express yourself more effectively, you will need to examine your words and the way you deliver them. Then you can master new techniques to get your message across.

As you work to become more proficient, you may occasionally feel awkward if you fail to make the impact you hope to make in a particular situation. But if you stick with it and continue to practice, you will gradually develop fluency with winning verbal skills.

In business, the success of many deals is determined by such considerations as price, quality of product and services and availability of resources and manpower. When all of these elements are relatively equal, however, what swings a decision in favor of a particular person or company is often the intangible . . . the human factor.

Businesses, big and small, are conducted by people talking to people, enjoying people and caring about people. Being able to convey to others what a good and likeable person you really are will be of enormous benefit in bringing you the business contacts and personal relationships you are seeking.

My work in communication really started at UCLA in 1962, before I had any degrees. The first patient I worked with was a child named Betty. Though she was nine years old, her communication was no more advanced than that of a toddler, trying to imitate a parrot. If I said to her, "Betty, would you like a cookie?" she would repeat endlessly, "Betty, would you like a cookie? Betty, would you like a cookie?"

Betty's problem had been diagnosed as "early infantile autism" or childhood schizophrenia. Her repetitive speech was labeled "psychotic." But many "normal" people are also repetitious, though to a far lesser degree and with greater subtlety. Yet they, too, are unable to express themselves effectively. Because they tend to "repeat and repeat" the same things "over and over" again, they are losers who are unable to communicate in a more direct, simple manner.

In this chapter, as a first step toward transforming your verbal abilities, we'll examine a variety of weaknesses in communication, some of which may currently be preventing you from reaching your goals.

The first verbal style we'll analyze is the highly ineffective . . . but attention-grabbing . . . style of the lengthy and loud, short-tempered screamer.

DEALING WITH THE SCREAMER

Some people are unable to express themselves when they are hurt, feel anxious or disappointed. They have been taught that these feelings show "weakness," so in order to cope, they must find substitute behaviors that allow them to hide these emotions. When situations become tense and highly charged, or they become frightened, one of the ways they cover their feelings is by screaming and shouting.

Are you a screamer . . . or are there people in your life who fit this description? Do you often wonder what causes their seemingly unreasonable noise and rage? Be assured that cowering behind the fury and stomping of the screamer is a very small and frightened child.

You may be saying to yourself now, "You'll never convince me that when my mate acts like a raving lunatic, he's really a frightened child! The only one who's frightened when he carries on like that is *me!*"

The screamer hides behind the intensity of his ferocious bravado, so no one will ever guess he feels little and fragile. He is so preoccupied with his deafening outbursts, he is too terrified to even recognize his own true feelings. Instead, he denies his fears, sadness and disappointments and resorts to the expressive vehicle he has been conditioned to use . . . loud, assertive talk and excessive displays of anger.

When the screamer was small, his parents probably felt too inadequate to deal with his problems . . . perhaps they were overwhelmed with difficulties of their own. By shouting instead of showing his hurt or pain, the screamer could have caused his parents to misinterpret his noisy call for help as a show of strength. The parents could handle his yelling; for them it was reassuring and demonstrated that their child was capable of taking care of himself. Relieved, because they misjudged his message, they could then feel free to focus on their own conflicts.

Had the child revealed his sadness and frustrations to his parents, it might have signaled them that he needed their help, attention and support. But they were unable to help him. Because they were swamped themselves with problems, their emotional resources were already spent in attempts to deal with their own pain and trials.

When the screamer becomes an adult, his tirades continue.

They are so discordant and so intimidating that others' ears tend to protectively close in fear. The people to whom his messages are directed are seldom strong enough to listen to his sudden blasts of intense fury. No one knows he is in trouble. So the screamer might as well be silent, because his true message . . . HELP . . . is rarely heard.

THE SILENT ONE

Another extreme example of an unsuccessful communicator . . . the apparent opposite position of the screamer . . . is "the silent one." He is the person who goes dead in verbal interactions. Whenever emotional temperatures rise, he freezes. When he feels wounded because someone has been inconsiderate or irritating, he clams up. He is just as frightened as the screamer, but he reacts to his frustrations, hostilities and annoyances by becoming verbally paralyzed.

The silent one doesn't fare any better than the screamer. Neither one of their communication styles is very effective. In the case of the silent one, his messages can't be heard because they aren't even delivered! When he withdraws into his own world for escape and protection . . . no one can possibly understand what he's feeling . . . no one can help him or meet his needs, either.

Often, his early training as a "people pleaser" has taught the silent one to be nice and quiet whenever a conflict flares. He is "the good one," the peacekeeper. Even if he's seething with anger, he is rarely able to express it. But slowly, the pressure builds . . . his resentments multiply and his inner tension increases. He's like a balloon that keeps expanding until it bursts: His pent-up fury stretches to the breaking point until he finally explodes in an outpouring of resentment and fury. The person on the receiving end of his communication is then left bewildered by the sudden overreaction on the part of the formerly silent person.

Holding in strong emotions for long periods is only one pattern that "silent ones" learn during childhood. In some cases, their anger is veiled in psychosomatic symptoms that are cloaked in an endless variety of aches and pains that keep them visiting psychologists' and medical doctors' offices. Their symptoms can be expressed in a variety of ways including asthma, colitis, spastic colon, acne, piles, ulcers, headaches etc. Still other "silent ones" learn their families' style of using disguised verbal attacks such as sarcasm, criticism, gossiping or boredom as their indirect modes of sounding off.

The self-destructive substitutes for expressing anger are almost unlimited. Sometimes buried hostility is expressed as depression, overeating, gambling, alcoholism, drug addiction, losing money, laziness, sexual impotence or frigidity. In each case, the results are the same. The avenue used to conceal anger serves as a smoke-screen, obscuring the true nature of the silent person's feelings. When this happens, useful and effective communications are blocked . . . and they can neither be transmitted nor received.

IF I WERE YOU, I'D LEAVE!

Carl and Maxine, a couple in my Tuesday night group, had "loser" verbal skills and difficult problems communicating. During one session, they reported that they had gotten into a terrible fight while driving home from a party one evening.

Maxine said that Carl had humiliated her, by "flirting all night with someone else!" Her method of dealing with this was by screaming, criticizing him severely and name calling.

"How could you have been so *stupid* at that party!" she raged. "You were acting like an *idiot!* Everyone there was talking about you! They were all coming up to me and saying, 'That husband of yours is really making a *fool* of himself! I wouldn't put up with it! If I were you, *I'd leave him!*'"

Maxine's communication was so full of accusations and blame that her real feelings—"I love you and I'm so terrified that *you will leave me*"—couldn't be heard.

Marriage partners use insulting verbal attacks all too frequently. When this happens, neither one knows that he is valuable and important, or that the other person cares. When there is a lot of name calling, all that registers are words like "stupid," "idiot," "fool," and threats like "leave." No one has the ego strength to hear the buried message, "I love you and need you."

In the long-established pattern of their marriage, once Maxine had dumped on Carl she was ready to get back to normal . . . but Carl wasn't. Now it was his turn: He would torture Maxine with silence, and his lack of response would force her to begin guessing what was wrong.

For Maxine, once she had unloaded her angry feelings on Carl during their argument in the car, she felt relieved and was finished with the entire episode. She was ready to be friendly and go on. It never occurred to her that Carl was still smarting from her verbal attack. So when he started his silent act, she failed to realize that it was a direct result of their quarrel.

If Maxine and Carl had *not* been in therapy, they would have spent the next two weeks putting their energies into dealing with *his refusal to talk* and *her guilt about her vengeful words.*

Instead, we worked on communicating their true feelings. Maxine shared how threatened she felt when Carl was talking to the other woman at the party. She was afraid he didn't love her anymore. And Carl explained that he had similar worries . . . Maxine often frightened him!

He became aware that the only time he felt secure with Maxine was when he made her jealous. It was when she got so angry about his talking to another woman that Carl felt reassured. Then he believed she *really did love him.* There was a distinct pay-off for him to engage in these jealousy ploys. Otherwise, Maxine rarely expressed positive or caring words directly to Carl.

When he remained silent after a fight, Carl received still more reassurances from Maxine. It was at these times that she was so intent on making up with him that she would show great concern for him and become overtly loving and affectionate.

In therapy, Maxine and Carl learned to be direct and express more physical affection and verbal positives to one another. Eventually the jealousy maneuvers became unnecessary as both partners felt safe and stable within the marriage.

* * *

When jealousy is employed by lovers as a tactic, it is usually an act of aggression in retaliation for hurts received. So if your mate tries to make you jealous, instead of becoming nasty or accusative, stop and think for a moment: "How did *I* provoke it?"

Are you "low" on being attentive and loving, and "high" on frightening your spouse or making him jealous? Have you fallen down on delivering your honest positives, thinking, "It isn't necessary. He already knows that I *love* him."

He *doesn't* know!

Even if you mentioned that you loved him yesterday, you need to repeat it today. Remember that the long-legged, adult person that you are in love with is *only* two years old emotionally.

When your mate feels confident that you cherish him, his actions and feelings will take a different direction. People develop a strong sense of responsibility and a dedication to behave more lovingly when they know they are adored.

Most people tend to mirror back the communications that are delivered to them. If you extend loving feelings, they are more apt to be returned you . . . *quid pro quo* . . . measure for measure.

Be watchful. If you are attracting a good deal of hostility . . . WAKE UP . . . and check your *own* behaviors. Accept that *at least half* of the problem lies in your *ineffective* verbal interactions.

EXERCISE 10: USING YOUR "PASS-THE-BUTTER" VOICE

This exercise outlines a method for you to use to increase your winning verbal skills. It can be used as a guide for handling all kinds of conflicts and resentments in your life. The skills listed here build on those you've already practiced in Exercise #9, "The Positive Swim."

Your manner of speaking is *learned*. Whatever your verbal mode is now, you can *learn* to expand the power and scope of your communicative ability and drop your ineffective verbal styles.

This exercise provides a simple formula that you can rely on in a heated situation when your mind tends to go blank. The pattern to remember is:

First deliver three *honest positives* (+ + +).
Then deliver the problem briefly (−).
Then deliver another *honest positive* (+).

Whether your "conference table" is in a multi-million-dollar corporation or in your own breakfast nook, it is important for you to find healthy ways to express yourself. Remember: While the people you are hoping to influence may be capable and even brilliant in many areas, emotionally they are small and very fragile. Always start with words that are kind and warm, so their ears will open and they can hear you. Then express yourself honestly.

The voice you will need to use is similar to the voice that would be appropriate if you were asking someone to "please pass the butter" at your dinner table. This voice is free from sarcasm or innuendo. It is pleasant to listen to . . . the sound is agreeable.

If the person were your spouse, you might start off this way:

POSITIVE 1: "Honey, you are so important to me."

POSITIVE 2: "You are the center of my love life."

POSITIVE 3: "Everything you do has meaning to me, because I love you so much."

PROBLEM: "I was very hurt when you spent so much time talking to that woman at the party. I felt so frightened that I began worrying, 'Would you ever leave me?'"

Before you finish this communication, give your mate another positive:

POSITIVE 4: "Honey, I love you and I need you. You are so precious to me."

SPEAKING UP

The formula in Exercise 10 provides a technique for speaking up. You will find it useful not only in love relationships but in any interaction with others . . . business associates or friends . . . in which a conflict may develop. Just remember the formula: three honest positives . . . then the problem *briefly* . . . then another honest positive.

People who don't speak up often complain that they are afraid to try, because they believe that there is little hope of changing their situation. Winners know they won't always be able to create the changes they would like to make in their lives, but regardless of what the predictable results may be, *they are committed to taking a stand*. They make an effort to influence the course of events.

WINNERS SPEAK UP EVEN WHEN THE ODDS ARE SLIM THAT THEIR COMMUNICATION WILL EVER CHANGE THINGS.

I helped one patient, Doree, discuss a grievance with her lawyer. She was aggravated with him about a bill she had received. Doree had not been warned in advance that her lawyer's fees had gone up. Without notice she had been charged at a higher rate for her last three visits to his office.

Annoyed, Doree decided to call him. As she was dialing she thought to herself, "I may not be able to do anything about this, but I'm so furious, I want to at least try."

When Doree reached her attorney, she began following the script we had worked on together. Remembering her lawyer was only "two years old," she used her "pass-the-butter voice" and her honest positives:

POSITIVE 1: "I really admire and trust your abilities."

POSITIVE 2: "I wouldn't dream of going to anyone else."

POSITIVE 3: "Your work is excellent!"

PROBLEM: "I was angry that without telling me in advance, you charged me 25 percent more than the fee I've been paying for years. When I came to see you last week, I assumed that I was still being charged the old rate. This isn't fair, and I would like to have my statement adjusted for those three visits."

POSITIVE 4: "I want our good feelings to continue because I really respect you as my attorney . . . you're the best!"

Doree's attorney returned her warmth and good feelings. He admitted that his bookkeeper had made an important omission and agreed to have her account corrected.

PROGRAM YOUR REQUEST IN THEIR COMPUTERS

When something is bothering you, if you can go straight to the person involved and openly discuss the problem, your efforts will *always* result in a win. Even if you don't get what you want, you *will get you*. You will enjoy strong feelings of self-respect because you moved into action and tried.

In addition, when you make a direct request, it's as if you've programmed a computer card into the mind of the other person. He may say "No" at the moment, but by expressing your needs, you have registered them in the filing system of his thinking. Sometime in the future this could work to your advantage. Your genuinely open and positive approach will probably leave a favorable impression on him, and if circumstances change, he will be inclined to call back and help you.

If you didn't "program" his computer in the first place with your message, that person would never know a problem existed, and there would be no chance of his changing his mind in your favor.

UNBLOCKING YOUR ENERGY AND CREATIVITY

There's yet another reason that it's very important for you to learn to speak up: Repressed emotions can cause a bottleneck in your thinking. When you withhold intense feelings, you may pay a high psychological price.

Emotions like anger, for example, rarely lie dormant. Instead, they swish back and forth in your mind, like clothes in a washing machine. As you churn the same thoughts and feelings around and around in an ongoing internal conversation, the problem expands and becomes all-consuming. It's on your mind as soon as you get up in the morning. Indeed, it doesn't matter what you're doing . . . eating, driving, exercising or working . . . the unresolved feelings invade every corner of your consciousness. There is no rest as the anger in your mind keeps churning and multiplying.

When problems become obsessions, so much time goes into replaying your painful thoughts that you have little vigor left for being creative, energetic or happy. Your resources have already been spent on the replays.

Sometimes people who are unable to express anger directly do so passively by holding grudges. They collect injustices and hold onto them indefinitely. Their minds are virtual storehouses for grievances . . . accumulating gripes about even minor incidents and brooding about them endlessly. Because some people seldom communicate their feelings and dispel their fury, they remain stuck. They are the perpetual victims who count their injuries and complain how they are "always" abused and mistreated.

When *you can speak up* and release yourself from the festering burden of angry grudges, the atmosphere surrounding your life will stay sweet and pleasant. Under these conditions, and with your mind at peace, you will have more energy and time to create. Then you will find more opportunities to be successful.

EXERCISE 11: LETTING GO OF COLLECTED INJUSTICES

If you have collected injustices over the years, it is time to break free and let go. Stop counting all of the times when you were slighted, humiliated or otherwise treated badly. Realize that you are the one who is now inflicting the injustices . . . on yourself.
YOU CAN STOP YOUR SELF-
DESTRUCTIVE THINKING NOW!
Whenever you feel that you have been unfairly singled out, abused or rejected, read the following suggestions over and over:

• *Stop the action in your head.*
Instruct yourself to cease and desist your endless annoyances and complaints. Imagine that you are the very person with whom you are angry, remembering that you are probably 50 percent responsible for the problem. Explore the other's inner feelings, and see if you can take *his* side. Force yourself to be sympathetic with *his* cause. This will help you understand the point of view that he is struggling with.

• *Recognize that there are good people out there who are different from you.*
Don't expect everyone to conduct himself in the manner you do, or think and evaluate situations in your way. Realize that when you expect others to respond to you in kind and do for you precisely what you have done for them . . . you are setting yourself up to be disappointed. No one will look at reality exactly the way you do. No one has had your exact upbringing or your precise life experiences.

• *Be assertive.*
You can be more assertive without being hostile or intrusive. When you feel slighted, say so, remembering that no one has intentionally set out to hurt you. Too many people find it easier to hold grudges than to ask directly for what they want. Let your wishes be known.

For example, you could come right out and say, "I would love to be included in your guest list." While you may sometimes meet painful rejection, it is often wisest to take a stand and let people know what you want. But do this gently and warmly.

• *Examine whether you are making unreasonable demands on others.*
It will not always be appropriate for you to be assertive; you will need to use your judgment. For example, it's childish to imagine that you will be invited to every occasion by your friends or relatives. You don't include *everyone, every time,* and you need to know when *not* to complain when you're excluded. Realize that you can be truly admired and well liked and still be left out. Deal with your disappointment by understanding that no setting is large enough to accommodate everyone.

• *Remember that no one is out to get you.*
People are rarely deliberately cruel. More often they are unwittingly neglectful or inconsiderate. When others are troubled or preoccupied with their own problems, they can be insensitive to your feelings and unable to recognize their errors or omissions. It

will be healthy for you to assume that others are well meaning when they have hurt your feelings. Chances are they slighted you unconsciously, so before you respond to them, remind yourself that their intentions were probably very good.

• *Give gifts for your own satisfaction.*

Extend your love or give presents to others because you derive pleasure from doing so. Throw your rulers and measuring scales away and work at enjoying whatever it is that you receive. Don't get caught up in expecting equal gifts in return.

THE GOOD LISTENER

A winning communication, which will keep the interest of the person you are talking to, is a conversation that moves BACK and FORTH between the two of you. Part of your responsibility is to speak up and let the other person know who you are. The other part is your ability and willingness to *LISTEN* to the other person.

It is important to learn how to focus your full attention on the speaker without interrupting, and to answer what has been said directly once that person has finished sharing his ideas. Don't bring up another topic that is on your mind without first responding to him.

Sometimes you may encounter people who seem to be deaf to your words and ideas. They are what I call "train talkers," poor listeners whose communication skills are almost nonexistent. When you speak with them, you feel like you're trying to catch a moving train that speeds along, spewing out steam. No matter what you say, train talkers just keep going, seemingly oblivious to your input and suggestions. They carry on a monologue, ignoring your comments, as though you weren't there.

Research has suggested that "train talkers" are not liked. A study by Dr. Chris Kleinke at the Edith N. Rogers Memorial Veterans Hospital in Bedford, Massachusetts, showed that the amount of time you spend listening strongly influences the impression you make on others. Dr. Kleinke's experiment revealed that people who speak 80 percent of the time and listen only 20 percent of the time are not as well liked as those who speak and listen in equal proportions.*

* Chris L. Kleinke, "First Impressions," (Englewood Cliffs, N.J.: Prentice-Hall Inc., 1975), p. 84.

TANIA THE TRAIN TALKER

One of my patients, Tania, came to see me with her nine-year-old son, Judd. During their first visit, she complained that Judd rarely conversed with the family and spent most of his time alone in his room.

Observing the interplay between Judd and Tania, it soon became obvious to me how the boy's silence had been shaped and nurtured by his mother.

This is a typical example of how they spoke to each other during one of their sessions with me. Soon after they arrived, Tania explained that they had just eaten lunch:

TANIA: The gorgeous restaurant we went to served the finest poached salmon I have ever eaten! It was so fresh, succulent and well prepared that I could have had twice as much!

JUDD: Mom, what was the funny French name of that apple dessert I had?

TANIA: And the fish sauce! What a culinary dream. I have never enjoyed a better lunch. Don't you agree, son? *(She turned toward Judd.)*

JUDD: Mom, was it a Tarte Tartan?

TANIA: We both ate like horses, didn't we, dear? *(The boy lowered his chin onto his chest and stared silently into his lap, without responding.)*

TANIA: See what I mean, Dr. Kassorla? He hardly ever talks to me.

Tania was completely unaware that during this brief exchange she had *ignored* Judd *twice* when he had spoken to her. Each time the boy asked about his dessert, she had gone right on elaborating about the fish, acting as though he weren't even there.

No wonder Judd didn't talk! It's predictable that a child who is forced to interact regularly with a "train talker" will be molded into a "silent one." Because Tania treated Judd as though he were invisible, it was reasonable for him not to respond, remain silent and try to escape to his room when they were home. Though he may have been too isolated, it seemed better to him than sitting beside his mother feeling lonely and ignored.

Understandably, Judd was learning to behave exactly the way his mother did. During their conversation about the restaurant, when Tania finally did speak directly to him, saying, "Don't you agree, dear?" Judd had completely ignored her comments about the fish sauce and their lunch. He wasn't listening, either, and had responded with a question about his dessert!

In our sessions together, Judd revealed that he felt extremely inadequate. He believed that his mother never listened to him because what he said was unimportant.

In time, I was able to help Judd and Tania understand the dynamics of their interactions. At first, Tania couldn't accept that she was the one who actually stopped her son from joining in conversations.

This is yet another example of how people pass on neurotic family patterns from one generation to the next. Tania, who was shaped by her parents to be a "train talker," was now raising another noncommunicator. Had she not sought help, Judd was quickly developing into a non-effective communicator who would probably have grown up to raise "train-talking" children of his own!

BE CAUTIOUS ABOUT PROJECTING

Another type of communication that weakens your effectiveness involves projecting your feelings onto other people. Most of us tend to do this at times. For example, when we are in emotional pain, we perceive that everyone "out there" seems to have a sad face; when we are exhausted, everyone we observe seems to be fatigued.

When I was a youngster, I can remember that when my mother felt cold, I had to put on my sweater! Parents rarely check their children's needs. They believe they know us so well that they can accurately read our minds. Often the line between their projections and what is really happening to us becomes blurred. We are so accustomed to being told what we are feeling that we may have difficulty getting in touch with our own realities and thoughts. Then, when we are adults, there is a real danger that we will incorporate our parents' projective techniques into our own conversational styles.

One way you may project your ideas onto others is by giving them limited conversational choices and controlling the parameters of their responses. For example, you may ask, "Are you feeling tired or cranky?" But it could be that *neither* of the choices you offered is accurate! You would increase your verbal effectiveness if you ask, "What are you feeling?" This would permit the other person to scan the range of his emotions and respond with the most accurate information he possesses. Then the answer would come from the source, the person involved, and not from your projections or the two limited alternatives, "tired or cranky," that you presented.

"ARE YOU ANGRY, MOMMY?"

Years ago, I was driving to the market with my daughter Jackie, who was then two years old. I was unusually quiet, and she looked at me with a troubled expression. Touching my arm, she asked, "Are you angry, Mommy?"

I was startled, because at that moment I had been thinking something like "Should I buy lamb chops or chicken? No, I think I'll make veal tonight."

I wasn't a bit angry, just deep in thought. But after Jackie's question, I realized that my "thinking face" delivered another message. Apparently, I did look angry and gave Jackie the impression that I was thinking "You are the naughtiest little girl in the world. Boy! Am I angry with you!"

Fortunately, Jackie checked, so she didn't have to rely on what she had *guessed* my face was saying. Had she acted on her assumption and related to me as though I were angry, I might have been so confused that I *could* have become annoyed and started a fight with her!

Instead, by finding out on the spot what was on my mind, Jackie helped me to be more aware of the way I was relating. Her question made me realize that I needed to be more cognizant of my behavior and more sensitive to how I was treating her. It helped me to be careful about my communication, not only with Jackie, but with everyone.

My daughter is a young woman now, and I'm *still* concerned about my thinking face! I try to monitor that I don't look angry when I'm with people . . . when I'm really silently thinking about lamb chops!

* * *

To maximize effective communication, a winner gathers all of the cues at his disposal to help him understand and reach someone else. He *does pay attention* to every nuance of the other person's behavior . . . his expression; his body language; the tempo, tone and frequency of his words; changes in the sound of his voice . . . every hint he can gather for feedback. But having done all this is still not enough! You need to check out verbally the meaning of your data, rather than jump to a conclusion and imagine what the other person is thinking and feeling.

WINNERS REMOVE THE GUESSWORK
FROM THEIR
INTERACTIONS BY ASKING DIRECT QUESTIONS.

Losers do the reverse. They tend to make almost instant judgments based on subtle expressions or gestures. With very little to go on, they assume that they can read the other person's mind. Then they act on their assumptions. This approach offers about the same validity as consulting a crystal ball or a Ouija board.

BECOME A WINNING COMMUNICATOR.

Ask questions and check out your hunches with the person involved. Go directly to him, so that you can get the most reliable information available . . . free from your projections.

SIXTY DIFFERENT INTERPRETATIONS

The futility of making assumptions based on a few visual cues was dramatically pointed out to me in an undergraduate psychology class I attended when I was a student. The course was abnormal psychology and was held in a room laid out like a small theatre. I sat with approximately sixty other students in seats that rose in steplike fashion toward the rear of the room.

One day, about thirty minutes into the class, the door suddenly flew open and a man who was being chased bolted into the lecture hall screaming, "You're crazy! You don't know what you're doing! I'm innocent!"

It all happened very quickly. The man ran in and out of the room in a flash. He was followed closely by another man who was shouting, "I hate you! You'll never get away with this!" The second person had a gun in his hand, which he fired twice.

The entire episode was over in perhaps eight seconds. Right after the shots were fired, the professor said, "This was a planned event. Get out your pens and paper and start writing about what has just occurred."

We were asked to turn in our reports at the end of the class. A week later the professor informed us that though we'd all seen the *same* incident, we had expressed a variety of *unique* accounts of what we perceived as having taken place. The descriptions were so disparate, it seemed as though each of us had witnessed different events in entirely different settings!

At the next class meeting, our teacher handed out a series of pictures and a multiple-choice questionnaire. We were to check the box alongside each photo that best described whether the person in the picture was feeling sad, happy, disappointed, angry, jealous—or whatever emotion was indicated on the paper. There were five choices for each snapshot.

The professor reported the results during the next class. Again, there had been little agreement among us. The details of the experiment were explained to us. The professor said that at the time that the pictures had been taken, the photographer had called out an emotion to the subject, and the person posing had tried to portray it.

Each of us had seen different emotions portrayed in the very *same* pictures. When we compared what the person in the picture was *trying* to convey with what we had *guessed* he felt, few of us could accept the so-called "correct" results.

* * *

These studies suggest that in real life the probability of guessing what the people in your world are feeling is very low. Using the "look-on-his-face" method to guide you in how to behave or react toward others is foolish.

When patients say to me, "I *know* what my spouse (child, parent) is feeling," I stop them.

"You *don't* know," I point out. "You are only guessing! And the probability of your guessing right is so small that it's nonsense to try. Why speculate? When the person is alive and able to answer for himself, drop your assumptions and *ask questions.* Then you can improve your communication and your verbal effectiveness. And when you get the answer . . . BELIEVE THEM . . . ACCEPT IT!"

USING THE INFORMATION YOU HEAR

Once you invite the person you are communicating with to share what is on his mind, it is important to *believe* what you hear.

Suppose you're talking to your business partner. While explaining your reasoning about a venture you're planning, you observe what you think is an annoyed expression on his face. You want to be verbally effective, so you quickly and warmly ask, "What are you thinking?"

When he responds, listen! Don't interpret . . . don't argue . . . don't correct.

JUST LISTEN AND BELIEVE WHAT YOU HEAR.

We've already discussed the fact that losers are "do-it-your-selfers." They think they can rely solely on their own judgments and evaluations. Winners are different. They want and *use* the feedback they get from the people they're talking to. When you can hear another person's point of view, it's like opening a library of new books. There are many new concepts to explore, and many new ideas to absorb.

Most of us limit ourselves; we use *only* our own perceptions, feelings and thoughts. Consequently, we benefit from *only* a portion of the input that is available, as compared to what we could gain if we listened to what the other person can offer us.

BE STILL AND LISTEN.

Don't try to defend your point of view and argue someone out of his feelings or push him toward your position . . . or you will lose his fresh point of view.

When you listen to everything he has to say, a fact that you may have left out, forgotten or overlooked in your reasoning may come up. Don't miss this opportunity for enlightenment.

Winners exist in a world of other people. You do, too. At home and at work, you need to be able to share your feelings and your needs with others, and . . . above all . . . hear about their feelings and needs. The time, effort and energy that you put into learning to communicate better with those around you will be returned to you many times over.

Increasing your verbal effectiveness will produce *multiple* benefits. You will:

- learn to voice your feelings in situations of conflict.
- free yourself of the burden of repressed anger.
- start changing circumstances that make you unhappy.
- preserve and enhance your relationships with others.
- learn to listen.
- become more likeable.
- avail yourself of new sources of information.
- help yourself move closer to your goals.

All of these rewards are available to you. No matter what your present communication skills may be, you can begin improving your verbal proficiency today. Get to work practicing new, more effective communication techniques.
START LEARNING TO BE A WINNING COMMUNICATOR.

WINNER SCORECARD #12

Are problems in your communication style keeping you from getting what you want? Are you ready to start learning to express yourself in ways that will help you move closer to your personal objectives and at the same time improve your relationships with others?

Good! Keep these key points in mind:

LOSERS	WINNERS
1. When situations become highly charged and losers are unable to share their pent-up feelings, they may substitute screaming and shouting. The emotional outlet they have been conditioned to use is loud, assertive talk and excessive anger. They believe that their point has been won when they have silenced everyone else.	**1.** Winners don't deny their feelings, they communicate them to others. Because they are more secure with their sense of adequacy, they can recognize, acknowledge and share their true experiences and emotions.
2. Losers may react to frustration, hostility or annoyance by becoming verbally paralyzed and withdrawing into their own world for escape and protection. Eventually, their feelings may be overwhelming and they explode into a rage or other self-destructive behaviors.	**2.** Winners speak up when something happens that annoys or frustrates them. They go directly to the person involved. They don't let negative reactions collect, fester and grow.

LOSERS

3. When losers are angry or hurt, they often resort to name calling, accusations and blame. Their insulting messages obscure what they really want to communicate. All that registers are their vengeful words which can create irreparable damage to the relationship.

4. Losers don't speak up because they believe there is little hope of changing their situations. They are afraid to even try, because they dread being rejected. Consequently, there is no chance for them to alter their circumstances.

5. Losers let repressed emotions create a bottleneck in their thinking. They churn their anger and resentment over and over in their minds, and their problems expand and become all-consuming. This leaves losers little vigor to be creative, energetic or happy.

6. Unable to express their anger directly, losers hold grudges. They accumulate gripes and collect grievances concerning even minor incidents and brood about them endlessly. They remain stuck . . . perpetual victims, counting their injuries.

WINNERS

3. Winners handle conflicts and resentments by surrounding their complaints with expressions of honest kindness and warmth. In this way, they have a chance of changing things, while still preserving their relationships with the important people in their lives.

4. Winners ask directly for what they want, even when the odds are against success. They know that a direct request programs a computer card into the mind of the other person. While the initial response they receive may be "No," if circumstances change, the other person may call back to grant their request.

5. Winners speak up and release their anger. By surrounding their messages with honest positives and using their "pass-the-butter" voice, they are able to maintain friendships and still be able to discuss and dispel grievances.

6. When there are misunderstandings or disagreements, winners are willing to talk things over because they believe that no one has intentionally set out to hurt them. They also realize that they may have contributed to the conflict themselves.

7. Losers who are "train talkers" ignore other people's efforts to add something to a conversation. Carrying on a monologue, they fail to respond to others. Rather, they continue speaking as if they didn't even hear what was being said.

7. Winners focus their full attention on what the other person is saying to them without interrupting. They listen, then answer directly once he has finished sharing his ideas.

8. Losers project their own feelings onto others. When they are sad, they see pain on others' faces; when they are exhausted, everyone seems to be fatigued. They control conversations by limiting the other person's choice of responses.

8. Winners avoid projecting their feelings onto other people. In conversation, they ask questions, seek feedback, then listen to the other person's words and learn.

9. Losers make almost instant judgments based on subtle expressions or gestures. With little to go on, they assume they *know* what the other person is thinking and feeling. Then they act on their incorrect guesses and speculations.

9. Winners use all the clues at their disposal for information. They observe the other person's face; his body language; the tempo, tone and frequency of his words; and changes in the sound of his voice. But then they *question* the other person to check out the accuracy of their hunches and interpretations.

10. Losers believe they can rely solely on their own judgments and evaluations. They try to argue others out of their feelings and push them toward their own point of view.

10. When winners ask someone else what he is thinking, they hear their messages, without judgments or interruptions. They explore the other person's perceptions. They can tolerate differences . . . they know that theirs is not the only way of looking at life.

CHAPTER 13

Face Up to Conflicts and Be Verbally Effective

I was angry with my friend;
I told my wrath, my wrath did end.
I was angry with my foe;
I told it not, my wrath did grow.
—WILLIAM BLAKE

At no time is the ability to communicate more important than when you are angry or in conflict. Yet many people find that it is in precisely such circumstances that they haven't the skills to cope. When there is a need to say "No" to another person, to face their anger or point out their mistakes, many people are so filled with fear that they are almost immobilized. In this chapter, we'll continue to work on improving your verbal effectiveness, by providing you with new techniques to get your message across . . . even in the most difficult situations.

HOW TO SAY NO WITHOUT SAYING GOODBYE

Part of learning how to be a winner is acquiring the ability to say "No."

Without being able to say "No," you can't be a complete person. Instead, you'll become an unwilling slave, the constant victim of others' wants and desires.

How often do you say "Yes" when what you want to say is "No"?

Are you afraid you might hurt the other person's feelings? Do you say "Yes" quickly and almost automatically, then hate yourself later for doing so?

If you can't say "No," are you the resentful "sacrificer" who always says "Yes" . . . the person who gives all and reminds everyone about it later? Or are you the one who fails to take care of yourself and becomes a burden to everyone you dominate with your guilt and tortured sighs? If so, their resentment toward you will grow, and their feelings of love for you will dwindle and die.

Whether the requests you receive are frivolous whims or matters of critical significance to your loved ones, your communications must include the ability to say "no" so that *your needs will be considered.*

At the opposite extreme from the "sacrificer" who never says "No" is the person who says "No" all too often and in an angry way. Can this be you? If so, you're playing an emotional tennis match. When you hit an angry "No" to someone, you may be sure it will be returned in kind.

Losers use harsh and abrupt "Nos." Their delivery conveys an insulting quality and a finality that not only alienates the receiver, but sets up a situation of reciprocal animosity. This is how the tennis game starts; your angry volley today guarantees that tomorrow, in another situation, the other person will feel he "owes you one" and will "get you back."

All too frequently, people who have trouble saying "No" say "Yes," then change their minds at the last minute because they didn't want to consent in the first place. They let you down at the very last minute when it is too late for you to make other plans.

The oldest, shortest words—"yes" and "no"—are those that require the most thought.

—PYTHAGORAS

Saying "No" is a difficult communication skill to put into practice, because most of us have early memories of being scolded or rejected whenever we dared to say "no" to our parents. From our childhoods, we remember that "No" was associated with pain and punishment, long periods of silence, emotional discomfort and withdrawal. In some cases, "No" meant a complete severing of a relationship. This was true because often the "No" was delivered under circumstances of intense anger, with disastrous results.

But where is it written that "No" has to be spoken in rage, with a snarling face and gritted teeth? You can learn to say "No" with a friendly expression on your face. Your delivery can be similar to the easy attitude you have when saying "Yes."

THIS DYNAMO KNOWS HOW TO SAY "NO"

Sherry Lansing, the first woman to head a major Hollywood film studio, was president of 20th Century-Fox while in her early thirties. Quickly labeled a dynamic decision maker, her word had meaning . . . much the way a handshake sealed an oral contract years ago.

Agent Irving Paul Lazar said of Sherry that she is appreciated and highly respected by the people she works with. He told one reporter, "When I ask Sherry to read a script or a book, she reads it right away and *calls me back.* Do you know how many cowards there are in this town who don't call back, and just let you hang there if they don't like something? Silence is the answer they give about 90 percent of the time. But Sherry reads the material I send her and she calls back with a definite answer. She says 'yes' or 'no' —and when it's 'no,' she still keeps you as a friend. Every writer in town will tell you that. She's the best thing writers have had here in years—a breath of fresh air."*

EXERCISE 12: DELIVERING A WARM BUT FIRM "NO"

Whatever your current style of dealing with saying "No" may be, you can learn to be far more effective and do so warmly without losing friends. Whenever you're having trouble, to become more of a winner and deliver a warm but firm "No," review these guidelines:

Step One: Stop Being a Perennial Child

Everyone who demands something of you is *not your mother.* You are not desperate to be parented now . . . you are an adult . . . with independent resources. You no longer require a pat on the head and constant approval from every authority figure. You can say "No" today and you won't be spanked . . . you won't lose approval.

* Budd Schulberg, "What Makes Hollywood Run Now?" *The New York Times Magazine* (April 27, 1980), p. 52.

Step Two: Rule Out Negotiations

By stating your "No" in a friendly, brief and firm way, you will silently communicate, "I have spoken. This is not open to negotiation." Your friendliness shows that you are completely self-assured, and your firmness and brevity signal that the issue is closed.

Step Three: Face the Other Person Nose to Nose

When you are saying "No," watch your body language. Your posture may speak for you in a negative way, contrary to how you want to communicate. Correct this by looking the other person straight in the eye as you talk. Your unspoken message will be that you are certain about what you are saying. If your subtle gestures suggest you feel awkward or lack confidence, the other person will pick up this clue and not believe you.

Step Four: Don't Give Explanations

When you provide reasons for your decision, you are implying that your motivation was capricious and needs justification. A long explanation raises false hopes and suggests that you may be feeling guilty and could be persuaded to reverse your decision. Coming up with a list of excuses and explanations is being disrespectful to yourself. You are a responsible and prudent person, and neither have to defend nor prove your reasons.

Step Five: Allow Yourself a Time-out Period to Think It Over

Even if you are a terrific decision maker, there will be occasions when you are unsure about your response and will need a few days to decide. Assume an attitude of confidence when you express this need. Smiling, say, "I want to think this over. I'll get back to you soon."

1. *Don't be pressured* into an immediate "Yes" or "No" before *you are ready.*
2. Take as much time as you need to arrive at a decision that *you can live with.*

Step Six: Surround Your "No" with Positives

Take advantage of the formula you learned in Exercise #10: "Using Your 'Pass-the-Butter' Voice." In that exercise, you surrounded your message with honest positives. Do the same with your "Nos."

Suppose a friend has asked you to lend him some money and you want to say "No." First state your *honest* positives. Then sandwich in a short "No," and then close with one more honest positive:

Positive 1: "I'm so pleased that you trust me and want to share your money problems."

Positive 2: "Our friendship is really important to me."

Positive 3: "I know my good feelings for you will go on forever."

Your "No" Message: "I don't want to bring money issues into our wonderful relationship."

Positive 4: "I value you so much, I don't want anything to interfere with our loving feelings."

Then add yet another positive by putting your arm around your friend, offering some alternative suggestions, if you can. Then move on to a conversation about something else.

EXERCISE 13: CORRECTING ANOTHER'S MISTAKES

What may be even more difficult than saying "No" is pointing out another person's mistakes in a friendly and productive way. Most of our childhood interactions with parents have taught us how to do this ineffectively by using large doses of negatives and scoldings. While this method may give you the temporary relief of unburdening your pent-up anger, it will cause others to flee . . . or to stay and sabotage you. Your old childhood techniques will prevent you from winning as an adult. Now you can learn another way to communicate when facing the uncomfortable situation of needing to "call someone down":

Step One: Start With Positives

Even though you are very upset with someone's performance (or mistakes), it is important for him to hear what you have to say. So start with your positives.

Let's assume your problem is with a valuable employee who is extremely late with a project. You want to reassure him about your appreciation of him, get out some of your feelings and still keep him productive, cooperative and happy.

Positive 1: "Your record of achievement has been remarkable."

Positive 2: "Your projects are so well organized and so detailed that I've used them as examples for our new people."

Positive 3: "You're a valuable part of our team."

(Now it will be time . . . after you have mentioned his strong points . . . to proceed with the troubling situation that is bothering you.)

Present the problem: "This project is the first commitment you've failed to meet since I've known you, and I'm concerned about the delay."

Positive 4: "I'd sure like to help you with the problem, because I know how dependable and capable you've always been."

It's wise to allow him to respond. Then a problem solving dialogue can ensue. Afterward you may change the subject to a topic that is mutually rewarding and go on to sharing some pleasant feelings.

You can use this exercise and adapt it to other relationships, inside and outside of your business life. Just be sure to make your criticisms and complaints concise. See to it that your honest expressions of esteem are generous. This will produce the winning changes in others that you're looking for.

I DIDN'T REALIZE

Sometimes, much to your surprise, you may find that you've upset another person with a remark that you made quite innocently, thinking it was fine. You didn't realize it was extremely negative or insulting. Here's a good way to handle the conflict that arises then.

Too often when we speak, we unwittingly hurt the people we care about. We are insensitive and don't realize how it feels to be on the receiving end of what we're saying.

Somewhere between the point where we organize ideas in our minds and the moment when we speak, distortions can occur. Sometimes the words leave our mouths in a different form than we intended and an idea can take an unexpected turn.

We believe that what we are saying is harmless. We imagine that we are just being honest, or perhaps teasing a bit, and having fun. We are shocked when our listener seems to think quite differently! Surely he is thin-skinned, has little sense of humor and is taking our remarks far too seriously. We are unaware that what we said was overly critical and probably very humiliating.

Suppose you are speaking to someone who is very close to you. You're certain that you're handling yourself in an easy, conversational way, but suddenly he erupts in angry, frustrated shouting!

Try to be still and hear what he has to tell you. The person with whom you are speaking is the one who can best describe to you how it feels to receive what you say. His perceptions can help you unravel the reasons for your ineffective communications.

Begin by realizing that you *may* have wounded him. The fact that you didn't intend to be cruel doesn't absolve you. Forget about your intentions. Instead of reacting with surprise to his anger, *use* the information he is offering you about how the interaction wounded him.

Say to yourself, "I thought I was just casually stating my opinions. I didn't think I said anything terrible. But judging from his reaction, something else must have happened, because I can see that I have really hurt his feelings!"

Don't attack the other person or defend yourself by saying things like "You misunderstood me. You're so touchy! I didn't say anything wrong. Can't you ever take a joke?"

Instead, slow down . . . pay attention . . . and then reply: "I really care about your feelings and I didn't realize that I was being inconsiderate. I don't ever want to do that."

Tell the person that you were feeling very good about him, and that you are concerned that your delivery fell so far from your intended mark. The healthier your personality is, the easier it will be for you to talk about YOUR MISTAKES and resolve the problem.

When you can assume your part in his negative reaction, he will be able to calm down. He will recognize that your intentions were not malicious, that you were simply unaware of the insulting effect of your words.

Become verbally effective and welcome feedback when you get too far off base. Get people to help you, to work with you and to support you.

DEVENOMIZING THE ENEMY

Imagine that you've just heard from a friend that Barry, an old business associate, has been criticizing you. He says that you're unethical and way out of line because you repeated something he had mentioned to you in absolute confidence. He's furious with you, because a leak now could cause him to lose a big deal.

Suddenly your pulse rate increases and your stomach starts tightening as you think to yourself, "Why is that fool Barry making such a fuss? I just mentioned casually that he had landed a huge account. What's so terrible? If I were in his shoes and *he* told everyone, I'd be proud of it! I didn't kill his mother . . . I just jumped the gun a little bit."

To reassure yourself, you run through all the reasons you think Barry is overreacting and all the reasons you just *know* you didn't do anything so wrong.

To give yourself an added boost and release some of the anger you're beginning to feel toward Barry because he is mad at you, you start a gossip campaign about him. You tell everyone who will listen every negative fact you can remember about Barry. This gives you a feeling of relief and the sense that you are "getting back at him."

No more sound sleeping . . . you're up every night now, imagining how you're going to "tell him off" and fantasizing about elaborate schemes to hurt Barry . . . everything from beating him up in a public place to insulting his wife.

Deep in your heart, you know that these are all ridiculous loser tactics, but you don't stop. One sleepless night, you visualize a scene in which Barry calls you. He is extremely friendly and insists on renewing his friendship with you. In your fantasy, he tells you that you are a genius and a great humanitarian. He apologizes profusely for having been foolish enough to criticize and reject you. Then, as your fantasy plays on, Barry is on *The Tonight Show*, telling the country how great you are!

Finally, after wasting a month being a loser, engaged in this unproductive gossiping and fantasy, you decide to do something more realistic to correct the problem . . . you reach for the phone to call Barry.

EXERCISE 14: GOING TO THE PHONE

Is there anyone in your life about whom you are carrying around unresolved angry feelings? Anyone with whom you have unsettled conflicts? Do you have fantasy conversations with this person when you're in bed at night? Stop wasting your emotional energy! It's time to try to reinstate the good feelings the two of you had before your misunderstanding!

Begin by moving into action. Be straightforward and call the other person . . . the sooner the better! Remember, winners work at quickly correcting their mistakes, without self-flagellation or guilt.

When you go to the phone, your goal is to be mature, warm and "big" enough to admit that you didn't handle an incident well.

Suppose it's the situation with Barry—though you didn't intend to be malicious, the reality is that you *did* disclose a confidence and it did hurt Barry.

Here are some pointers you can keep right in front of you when you are ready to make your phone call. While they are presented here to apply to your imaginary conflict with Barry, they will provide a framework to refer to when you are involved in any disagreement.

Step One: Be Vulnerable

The minute you hear Barry's voice, say, "I made a big mistake when I repeated what you told me. I feel foolish now. At the time I was doing it, I was just so excited about your good news that I never stopped to consider how irresponsible I was being in not respecting your confidentiality."

Step Two: Deliver Some Honest Positives

You can't be too generous when you bring in your honest positives. Praise three or four of the qualities you most admire in Barry: "You have an excellent reputation in our field, and I truly respect you, as does everyone else. In our dealings, you have always been honest and aboveboard. I value our relationship greatly."

Step Three: Arrange a Meeting

Extend yourself and say, "I've been thinking about you a lot this last month. I really miss our friendship and I'd enjoy taking you to lunch."

Step Four: Keep Repeating

Go back to steps 1 through 3 as often as necessary, until Barry agrees to meet with you.

Step Five: Greet Him Warmly and Share Your Feelings

When Barry appears for your lunch date, put your arm around him and extend your warmest greetings: "I'm so pleased you were willing to see me." Tell him how worried you were that you would lose his friendship. Describe how painful his rejection was to you, even though you know you deserved his anger.

If you express yourself genuinely, it will be possible for your relationship to mend almost instantly and become even stronger than ever.

Verbal effectiveness will be useful to *you* in reducing your daily conflicts, whether you are speaking to your own small child or to a group of business associates.

Learning to verbally negotiate the difficult moments and problems in your life will help you get what you want, make your life flow more smoothly and free you from the energy-sapping burdens of resentment or guilt.

Now you have more information to help you. Get busy putting these ideas into practice at every opportunity, and before you know it, you'll be reducing conflicts and communicating like a verbally effective winner!

WINNER SCORECARD #13

Winners face up to conflicts and disagreements and use polished communication skills to work them out. You can learn to do the same. Keep these pointers in mind:

LOSERS	WINNERS

1. Losers are afraid to say "No," so they become the constant victims of everyone else's wants and desires. Because of their reluctance to say "No," they sometimes wait until the last minute, then disappoint others when it is too late for them to rearrange their plans.

1. Winners consider their own needs and say "No" when appropriate. They deliver their "Nos" in a positive, easy-going manner with a friendly expression on their faces. Their attitude is similar to the one they express when their response is "Yes."

2. When a loser says "No," he often uses harsh, abrupt language, delivered in a rage, with a snarling face and gritted teeth. His underlying message is not only "No," but that there is something inherently wrong with the other person.

2. Winners rely on a simple formula when they want to say "No": First they deliver honest positives, then their message, and finally more positives. They face the other person nose to nose, without providing excuses or long explanations that would suggest that they could be persuaded to reverse their decision.

3. When losers want others to improve their performance, they demoralize them with sarcasm, innuendos, endless putdowns or embarrassing public comments. Then they fail to understand why they don't get the increased motivation and effectiveness they are seeking.

3. When winners want to alert someone that he's made an error, they first let him know they appreciate his strengths and past efforts. After several honest acknowledgments of past performances, they briefly discuss the problem. Before the conversation ends, winners make sure to shift to a topic that is mutually rewarding.

4. Losers react with surprise when someone becomes angry with their remarks. They just *know* that their intentions were good and conclude that the problem *must* be with the "other guy." The losers' response to criticism is attacking others and defending themselves.

4. Winners accept that when someone becomes annoyed with them, they have somehow invited that reaction. They welcome feedback and use the information they receive to try to change and be less insensitive.

CHAPTER 14

How to Make a Great Impression

There are a few times in your life when it isn't too melodramatic to say that your destiny hangs on the impression you make. Such times include the mating season and job hunting. At moments like these, you're not interested in second place.

—BARBARA WALTERS

Wanting to be in first place is a normal and healthy desire. It is fair to work for that status and it is a measure of winning to achieve it.

Introducing yourself to the world in the most self-enhancing way possible is a valuable skill that I want you to begin learning now.

Did you know that winners brag, boast and broadcast their excellence? Wherever they are, winners present themselves in the most flattering professional and social manner they can.

I remember the first time I met Armand Hammer, the illustrious financier, art collector and philanthropist. I was giving a party at my home in honor of Hammer's friend and legal counsel, Sir John Foster. I was very taken with Hammer's vitality and dynamic personality. I found him to be a stimulating conversationalist, and his friendly, boyish spontaneity completely captivated me.

Hammer told me wonderful tales about his past, and his enthusiasm was contagious. I was instantly caught up in the remarkable story of how he had engineered his career from medical student to oil magnate. Listening as he unfolded his personal history was like watching a documentary film of a heroic figure.

He didn't miss a single opportunity to fascinate and impress me. He described in detail episode after episode in which his brilliant strategies and aggressive pursuit of opportunities had enabled him to triumph over formidable obstacles. And as he related some of his experiences to me, I realized that his worth lay not only in his distinctive achievements, but in his genuine concern about people. I was truly touched by this caring humanitarian.

A casual eavesdropper might have described the way he spoke to me as self-centered and full of braggadocio. But my honest evaluation of his sharing his life with me was quite different. I felt privileged to know some of the details about the excitement of his genius . . . he was a unique and unforgettable man! I was content, intrigued . . . and thoroughly involved as I listened to him.

Hammer knew how to present himself. He didn't work his way up to the very pinnacle of the international oil and finance pyramids by keeping quiet about his abilities. He was skilled at presenting his exceptional credentials and talents to the person before him.

SHOW YOUR STRENGTHS

Broadcasting your accomplishments is one way to send honest positives in your own direction. This is appropriate and fair for you to do. I approve of positive reinforcements, whether you give them to yourself or to the person next to you. They work, and are a healthy way to create an uplifting atmosphere that will be motivating and energizing for everyone.

Many of my close personal friends are winners. They are special people who are high achievers, and they often discuss their work and their unusual, thrilling activities with me. I take pleasure in hearing their success stories, which are often filled with instructive and entertaining vignettes about how they made their mark.

Their lives are modern-day novels, and as they turn the pages, they happily offer the "how-tos" of their successes. I want to listen to every word and learn from what they have to say. I am grateful for the insights they are willing to share and I respect their struggles and their wins.

You can let others know how bright, energetic and hard-working you are. Advertise your fine qualities and talk about your excellence. It is important to show your strengths. If you're going to become a winner . . . you, too, need to learn how to present yourself in a dynamic and positive way.

You may be feeling uneasy now as you read this advice. Are you concerned that if you follow it, you will come across as egotistical or obnoxious? Just how uncomfortable you become when you think about presenting yourself positively will be in direct proportion to how strong a dose of training in mediocrity you received from your early training.

SARAH'S REMARKABLE DISCOVERY

As children, most of us learn that to boast or even to listen to a boaster will be judged with disdain. Our loving parents unwittingly teach us this by stuffing defeatist ideas into our impressionable minds. Their indoctrination in how to present ourselves as losers starts when we're very young. Over and over, our adoring guardians repeat hackneyed aphorisms like "Those who know don't talk, and those who talk don't know," or "People with fat heads have thin minds."

Our mothers and fathers discourage us from mentioning anything that smacks of superiority, even when the boasting is about our having earned good grades or performed charitable deeds. Their rule is: Maintain modesty at all costs! Any self-approbation is discouraged with sarcastic remarks like "This know-it-all is getting too big for his britches."

Many parents who are intent on preventing their children from acquiring a so-called "big head" fail to realize that they are denying them the very praise and positive regard that youngsters need to insure normal emotional development.

This happened to my patient Sarah, who was twenty-three years old. She suffered from severe feelings of inadequacy, which often develop when a child isn't given enough encouragement and reinforcement for his ingenuity, special qualities or sincere efforts.

When Sarah began therapy, she felt mediocre and uninteresting. She hoped that working with me would help her "get her life together."

A few weeks after her first session, Sarah made a remarkable discovery. When applying for a new job, she was asked to take an intelligence test. When the results came back, Sarah was amazed to discover that the scores indicated she had an exceptionally high I.Q. In fact, the test suggested she was a genius!

Laughingly, Sarah related this news to her family when she got home. She was convinced, however, that someone must have made an error in the scoring. But her mother assured her that the results were correct. Her parents had been told about her exceptional I.Q. when Sarah was only eight years old.

Sarah was incredulous! What! A genius?!!

Why had her parents kept this secret from her for so many years? Her mother's reply was "I didn't want you to get a big head or think that you were better than other children. I was afraid no one would want to play with you if they found out you were different, and I wanted you to be able to grow up normally."

Later, during her session in my office, Sarah sobbed bitterly as she confessed that all of her life she was filled with self-hate because she felt so ordinary. Her parents had complained and criticized her so often as she grew up that she never suspected she was superior in any way. In fact, she believed that the reverse was true. It was only after she received her I.Q. test scores that she finally became aware of her amazing endowment.

By withholding the facts about Sarah's intelligence, her parents prevented her from gaining the self-confidence and sense of dignity that she needed to mature into a healthy adult.

* * *

Whenever you discover that the people in your life are special in any way, or have done something particularly well . . . TELL THEM! When someone is helpful, considerate or exceptional, it is important for them to HEAR about it from you.

REPEAT IT TO THEM FREQUENTLY.

Give everyone you care about your positive feedback, whether they are family, friends or colleagues. Don't withhold your recognition and acknowledgments of them.

GIVE THEM THE OPPORTUNITY TO BOAST.

Everyone needs such information for their personal growth and emotional stability.

STOP THE EDITING

When you want to make a great impression, you've got to speak up and let people know who you are. In Chapter 12, I talked about "silent ones" who are unable to express themselves when they are angry or frustrated. Now I want to describe another group of people who can't speak up . . . people who remain silent in social or work situations because they feel so inadequate and self-conscious. They know of nothing to boast about and are constantly editing what they do have to say.

Before they even open their mouths, they correct the content of what they are about to express . . . and judge it as unimportant, uninteresting, boring and simply not worth saying. These people are losers because they are so afraid to share their thoughts and ideas.

They are so cruel to themselves that frequently their self-criticism destroys their motivation to speak. They are particularly self-punishing and demeaning when they are among a large group of people.

Has an incident like this ever happened to you: You are with four or five acquaintances at a social gathering, and someone in the group is speaking. You are listening intently to the story, when something that is said triggers an idea in your mind that would fit right into the conversation. But rather than make a comment as a winner would . . . you stand there frozen, feeling foolish and embarrassed.

Instead of speaking up, you start editing. You hold back your ideas because you are certain that they are foolish and inappropriate. You believe that if you utter them, everyone will think you are stupid! Looking around, you observe that all of the others seem to be having fun and enjoying the story.

Suddenly the person next to you blurts out exactly what you were thinking, and a roar of laughter praises his wit. While you stand there seething because you didn't grab your chance to participate, all of the group's attention and approval is focused on him. The others are patting him on the back and saying he is clever, humorous and bright . . . while no one even notices you.

Even worse, rather than acknowledging yourself and silently applauding the fact that you at least thought of the same funny idea, you start scolding yourself for being quiet.

You are so preoccupied feeling miserable that you can't even concentrate on what the group is saying now. You notice that your body temperature has risen and you hope no one sees that you are wet with perspiration.

As you experience all these uncomfortable feelings, the conversation moves to another topic. People are laughing, asking questions and offering their ideas about something else. Everybody seems to be having such a good time.

But you're missing the whole thing, because you're still back several beats, remembering what you didn't say and suffering from your self-punishment.

This "judging yourself" behavior can cost you the fun of the entire party. You have set in motion a negative cycle that gains momentum as the night progresses. You look so depressed that people are put off and avoid talking to you. This gives you still more fuel for self-criticism, and your miserable mood accelerates.

Winners, too, are afraid to be rejected or labeled inadequate. Even so, they take a chance . . . they speak up . . . and edit *afterward*. If their words miss the point or have little meaning once they are spoken, winners correct them as best they can, later. Winners don't worry so much about how they will come across. They trust themselves and say what is on their minds. With this attitude, in the long run they are the ones who earn the most approval.

EXERCISE 15: GETTING IT SAID

A key factor in becoming a dynamic and spontaneous speaker is stopping your self-defeating mental editing. Here is a formula that will help to increase your verbal output, make you feel better about yourself and keep you actively in the conversation:

Say It

When an idea comes into your head, say it! Don't start monitoring your words, because by the time you're through, the whole crowd will be into another conversation, and you'll find yourself standing there alone with your well thought out ideas.

Speak up and get your thoughts out!

Stop Analyzing

Stop analyzing your reactions and noting that your pulse rate has increased, your knees are shaking, your palms are getting wet and there's a lump in your throat.

Stop your judgments. Decide in advance that what you want to say is fine, sensible and worthwhile . . . so say it!

Be Spontaneous

Remember that your goal is to be spontaneous. Deliver your words with confidence as you present *you*. Your audience will accept and believe you when you are authentic and self-assured.

Most people are preoccupied with judging and criticizing their *own* behaviors and beliefs. They are so unsure of themselves that it doesn't much matter what you say . . . they might be so troubled, they may not even be listening!

Edit Afterward

Once you have spoken, there's time to begin editing, when it is necessary. If what you said doesn't sound just right to you, you will have a chance to correct it afterward.

Whenever you want to, you can alter your words with phrases like "That didn't quite come out right. What I *wanted* to suggest is . . ." or "Actually, what I'm trying to say is that . . ." or "That sounded funny! What I meant to add is . . ."

You *do* get a second chance! New opportunities to express yourself in another way are available to you.

Mistakes Are Normal

Remember when you are talking that mistakes are normal. They are indications that you are alive and trying. Good!

No One Is Better

Don't glorify the next fellow. Most people think that everyone else is smarter, sexier, better, stronger and funnier than they are. This kind of thinking happens because as children, we learn to extol the superior virtues of the authority figures who raise and teach us. They are more wonderful in our eyes . . . taller, more capable, older, more effective. That was true then. As adults we continue to unrealistically idealize the foibles and frailties of others while severely condemning our own.

Get Involved

Right or wrong, get into life! Feel proud and be nice to yourself when you are willing to get involved. Don't worry about the consequences. Trust yourself and remember to say what *you want to say.*

PUT YOUR WINNING FOOT FORWARD

When you walk into a room, do you immediately say something negative and present a poor image of yourself? Is your initial greeting a collage of self-chastisements and excuses? Instead of offering a warm "Hello," do you arrive with a troubled, aggravated look and complain, "I feel like such an idiot! I set my alarm clock incorrectly and it never went off! I'm sorry for being late. How foolish of me!"

The mind can only absorb the data it is given. If you put yourself down in any one of your conversations, you place negative data about yourself in the minds of others. You program them with information that degrades you and is insulting. This sets up a reciprocal cycle, and these negatives will be played back to you by others, later.

When you present yourself by walking into the room, calling yourself a fool and dumping out all of your mistakes, the computer cards in their minds will read, "This is a stupid fool. He forgets to set the alarm clock and is always late."

On the other hand, when you provide others with information that says that you are intelligent, fun, sensitive and caring, you fill their memories with positives about you. At a future time, when someone asks their opinion of you, they will mentally run through the information you gave them. Pulling out the data you offered them earlier, they will play back what you told them . . . that you are intelligent, fun, sensitive and caring.

Winners present others with a long list of their talents and accomplishments. They remind everyone of their past successes, the good things they're doing now and the positive things they are planning for the future.

GIVE OTHERS THE CHANCE TO SEE *YOUR* EXCELLENT QUALITIES.

Be sure to fill their heads with honestly positive ideas about you, because people quickly form an impression of you that can be very long-lasting. The sound of your voice, the way you organize your thoughts, your posture, your energy . . . every gesture you make will be recorded in the minds of those you meet.

The total essence of your personality, the gestalt of who you are and the person you wish to be, is in YOUR HANDS.

IT IS *YOU* WHO WILL DETERMINE HOW OTHERS ASSESS YOU.

IT IS *YOU* WHO PRESENTS WHO YOU ARE.

The favorable or unfavorable first impression of you will happen within minutes. If you act like a loser when you go out on a job interview, for example, you will probably be finished before you ever get started. The people assessing you will be closely observing everything you do. Just your body language, the way you move, can tell them whether or not you are a likely candidate.

If you walk into a job interview feeling depressed . . . perhaps in a black funk because you are desperate about being out of work . . . these cues will be picked up. Unfortunately, your glum attitude may be misunderstood by the interviewer. He may think you feel negatively toward him, and in defense, he could turn it around and reject you. His unconscious decision would be "If this person doesn't like me, then the heck with him. I don't like him, either!" He could then follow this thinking with a conscious decision that would hurt you: "This applicant looks like he won't be able to get through the day. I certainly don't want to give him the job. I wonder how fast I can get rid of him."

If you want to be a winner in a job interview or similar important meeting, remind yourself before you open the door that the person you're going to see feels inadequate and frightened, too. Put a smile on your face and remember to be kind to him.

Be enthusiastic! Before the interview, count up all the positives in your life. Talk yourself into feeling good. Say out loud, "I'm a worthwhile human being! I'd be terrific for this job. I'm going to go in there and sell what a fine person I am."

Because people can form a lasting impression of you very quickly, it's important that you thoughtfully prepare a positive presentation of who you are. Your bearing and your facial expressions, as well as your words, will contribute to how you will be evaluated and whether you will be accepted.

Carl Sandburg cautioned that what you say will convey to others who you are:

> Be careful what you say
> When you make talk with words . . .
> for words are made of syllables
> and syllables . . . are made of air.
>
> When you speak greetings,
> tell jokes, make wishes or prayers,
> be careful, be careless, be careful . . .
> be what you wish to be.

JEREMY WAS A LOSER

After several months of job hunting, Jeremy, a recent college graduate, was feeling very depressed and discouraged. He blamed his lack of success on the economy, the entrance of masses of teenagers into the job market, nepotism in the companies that refused to hire him and a consistent run of hard luck.

Finally, Jeremy decided to come in and talk over his problems with me. Before long, it became apparent why he was having so much difficulty.

In terms of his job-hunting skills, Jeremy was a loser. He introduced himself to his future employers in such an unflattering way that there was little chance he'd be hired.

In most of his interviews, without being asked any direct questions, he volunteered a series of negative remarks. "You can't trust people in this day and age," he'd comment. "In big corporations, there is so much back-stabbing and competition that you have to protect yourself every time you go to the water cooler." Or, "With all of my education, I certainly hope that I won't find myself answering to a female boss!"

As if that weren't enough, he also gossiped about former employers, suggesting that one was dishonest, another made promises he didn't keep and a third was having an extra-marital affair with his secretary. Anyone who had heard him making insulting remarks about his previous employers might have thought that Jeremy was trying *not* to get the job.

Jeremy believed that his comments would give the impression that he was sophisticated, keenly aware and knowledgeable and had a droll sense of humor. In reality, however, he came off as a potential troublemaker who would probably create interpersonal conflicts, be resistant and argumentative with his superiors and try to buck the company's policies.

* * *

In a job interview, a winner withholds negatives about himself and others. He works at being cordial and concentrates on showing how his skills, attributes and experience will benefit the company.

JOHANNA BECOMES A STAR

In Britain, I treated a young actress, Johanna, who complained that she was usually out of work. She was relatively unknown and was finding it difficult to get started. She went out on many auditions for parts on television shows and commercials, but she rarely landed a role or even got "called back." She did get hired occasionally, but it was only four or five times a year.

Once Johanna was in therapy with me, part of her work focused on learning to present herself more favorably to the people in her industry.

I encouraged her to emphasize her professionalism by having pictures taken with the lead every time she got even the most insignificant part on a television show. From then on, Johanna made sure that there was a photographer present on every set where she worked. She had $8'' \times 10''$ glossies printed with attached captions listing the name of the show, the star, the channel, the date and time the program was broadcast. They also listed Johanna's name in bold capital letters: "JOHANNA STEVENSON PLAYING GENEVIEVE." I suggested that these photos be mailed out to the various studios, casting directors and producers who hired talent.

Even though Johanna played only a few bit parts a year, she worked alongside a well known star in every case. When this was shown pictorially, it looked very impressive.

When you want to present yourself like a winner, it's important to think about the people who are going to judge and evaluate you. They are often under great pressure themselves. Their own jobs may be on the line, so they're cautious about the choices they make. Johanna needed to make the people who were in a position to hire her feel confident about her abilities.

Though her first set of photos and captions represented only five very minor roles, they were so well presented that there was a tendency to think, "This woman must be a very good actress. She's had parts in major productions."

Johanna made no incorrect or exaggerated claims in her publicity brochures. She never lied or said that she had been the major attraction in a show. Had she been asked, she would certainly have been truthful.

To further enhance Johanna's chances for success, I helped her to do research in the library. Before every interview, she checked to see if there were any magazine articles about the director, producer, star or writer of that particular program. She read everything she could find, to familiarize herself with the people who would be behind and in front of the camera. This gave her additional material to discuss that would separate her from the crowd. I believed that by preparing well in advance, Johanna would feel informed, capable and more self-assured. I wanted her to be able to project a proud and energetic image.

I explained to Johanna that winners are animated in their movements and emphatic in their speech. Even their walk is determined and forceful. When you are with winners, you can *feel* their spirited, dynamic personalities.

She worked for hours on each phase of how to behave in an interview: her communication skills, her makeup, hair, clothing, posture and appearance, and her general attitude and output of energy. Together we rehearsed what she would say. When speaking to casting directors, Johanna needed to come across as friendly, enthusiastic and self-confident. To accomplish this, she was to walk in smiling with a lively air, and extend her hand, first, to clasp theirs. She was to remember at all times that she was a person of value and that the people who had the power to accept or reject her felt insecure and vulnerable themselves.

Johanna put forth the effort and it paid off in one of the most competitive industries in the country. By the end of our first year together, she had eighteen more performances to her credit. Now there were a total of twenty-three captioned photographs in her portfolio which she brought along on every interview to show the casting director.

The number of call-backs Johanna received kept increasing. During the second year we worked together, Johanna made thirty-two guest appearances. By the end of the third year, she had a steady part on a TV series.

Before therapy, Johanna's acting income had been a little more than the British equivalent of five thousand dollars a year. Today she is a happy and hard-working actress who commands many, many times that figure.

THE STAKES WERE HIGH

As you become more successful, you will realize that the need to present yourself positively and establish yourself as a winner never ends. Even when you become well known and have been internationally honored and acknowledged by peers, the media and the general public . . . there are still daily challenges that make it necessary to keep exerting that winning effort.

I was confronted with this reality when I received a frantic call one afternoon from my paperback publisher's head salesman. He sounded almost out of breath. "I'm worried that one of the major grocery chains in the United States is wavering about ordering *Nice Girls Do,*" he said, referring to my last book. "They have over two thousand stores, and we need that kind of distribution to get your book out to the public. Please come with me next week to meet Robert Hancock, the head of marketing, because there is a great deal at stake!"

He went on to explain that this particular chain was probably the largest in the country, and if they agreed to handle the book, it would establish a precedent that smaller stores would surely follow.

A week later, I walked into the national headquarters of the grocery chain, accompanied by four representatives from my publishing company. As we approached Mr. Hancock's office, I suddenly felt very anxious.

"What am I doing here?" I asked myself. "I'm a psychologist, not a salesman! What if he doesn't like me? I shouldn't have let them persuade me to leave my family and fly here. I don't need to audition anymore. My book can speak for itself!"

I hated being in that position, but I was determined to make the best presentation I could, because I believed in my work, myself . . . and in my book.

We entered a large office, and Mr. Hancock greeted us warmly. I was pleased when he said that his wife had my first book, *Putting It All Together,* on her nightstand.

He invited us all to sit down and offered us coffee. Then there was a sudden hush. I felt uncomfortable as I broke the silence and started speaking. I wanted this man to know my background, and to understand how much I really cared about people. So I talked about my earliest days as a psychology student working with autistic children. I explained the methods I had designed to get mute children to speak. I described how their mothers had reacted at the end of the first week when they heard them utter their first word: "M-o-m."

Mr. Hancock was friendly and seemed to be genuinely interested in my story. He asked many questions as I presented every miraculous transformation I could remember. I told him about the totally mute twelve-year-old named Rachel who had come from London with her parents to see me and returned to England three months later with a vocabulary of three hundred words; I described Milou, another mute child who had traveled from Iran with his mother and left for home speaking almost normally; I told him about the mentally ill patients I had treated in various countries who were able to leave institutions and return to normal life. I discussed the lectures on schizophrenia that I had delivered around the world, and the small armies of lay and professional people on various continents whom I had trained to carry on my methods. I talked about the documentaries that the BBC made of my experiments.

Then I explained that in 1967 the focus of my research studies had moved from schizophrenia to family therapy, and that since then, I had treated thousands of normal people. I said that my special expertise was with couples and that the acclaim I prized most was being called "The Marriage Saver." I wanted Mr. Hancock to understand that my book was intended to help people get closer in marriage and deal with their fears of intimacy and sexual commitment. This was a core theme in *Nice Girls Do.*

It was important to me that he know who I was and what I believed in. Every minute that I was speaking to Mr. Hancock, I was presenting myself honestly . . . and positively . . . as a dedicated scientist, a hard-working therapist and a good person.

After our conference, Mr. Hancock took us all out to an elegant restaurant for lunch. We had a beautiful meal, and I valued every moment of our time together.

Before I left, Mr. Hancock said he wanted to have *four displays* of my book in *every one* of his stores in the United States and Canada!

On the plane going home, I reflected that I had spent a meaningful afternoon with a very bright and caring man. I sincerely liked Robert Hancock, and I had enjoyed his company tremendously. It was rewarding for me to present myself positively and share my work experiences with him.

* * *

LET THE WORLD KNOW

No matter how much success you achieve, you can never assume that other people have an accurate understanding of what really matters to you or what you have accomplished. It is worth your time and energy to convey who you really are to them.

To help yourself move closer to your winning goals, start closely observing your own behavior today. Pay attention to how you present yourself in every setting . . . whether you're at your job, at home, in social situations, speaking in person or by phone. GIVE UP APOLOGIZING AND PUTTING YOURSELF DOWN.

GIVE UP WORRYING THAT YOU'LL BE
SELF-CENTERED OR VAIN.
GIVE UP THE LESSONS IN MEDIOCRITY THAT YOU
LEARNED WHEN YOU WERE YOUNG.
When you start talking more about the good and happy things
that are happening in your life, others will be attracted to you.
They will be fascinated and want to get more involved. You can
become a positive, magnetic force. Remember . . .
YOU ARE RESPONSIBLE FOR HOW
OTHERS SEE YOU.
WHEN YOU DO SOMETHING WORTHWHILE . . .
LET THE WORLD KNOW!

WINNER SCORECARD #14

How do you present yourself? When you converse with other people,
what do you tell them about you? When they have the opportunity to
play back the information with which you've "programmed" them, do
they say that you're a winner or a loser?

LOSERS	WINNERS
1. Losers have learned that to boast or even to listen to someone else boasting must be judged with disdain. They spout hackneyed aphorisms like "Those who know don't talk, and those who talk don't know."	**1.** Winners brag, boast, and broadcast their excellence. They are interested and caring about others, but whenever they talk about themselves . . . they do so in the most self-enhancing manner possible.
2. Losers don't acknowledge the special qualities and assets of the people in their lives. This could inhibit and sometimes prevent others from gaining the self-confidence and sense of dignity they want.	**2.** Winners give everyone . . . family, friends or colleagues . . . their positive feedback. They readily and generously offer recognition and acknowledgments in every possible situation that is appropriate.

3. Losers are often afraid to share their thoughts and opinions. They sometimes stand silently frozen in the middle of a conversation, feeling foolish and terrified. Before opening their mouths, they edit every word they are about to say . . . judge it as not worth hearing . . . then they keep quiet.

4. Losers present themselves negatively. On first meetings they seem to insist on laying out every mistake they've ever made. They program the computer cards in other people's minds to read: "This is a person to ignore. He is a fool who makes too many mistakes."

5. Losers don't think that appearances are important. They want to be "accepted as they are." They resent dress codes or demands that they alter their familiar and comfortable modes of grooming and behavior. They are resistant to change. They look today much as they did yesterday.

3. Although winners fear disapproval and rejection, too, they take a chance and speak up. Believing in their goodness, they don't worry about how they will come across. If what they say misses the point, is incorrect or has less significance than they had hoped, they correct it . . . *after* they've said it.

4. Winners know that the mind can only absorb the data that it is given, so they provide others with *honestly* positive information that depicts them as intelligent, worthwhile, sensitive and caring. The people listening to them fill their "computer cards" with positives about them and play these back to themselves, and others, later.

5. Winners work to improve many areas of their total presentation: their communication skills, grooming, hair, clothing, posture and general appearance, and their intellectual capacity. They concentrate on changing in ways that will earn them more self-pride and dignity, as well as approval, recognition and praise from others.

LOSERS	WINNERS
6. Losers have a hesitant and tentative attitude. They have an apologetic aura about them that suggests, "I'm not sure . . . I'm afraid to try." They tend to be shy, look at the floor rather than at the people they are addressing, so they seem insecure in their manner and speech.	**6.** Winners project an aura of solidity. They are animated in their movements and in their speech. Even their walk is determined and energetic. When you are with them, you can *feel* the spirited essence of their personalities.
7. When they are uncomfortable, frightened or anxious in a situation, losers tend to quit. They make little effort to reverse the circumstances when a decision goes against their interest. Even when an important deal hangs in the balance, they are willing to lose rather than exert the effort needed to turn the tide in their direction.	**7.** Even in tense or humiliating situations, when the stakes are high, winners are determined to hang in and do their very best. They present themselves in the most favorable way that they can and persist in their campaign to actively shape the outcome of their careers and lives.

PART FIVE

Winners Face Their Fears

CHAPTER 15

Follow the Frightening Arrow

When everything seems to be going against you, remember
that the airplane takes off against the wind, not with it.

— HENRY FORD

Have you ever had doubts about your capacity to cope? When
you're trying to do something new . . . or solve an important
problem . . . do you suffer from disconcerting physiological
symptoms? Have you been troubled with problems like sweating,
increased tension or a rapid pulse rate? Are you worried that you
might not have what it takes to deal with the situation?

If so, you're normal!

Such symptoms are common manifestations of anxiety and occur regularly with most people. Winners may experience even
more of these discomforts than others, because they take on so
many new challenges. But winners tend to ignore their anxiety
and focus their energy on getting the job done. Though they are
often frightened, they don't run for tranquilizers to reduce their
fears. Instead, they *use* their anxiety as fuel . . . as "go-power."

You, too, can learn how to turn your anxiety into a force to
provide you with the thrust of a rocket and launch you into the
orbit of your goals:

Fear is a catalyst. People without fear get nowhere. Fear is the single
strongest motivating force in our lives, so whatever you do, don't try to

calm your fears. Encourage them. . . . The more frightened you become, the better your chances of achieving success.*

UNLEASHING YOUR SUPERPOWERS

Fear has the amazing power to both build and destroy. Sometimes it has an "atomic" effect . . . it can temporarily enable
people to tap into amazing hidden potentials that transform them
into supermen and -women:

—"An 80-year-old man, partially paralyzed, used his cane to
   beat off a gunman when the thug attacked the old man's
   granddaughter."

—"A man backing his car out of the driveway accidentally ran
   over his young son. The father singlehandedly lifted the car
   off the ground to free the boy."

—"A woman with a terrible fear of dogs successfully wrestled
   with several of them when a dog pack attacked her baby."**

Under normal circumstances, we don't possess such resources.
But fear and anxiety can be potent energizers, stimulating Herculean strengths and moving us toward miraculous feats.

The amount of drive unleashed in emergencies can also be
harnessed for everyday use! Just the knowledge that such incredi-
ble power is available to us can inspire more motivation and activity in our daily lives.

There are many adults, unfortunately, who have few skills with
which to help themselves cope in times of danger. In fact, they
become immobilized and abdicate their responsibility for action
and self-preservation to others. There have been reports of people
who stood rooted to the ground, in a fixed stare, when standing in
the pathway of an oncoming vehicle. This kind of tragic ineffec-
tiveness is a learned behavior, which is established during the
formative years.

In their zeal to be protective and caring, parents sometimes
infantilize their children by doing everything for them. They neglect to demand the cooperation of their offspring in age-appropri-
ate tasks and duties. Their children learn to plead, whine, demand

* Lois Korey, "How to be a Phenomenal Success . . . First You Gotta Be Rotten,"
Mademoiselle (September 1976), p. 248.
** Dr. Herbert Hoffman, Director of the Hillside Psychological Guidance Center,
Queens Village, New York.

and insist when they need or want something. They don't acquire the ability to take control of their environment and act independently or develop problem-solving behaviors. These are the people who, when they grow up, can't function in a crisis. They sit back and wait for someone else to act and rescue them, rather than risk trying or failing.

THE FEARED ENEMY

Losers are taught that anxiety is the enemy . . . to be avoided, no matter what! It must be feared and destroyed. Over the years, losers learn to employ a variety of different weapons to eradicate their anxiety. These include alcohol, drugs, oversleeping, overeating, habitual talking, excessive arguing or fighting, cigarette smoking and compulsive sexual patterns.

Such anxiety-reducers tend to be self-destructive. Using them is like cruelly smashing your own energy in the face, because you are killing a potentially powerful source of fuel.

Winners try to endure their anxiety. They accept it and acclimate themselves to the accompanying sensations and discomfort. When they attempt new behaviors and feelings of anxiety surface, they think, "Here it is. I can almost taste it . . . but I'm going to hold on! This is a change that I set out to make in my life, and I'm going to stay here and face it, no matter how uncertain and frightened I become."

When losers are trying to change and their anxiety surfaces, they use verbal escape hatches. I call this the mañana method of evasion:

—"I'm getting tired. I'll just postpone this new project I wanted to do until *tomorrow.*"

—"I feel queasy. I think I'll wait until I'm a little better, perhaps *later.*"

—"I can't concentrate now; there is too much distraction. I'll get back to this *afterward.*"

—"I have so many important errands to run. I'll leave this now, and try to finish it *in a few days.*"

Stop your postponements and rationalizations! They are harmful, and you don't need them. Instead, risk becoming acquainted with your fears . . . and do it *today!*

PUT YOUR GHOSTS TO REST

Many of the fears that you carry around with you as an adult were established when you were very small. Today, when even a subtle cue arises from your past that in any way resembled a situation you feared when you were a child, you may be thrown back to experiencing the same symptoms that you had when you were young. They will be the uncomfortable feelings that are called "generalized anxiety."

As an example, let us imagine that as an infant you were startled by a barking dog as you sat on your yellow blanket. Frightened by the loud noise, you began crying. Afterwards, the entire unpleasant event became buried deep in your unconscious.

Now that you are an adult, even though you may not know why, furry objects, animal noises and anything colored yellow make you feel uneasy and anxious. You want to get away from them . . . fast!

Even though you may be chronologically more mature now, you are still emotionally crippled by these unrealistic old childhood fears. But since the process is unconscious, you never consider it an advantage to tolerate the discomfort of your anxiety and face yellows or furs again as an adult. Instead, you have another cigarette or take a drink and anesthetize yourself. You live your whole life through, and eventually die with these paralyzing anxieties preventing you from enjoying so many experiences.

When you try to reduce or avoid your anxiety by popping pills, food or liquor, it will probably work for you temporarily. But why do it? _Most of your anxieties are based on fears that will *never* materialize!_ They were planted in your unconscious when you were so small and have their genesis in dangers that you *believed existed then.* But they were probably only a toddler's distortion of reality.

These old fears no longer have the power to hurt you. The boogie-man is history, now that you are older and more capable. You can put your childhood ghosts and archaic myths to rest.

RISK, RISK, RISK

Take a chance now and change your life. The venomous horrors from your childhood are gone; the dangers are past; the barking dog is silent. Force yourself to embrace the yellow blankets in your world and risk becoming acquainted with your anxieties. Then you will find their fearful powers have vanished.

George Patton, the four-star general who was instrumental in the victory at the Battle of the Bulge during World War II, counseled his soldiers about dealing with their anxiety. He believed that "fear holding on a minute longer" was the key; to face the anxiety was the best way to overcome it.

I teach my patients to confront their fears and "follow the frightening arrow." Let me explain. Imagine that you have come to an emotional crossroad. You must choose between two equally compelling directions. There are two signs facing you, with arrows pointing toward different paths. One reads "Comfortable, No-Anxiety Road Ahead." This arrow points down the *familiar* path that you have taken many times (i.e., being a failure, overeating, smoking, arguing, being afraid to say "No," etc.). While you may hate that road and even despise yourself for following it, you have been traveling there for so long that you know the way . . . it is second nature to you.

The other arrow at the crossroad is labeled "Uncomfortable, Anxiety Road Ahead." It points to an *unfamiliar* path . . . and a new behavior (being successful, slim, calm, speaking up, taking care of yourself, etc.). Going this way is healthier, and it is probably the most productive and challenging route for you to take.

If you decide to "follow the frightening arrow," however, and take this unknown path, your anxiety level is likely to rise, dramatically, at first. You may feel extremely ill at ease. But experimenting with a new approach to your lifestyle can lead to insights and ideas that you might never know if you play it safe on your old "Comfortable Road." And eventually, if you stay on the winning road, your anxiety level will lessen and finally the fear will be gone.

Robert Frost wrote about the positive impact that taking a less-traveled direction can make on a person's life:

> Two roads diverged in a yellow wood,
> And sorry I could not travel both
> And be one traveler, long I stood
> And looked down one as far as I could
> To where it bent in the undergrowth;
>
> Then took the other, as just as fair,
> And having perhaps the better claim,
> Because it was grassy and wanted wear . . .

> Two roads diverged in a wood and I—
> I took the one less traveled by,
> And that has made all the difference.*

As soon as you risk the anxiety of trying an unfamiliar pathway, you will become far more aware of your apprehension and uncertainty. Your anxiety may express itself physically in a loud and piercing voice that will advise you: "This may be dangerous." Perhaps it will be your squeamish stomach, increased heartbeat or sweaty palms that will signal you. When you feel and hear these sensations, let them act as your coaches, urging you on: "Keep going. We know this is tough, and you are frightened, but don't stop. You are almost through this. Hang on a little bit more and you will be finished with this fear forever . . . then you will be *free* of it for the rest of your life!"

THE WAY TO GET OUT OF YOUR FEARS IS TO FIRST *GET INTO THEM!*

Stay with your anxieties. This is a new place for you. And it is better to be a little frightened and give yourself an opportunity to develop some healthy new behaviors . . . than to keep traveling on the same old comfortable path which is going nowhere!

The willingness to take a chance is often the key to finding qualities within yourself that will help you to become a better integrated person.

> To venture is to risk anxiety, but not to venture is to lose yourself.
> —KIERKEGAARD

Once you make the decision to follow your frightening arrow and unleash the fuel of your anxiety, the range of possibilities for discovering who you are can be endless. No one knows what the outer parameters of his own potential may be. There are no ceilings on talent, no boundaries on excellence and no limits on creativity. Whether your goals are small or of Olympian proportions . . . you, too, can take the risks that could change your life to a win.

---

* Robert Frost, "The Road Not Taken," *Complete Poems of Robert Frost* (New York: Henry Holt and Company, Inc., 1949), p. 131.

RUN FOR THE GOLD

Bruce Jenner became the "World's Greatest Athlete" on July 30, 1976, when he compiled a world-record-setting score of 8,618 points in the decathlon and won the Olympic gold medal.

That day, fans all over the world were caught up in the excitement. Do you remember the broadcast image of Jenner throwing himself into the air at his moment of triumph, while his wife, Chrystie, ran across the field and hugged him, laughing and crying with elation? It was a picture of absolute exhilaration.

Jenner's "run for the gold" began in Ossining, New York, where he was born on October 28, 1949. His school years were difficult for him because he suffered from dyslexia, a learning disability. Because he was a poor reader, Jenner was assigned to classes for slow students.

"I don't think I ever had that much confidence in myself, intellectually, or as a person," Jenner says today. "I think that one of the main reasons I got into sports was that it was a place that I could prove myself as a human being, because I didn't feel I was respected at school. I may have been slow in the classroom, but I'd go out on the basketball court and take on anybody."

After graduation from high school, he accepted a partial track scholarship from Graceland College in Iowa. It was there that his coach, L. D. Weldon, recognized Jenner's athletic promise and convinced him he should train for the Olympic tryouts in the decathlon.

"From 1973 to July of 1975," Jenner recalls, "I had been undefeated. I trained very, very hard for that 1975 season, but I wasn't even close to 8,500 points. Although I was winning meets, there was something wrong, something missing. I went to our national AAU contest in Santa Barbara, at UCSB. But still something was lacking."

At the Santa Barbara meet, Jenner totally blew the pole vault . . . the steps he had followed for years in training were off. "If you don't make the opening height, you lose; you can get up to a thousand points in that one event. But my steps were wrong and I wasn't able to get off the ground. I was very upset. I said a few words, ran outside the gate and found a big clump of trees. There I started crying my eyes out. It wasn't so much missing the height, but this was one year before the Games.

"I had a million things going through my head: 'Maybe I'll never get any better; maybe I've reached my peak. No matter how hard I train, I'll never score.'

"I was emotionally protecting myself in case I *didn't* place first, because I knew it could be a tremendous disappointment."

Jenner didn't finish the meet. Instead, he went home to do some soul searching. "I had some conversations with my wife, Chrystie. She said to me, 'Do you want to get the gold medal at the Olympics? Is victory at the Games important . . . is it the most important thing in your life?' "

Chrystie's question struck a nerve. "I remember sitting in the big black chair in the living room. And I could not say, 'Yes,' because of all the things that were going through my head. Then I thought, 'PROTECT YOURSELF. Maybe keep the insurance business. Keep other areas of your life going, in case you fail.'

"Anywhere from second place down would be a failure to me, because I had the potential to win. So I sat back and thought to myself, 'If I say, "No, it isn't the most important thing in my life," then deep down inside I'm kidding myself.' Because I really thought it was. I was just holding myself *back*.

"So I thought, 'If I say to myself, "Yes, this is the most important thing in my life"—then it means *more* than just trying to make it to the Olympic Games! It's not just trying to compete in a meet! You have admitted to yourself that this *is* your life, and this *is* what you want to do. If you don't win, it's your *life*.' "

To Jenner, fully embracing this goal would mean that his whole existence would have to center around training. That would be *it* . . . "my reason for living and breathing."

"It was a tremendous risk. It's almost like risking your life. But I had to make that commitment, to get to that final step, which was winning the games.

"Because it *had* to be that important to me. If it wasn't, I would be out there with 98 percent, instead of 100 percent.

"I sat back, and thought, 'I have enough confidence in myself as a human being that if on that day I fail, I can recover. It may take me days, weeks, or years of my life. But I can deal with failure if I have to on the 30th of July 1976. I will cope with it then.'

"So I finally said to Chrystie, 'Yes, I really have to admit that it *is* the most important thing in my life!' "

As Jenner remembers that moment now, he felt as though someone had turned on a valve, and his adrenaline had started to flow. "Just sitting in that chair, my attitude completely changed."

A month later, in August, 1975, almost a year to the day before the Olympic Games, Jenner competed in an extremely important meet and broke the world record for the decathlon with 8,524 points. "It was my attitude change: 'This is my life; this is what I want to do.' I went to the meet and I was so psyched. I went through the whole thing, every event, and I was *on!*

"That was a major change in my career. It came from failing and then taking a serious look at dealing with the prospect of failure in the Olympic Games."

* * *

I love this story because it describes so clearly how one can transform anxiety into personal fuel. Once Bruce Jenner decided to follow *his* frightening arrow . . . to embrace his goal of winning the Olympics despite his dread of failure . . . he could literally feel new power surging through him.

It is unlikely that you will aspire to become an Olympic gold medal winner. But even if the problems you face seem less formidable, or your objectives less grand than Jenner's, you can follow his example. By facing your fears you can energize yourself for the pursuit of your own goals. You don't have to wait for a crisis or a momentous event to learn the art of making that commitment . . . turning *your* valves on . . . giving it *everything* you have and letting your adrenaline flow.

You don't have to spend your life stuck in old patterns. At any age, you can follow the frightening arrow and dare to do the things that have caused you the most emotional terror in the past.

COME OUT OF THE CORNER

Perhaps when you were a child your mother always called you "shy." Perhaps you feel socially inadequate. Are you tired of being pigeon-holed? Would you like to change?

Then emulate Bruce Jenner and take a tremendous risk! Go for that 100 percent effort! *Stop* holding yourself back! Muster the strength to deal with failure and try a different path.

When you are at a party or meeting new people, do you usually move quietly into a deserted corner, hoping that someone more confident than you will come to your rescue? If this is your customary role, try exploring a brave new social skill . . . conversing with a stranger.

The next time you're at a social gathering, look around the room and find the person who looks the least intimidating.

THEN TAKE A RISK!

Go right up to him or her and extend your hand. Put on your smile and say something like "Hello, I'm Irene Kassorla. Isn't this a lovely party?"

Talk to him about the room, the food, your friendship with the host or hostess . . . anything you can think of. Take your cues about what topics to discuss from the environment around you. Be warm. Try to relax, remembering that the person you are approaching is as terrified and anxious about talking to you as you are about talking to him!

We are all in the same emotional boat. He is frightened, too, so be friendly. Ask him questions about his work, his tastes, his interests. After a while, excuse yourself to get some refreshments. Then you'll have another opportunity to recycle the entire plan with still another person. Do this as often as you can.

Each time you unleash your anxiety by expanding your style of interacting with others, you may experience renewed symptoms, such as rapid pulse rate and perspiration. These are good signs. Welcome them and KEEP GOING, because they are a warning from your unconscious, feeding back to you that you are blazing a new emotional trail.

Being stuck with an unflattering label like "shy" all of your life can be demoralizing. It will be invigorating for you to initiate changes and work at becoming the person you long to be.

IT GETS EASIER AND EASIER

Do the thing you fear and the death of fear is certain.

—RALPH WALDO EMERSON

Fortunately, every time you confront the areas you have always avoided and tolerate the anxiety that results, you will find that your fears will lessen. It does get easier and easier.

Let's assume that your fear of walking up to a stranger at a party can be analyzed in terms of weight. If this action provokes 100 pounds of anxiety for you, on your first try you may feel the impact of the full 100 pounds hitting you.

By the second time, you will already have risked carrying out this behavior once, so it will be somewhat more familiar. This will make the weight of the anxiety drop to only sixty pounds.

Your third trial will be even less frightening for you. Perhaps you will experience only thirty pounds of apprehension. By your sixth and seventh tries, you will be so practiced that your fears will have almost disappeared, and you will be a skilled, charming person who can approach strangers . . . anywhere . . . with grace, warmth and ease.

Not every effort you make will result in a win. You may frequently fail along the way. Winners know this, but they *still* follow their frightening arrows. By taking the risk of feeling anxious and continuing to try, eventually they travel on the road to more success.

> Research indicates that those who take risks rarely regret doing so, even when their choices work out badly. They feel they are learning valuable lessons, and they cherish the freedom to make their own mistakes.
>
> —DANIEL YANKELOVICH*

RISKING LARGE AMOUNTS OF EFFORT

Some of my patients have reported that it is especially painful for them to follow the frightening arrow when they are at school. When the threat of low grades and difficult subjects is looming over them, many students feel particularly anxious about doing their homework and preparing for exams.

Realizing that hours and hours of studying may not guarantee the best grades, winners still risk exerting every bit of energy they have to study diligently.

A loser behaves quite differently. He says to himself, "If I don't crack a book and I fail, I won't look so bad. If I do nothing and get nowhere, that's okay. It fits . . . it will all make sense. But if I kill myself studying and I *still* don't make it and I receive poor grades . . . I'll look ridiculous!"

According to a research study conducted in the Psychology Department at New York University by Michael Lenauer, such people are "self-saboteurs":

> They are so afraid of discovering inadequacies in themselves that they unconsciously undermine their chances of success by giving themselves a handicap. If they fail, they can point to their disadvantage: "I didn't start to write the term report that was due this morning until

* *Society Magazine* (July/August 1981), p. 2.

10:00 p.m. last night," or "I had such a hangover, who could think during that exam?"*

In order to save face and keep his risks to a minimum, the loser doesn't try, doesn't study and doesn't learn or change. And he certainly doesn't follow any frightening arrows! The consequences are that he can rarely win, but he foolishly decides that he is ahead because his investment in time and effort has been so low.

RISKING THE SLAMMED DOOR

Have you ever tried to look for a job? How many hours a day did you put into this endeavor? After weeks of searching, did you wonder why nothing promising happened?

Sometimes, on my talk-radio program, a listener will complain, "I simply can't find a job. The economy is so bad, a person like me hasn't got a chance to get to work!"

When I question the caller about how much time he has put into his job search, his reply is usually something like "Well, I went out on one interview last week. I also made phone calls one morning this week for *two* solid hours!"

This output of energy adds up to only four hours of job hunting in two weeks. No wonder he can't find work! Because his efforts have been small, so are his results!

The job-hunting activities of a winner would demonstrate a marked difference in risk taking, effort and performance. His daily schedule would look more like this:

6:00 A.M. to 8:00 A.M.: Be at desk checking all the want-ads in the local newspapers. Circle each potential job.
8:00 A.M. to 9:00 A.M.: Shower, dress, eat breakfast.
9:00 A.M. to 12:00 P.M.: Make calls to arrange appointments. Send out resumes whenever requested.
12:00 P.M. to 1:00 P.M.: Eat lunch. Travel to first interview.
1:00 P.M. to 5:00 P.M.: Meet with personnel managers, department heads and owners to discuss prospective positions.
Weekends: Spend at least six hours checking the classified ads in the Sunday papers.

A winner would also go through the steps involved in getting help from other sources, as described in Exercise 5, Chapter 6.

When they go out on job interviews, both winners and losers

* "Insecurity: Self-Saboteurs," *Psychology Today* (December 1979), p. 31.

feel anxious. The possibility of rejection is high, and so are their fears. Losers decide to postpone action until they feel more comfortable and less frightened. Not winners . . . they *get going frightened!*

Each time a winner pushes open a door to a job interview, he will probably have a big lump in his throat. But even though he feels very anxious, he follows the frightening arrow and walks right in. He will conscientiously visit the companies on his list, knowing that he risks having every door rudely slammed in his face.

Note the differences: The loser doesn't risk much, so he suffers little anxiety. He spends only two hours a week job hunting. The winner's risk-taking efforts fill sixty or more hours a week. With this dramatic difference in energy, who would *you* bet on as the likely candidate to land the job?

RON'S PSEUDO HEART ATTACK

Ron had been working for an international oil conglomerate for four years when he was promoted from Sales Representative to District Sales Manager.

His first major assignment was to organize the company's annual sales meeting, a two-day seminar that was the firm's biggest event of the year. Sales executives from offices all over the world would be present.

Ron was anxious about the huge task of providing accommodations, a comprehensive lecture program, banquets and entertainment for over *one hundred* visiting employees. With only ten days to go before the conference, he was so worried that he began to come down with sniffles and a head cold. Despite his physical discomfort, he threw himself into every detail of planning the meeting. Because he had a hunch his symptoms were related to his fears that something wouldn't be handled properly, he ignored his wife's advice to see a doctor and perhaps get some medicine.

On the Wednesday before the weekend conference, Ron awoke in the middle of the night in great pain. He was shaking and covered with sweat.

"I don't know what's happening," he said to his wife. "But I think it's something serious. I'm having sharp pains on my left side and under my arm."

Hearing this, his wife jumped out of bed and ran to the phone.

"Dear God," she cried in a voice filled with panic, "what if you're having a heart attack?!"

First she called the paramedics and then the family doctor. Within minutes, help arrived.

The doctor took his vital signs and examined him. He assured Ron he was well and that his symptoms were probably related to stress. However, he recommended running a series of tests on Ron the next day to confirm his diagnosis.

The tests verified the doctor's hypothesis that the pain in Ron's arm was caused by a muscle spasm related to stress and overriding anxiety.

During the next two days the jabs of pain in Ron's arm continued. However, the test results reassured him, so he wasn't worried. He ignored his discomfort and kept working. He didn't cancel the meeting or use his physical symptoms as a plea for sympathy. He was completely engrossed in making arrangements and didn't even think to discuss the problem with his co-workers.

When the conference finally took place, everything ran according to plan. The meetings were a great success. The president of the company was so pleased with the outstanding format that he personally attended every session, and congratulated Ron on a "superlative job!"

After the meeting, Ron and some of his colleagues sat around in his hotel room, talking about the successful weekend. It was then that Ron told them about his anxiety attack Wednesday night and the doctor's visit. "I was so terrified that I was risking my whole career and this thing would be a flop," Ron said, "that the other night I was convinced that I was having a heart attack! What with my terrible head cold, the last-minute cancellations by a couple of speakers and my pseudo heart attack, I can't believe I made it!"

Ron described what he had gone through during the preceding week, and all his fears came tumbling out. A sense of camaraderie and caring filled the room as the others began empathizing with him. One of the men shared his memory of giving a speech in high school and suffering intense feelings of stage fright. Then each man in turn talked about similar experiences. Ron was surprised when even the president remembered an anxiety attack he had experienced before giving the valedictory speech at his college graduation.

Most of the episodes shared by the men had identical components: Their stories concerned important events in their lives when they were frightened. They all talked about risking their fears and following their own frightening arrows.

Ron's openness served as a model that the men could identify with and imitate. As a result, they all felt closer and more relaxed. "It's great to let your hair down," the president laughed, "and find that everyone else has the same bald spot!"

Ron conducted many other conferences for his company. Fortunately, that was the last of his "pseudo heart attacks." Although some anxiety was present each time, by the end of the fourth sales meeting his fears had almost disappeared. They were replaced by Ron's excitement and exhilaration that his hard work would result in more successes, even when the task was new and his anxieties surfaced again.

DON'T GIVE UP HOPE!

In Chapter 7, I discussed the importance of maintaining a positive outlook. In support of this thesis, scientific studies have shown that your *attitude* toward life may be one of the most important factors determining your ability to win. Just as facing up to your fears can augment your personal power . . . self-doubts and feelings of helplessness can reduce your energy and your coping skills. Both mental outlook and your ability to maintain hope can have a powerful influence on your motivation to succeed.

These principles have been studied in research projects conducted by biologists and psychologists over the last thirty years. In a laboratory experiment conducted by Dr. Kurt Richter at Johns Hopkins University, the influence that hope had on behavior was studied. Dr. Richter carried out a simple study with two rats: In one hand he held a rat so firmly that despite all its efforts, the animal was unable to escape. After considerable struggling, the rat finally gave up its fight and remained almost motionless. Then the rat was placed in a tank of warm water, where it immediately sank without even attempting to swim and save itself.

In the second phase of the experiment, another rat that hadn't undergone the entrapment procedure was placed in the water. It quickly swam to safety.

The conclusion drawn by the experimenters was that the first rat had learned that it was helpless to change its situation, that no matter how much effort it expended, it wouldn't make a difference. Therefore, any actions it could make would be hopeless.

The second rat hadn't been subjected to conditioning that

proved there was no reward for struggling and trying. It hadn't learned that it was helpless or that its situation was hopeless. When confronted with a crisis that demanded an immediate response, it was able to act and survive.

Studies of college students have also shown that helplessness and hopelessness result from prior conditioning . . . they are *learned* behaviors.* And in working with terminally ill patients, hospital staffs have found that those who are highly motivated tend to live longer. In addition, patients who are filled with hope are more likely to recover from their illnesses than those who have lost faith. They are also happier.**

The clinical experience of therapists and the human and animal research projects suggest that those who try harder do better. Because helplessness and hopelessness are learned, they can be *unlearned* when you confront your anxieties. The more you face up to your fears, the more energy and motivation you will have to continue doing so.

AND WHAT ABOUT YOU?

Have you learned to be hopeful when encountering difficult obstacles in your life? This is another crossroad where winners and losers separate. The winner doesn't lose hope, he perseveres . . . he keeps going until he works things out . . . he finds other viable solutions.

Hopefulness and *humor* are the antagonists of fear . . . they can sustain you in your efforts to follow the frightening arrow. This was illustrated very vividly by the dramatic story that follows. It was told to me by a man who won perhaps the greatest battle of all . . . the fight for life.

PROGRAM YOURSELF TO LIVE

Norman Cousins is an Adjunct Professor on the faculty of the Department of Psychiatry and Biobehavioral Sciences at the School of Medicine, University of California, Los Angeles.

For thirty-five years he was editor of *Saturday Review* magazine. He has authored fifteen books, including *Human Options, An Autobiographical Notebook* and *Anatomy of an Illness.*

It was more than twenty-five years ago that medical experts first told Cousins that he had a short time to live. But with unrelenting

---

* Albert Rosenfeld, "Learning to Give Up," *Saturday Review* (September 3, 1977), p. 36.
** Ibid., p. 37.

hope and determination, he defied his doctors' advice and disproved their fatal prognosis. Over the years, he formulated a personal prescription for healing his body, using a combination of Vitamin C, positive thinking, joy, faith, humor . . . and hope.

Cousins was first alerted to his serious health problems in 1954, when he was refused a life insurance policy after an electrocardiogram showed evidence of a coronary occlusion.

The doctor for the insurance company told the then thirty-nine-year-old editor that he had eighteen months to live . . . and that was only provided he give up his job and all participation in sports and become totally sedentary.

Cousins wasn't willing to surrender his active lifestyle. Preferring to keep his heart healthy by exercising it, he decided to research alternate methods for staying alive.

Seven years later he *was* still alive. At that point, he was stricken with another deadly malady, ankylosing spondylitis, a collagen disease that causes progressive disintegration of the connective tissues in the spine and joints.

Again Cousins embarked on a bold self-rescue program. He took large amounts of Vitamin C and exposed himself to "humor therapy," systematically watching Marx Brothers movies and reading James Thurber's and Robert Benchley's comic writings. He later reported, "I made the joyous discovery that ten minutes of genuine belly laughter had an anesthetic effect and would give me at least two hours of pain-free sleep."*

Cousins believes that negative forces like tension and stress can weaken the body, and positive forces . . . joy, love, faith, laughter and hope . . . can have the opposite effect.

"No one can tell me that our ability to overcome depression does not result in positive biochemical changes in our body," Cousins told me. "We can program ourselves to live."

Cousins' third contest with death occurred in 1981, when he was struck down by a heart attack. Knowing that panic was the big killer in emergency situations, he talked to himself in order to remain as tranquil as possible: "The first thing you've got to do is to take care of that internal upheaval. So when I had my heart attack, I said, 'OK, Cous, hold on now . . . help is on its way. You'll be all right. We'll deal with this thing very calmly.'

"I was absolutely confident that I was going to make it. I knew

* Norman Cousins, "Anatomy of an Illness (As Perceived by the Patient)," *The New England Journal of Medicine*, 295:26 (December 23, 1976), p. 1461.

that confidence was essential. The price of fear was so great that I scared myself *out* of having any fear.

"When I got to the hospital, the dean and the cardiologist were waiting for me. I said, 'OK, men, just take it easy. I want you to know that you're looking at the damndest healing machine that's ever been wheeled into this hospital!' "

Cousins' experiences have led him to the belief that the mind is more powerful than medicine, a fact he says deserves more attention from health professionals. "If the mind can produce its own medications, then this is not only something that should not be ignored, but should be a basic part of all therapy."

But I was especially struck by his conclusions about fear. While Cousins may have been thinking about its effect on physical health, his words are relevant to all aspects of life:

"I can't think of anything more crippling than fear. When people act out of fear, they tend not to see how a problem can be turned around, right in that vital fraction of a situation.

"Fear produces something like an astigmatism of the intellect. You're not aware of what your options are. Fear is like pessimism: It's self-fulfilling, and the body has a way of following the expectations of the mind, so the fear tends to create situations that justify fearing."

* * *

By learning to confront his fears and supplant them with joy and faith, Norman Cousins was apparently able to set loose the remarkable healing powers of his own body.

By following the frightening arrow and facing up to *your* fears, you, too, can unleash extraordinary powers that will enable you to accomplish your goals and become a winner. By taking the road less traveled and experimenting with new ways of doing things, you can discover your full potential. By enduring your anxiety and consistently risking your best effort, you can achieve more than you ever believed possible.

If you respond to your fears like a loser and avoid taking chances, you will probably have to bear relatively little anxiety in your life. But you are not likely to achieve much, either.

As movie producer/entrepreneur Mike Todd said more than three decades ago:

Remember, you can't steal second if you don't take your foot off first.

WINNER SCORECARD #15

Winners know how to endure anxiety and transform their fears into fuel to accomplish their goals. Losers are so afraid of their anxiety that they use self-destructive methods to anesthetize themselves and in the process destroy their own energy.

How do *you* respond when you are assailed with doubts about your ability to cope with new or difficult situations?

LOSERS	WINNERS
1. When losers doubt their capacity to cope, they avoid their fears at any cost. Their weapons for eradicating anxiety include alcohol, drugs, oversleeping, overeating, habitual talking, excessive arguing or fighting, cigarette smoking and compulsive sexual patterns.	**1.** Winners are often frightened when they are attempting to solve problems or learn new skills, but they ignore their apprehension and focus on getting the job done. They turn their anxiety into fuel . . . it becomes their "go-for-it power."
2. Losers enlist few skills to help themselves in times of danger. They become immobilized and abdicate their responsibility for action and self-preservation to someone else. If no one is there to save them, they sit back and wait helplessly.	**2.** In emergencies, winners are able to tap into amazing hidden potentials. Their fear and anxiety serve as potent sources of energy that stimulate heroic efforts and enable them to accomplish seemingly impossible tasks.
3. When losers attempt new behaviors and feelings of anxiety surface, they use verbal escape hatches like "I'm just too tired and unable to concentrate now," or "I'd rather wait until tomorrow, when I will surely feel better," or "I've caught a cold or the flu . . . my doctor says it's going around. I'd better quit and rest."	**3.** Winners accept their anxiety and acclimate themselves to the accompanying uncomfortable feelings or physical symptoms. They get the anxiety-provoking task over with, *today,* rather than postponing it for some indefinite *tomorrow.*

LOSERS

4. When losers come to an emotional crossroads where they must choose between two equally compelling directions, they select the route that's marked "Comfortable, No-Anxiety Road." Even when they hate themselves for going along that route, they prefer this path because it's familiar. They have been traveling there for so long that they already know the way.

5. Losers are "self-saboteurs." They are so afraid of discovering inadequacies in themselves that they unconsciously undermine their chances for success by giving themselves a handicap, like starting late or not really trying. If they fail, they can point to this disadvantage as the cause . . . rather than their intelligence or inability to cope.

6. Losers sometimes become so overwhelmed by a project that they experience physical symptoms of anxiety such as body pains, fever, colds, flu, etc. When this happens, they moan and complain about it to everyone they know. Then they cancel the few plans they *have* made and spend their time recuperating.

WINNERS

4. Winners follow the frightening arrow and take the "Uncomfortable, Anxiety Road" that leads to trying a new behavior and change. They know that experimenting with different approaches to their lifestyle can result in insights and ideas they might never know by playing it safe.

5. Winners risk exerting every bit of energy they have, even when they know that increased efforts may not guarantee success. They eventually come out ahead as a consequence of hours of time devoted to trying.

6. When winners need to face a stressful task and they begin suffering aches and pains, they ignore them and keep going. They don't change their schedules or use their physical symptoms as a means of avoiding work or a plea for sympathy.

7. Losers are plagued with self-doubts and feelings of inadequacy. Because they lose hope and stop trying after only a brief struggle, they frequently fail . . . and their feelings of inadequacy increase.

7. When trapped in difficult situations, winners become even more highly motivated. They don't lose hope; instead, they persevere and keep working until they find a viable solution.

CHAPTER 16

The Fear of Success

. . . If you can meet with Triumph and Disaster
And treat those two impostors just the same . . .
And lose, and start again at your beginnings . . .
Yours is the Earth and everything that's in it.
—RUDYARD KIPLING

I often lecture about the fear of success. It's a popular topic, because most people want to know what it is that prevents them from achieving the success they desire. At first they find it almost impossible to believe that they may be undermining their own progress. They can't accept that they may be unconsciously sabotaging their efforts to win, because their *conscious objective* is to improve their lives.

When I discuss the fear of success, invariably someone in the audience will challenge me: "Dr. Kassorla, I can't believe that you are associating the word 'fear' with the word 'success.' Everybody I know *wants* to be successful. We're all striving for it! It's the big prize. In this world if you have it, you are good . . . and if you don't have success you are bad."

I get similar reactions from people who call me on talk-radio and TV programs. Listeners have difficulty believing that success has a strong component of fear. I hear the same skepticism when I work with new patients who are eager to acquire winning skills.

When they first enter therapy, some patients are in so much pain they say to me, "If I don't change, I'm afraid I won't be able to go on living." Yet, as the changes begin emerging and they become more effective, they find themselves in such an unfamiliar place that they want to quit therapy and stop their progress. While the process is unconscious, they actually fear that their new, successful behaviors will drive them into some vague and unforesee-able jeopardy . . . perhaps even death. After spending a lifetime of struggling with punishments, insults and criticisms, it's too diffi-cult for them to turn the emotional dial and switch to pleasure and winning. They don't have the tools or experience to deal with success.

Very few children receive approving comments on how well they are doing, how remarkable and talented they are or how proud their parents feel.

Whenever children *do* accomplish something notable, their par-ents' attention is quickly directed to what they *didn't do* or *don't have.*

For example, a young child returns home from school and elat-edly says to his mother, "I got the best grade in the class today in spelling!"

His reward is a fleeting "That's fine," followed by a long, nega-tive interval, such as "It's a relief to hear something good for a change. When you left this morning and I took a look at the mess in your room, I felt like crying. It was awful to find your clothes piled on the floor and all of your . . . etc., etc." Complaints and nega-tive feelings like these usually fill much of the parents' and child's time together.

When success finally does come into your life, it is almost as strange as having someone from a primitive, backward society move into your bedroom. You are uncomfortable and uneasy. You miss the familiar negative voices and faces. You long for your loved ones and even the painful ways you used to interact together, feeling lonely, left out, inadequate . . . awful. The fighting and verbal attacks, the humiliations and embarrassments you de-fended against and hated them for don't seem so bad now because you are trapped with this stranger . . . hoping he will leave so the family you know and love can return.

Success is this unwelcome, unfamiliar stranger, and all your unconscious motivation will be to escape from him and avoid your winning.

LOSING THE LOSER IN YOU

Whenever you abandon an old way of behaving, even when it has been harmful or self-defeating to you, there can be a deep sense of loss. A mourning period begins . . . you unconsciously yearn for your loser skills, in spite of the fact that they are the very habits that have hurt you. You miss them, just as you would long for dear departed family members or friends.

As you stop using your old patterns, you may feel an emptiness, a vacuum. During the time it takes to learn new, healthier behaviors with which to fill this void, the emptiness persists. It may take the form of a depression or an oppressive sense of anxiety that you aren't able to trace to anything specific. Even though you know that your old style had a negative influence on your life . . . even though it kept you from growing to your full potential . . . you still miss it and are sad.

You are in conflict, because your rational mind says it is perfectly all right, indeed desirable, for you to give up your loser habits, yet your ego continues to mourn the loss. Your intellect and your feelings are out of sync. You move into a vacillating position: "Yes, I'm longing to change," and "No, it is too scary," which prevents you from daring to take the chance and change.

IT IS TIME FOR YOU TO GO FOR IT . . .
TO CHANGE
AND RIGHT NOW.

Your discomfort and uneasiness with daring to be successful will be short-lived. The anxiety and mourning period will quickly pass if you can remember that being mediocre is not wonderful. Discard the life patterns that have kept you ordinary, miserable and resentful.

YOU CAN BE MORE SUCCESSFUL.

In order to become more effective in dealing with your problems and leaving behind your losing skills, you will need to contend with the persona of your stubborn ego.

Here is another analogy to help you to understand the rigid nature of your unconscious and how fearful it is of change.

THE CARETAKER IN YOUR CASTLE

Your ego resembles a strange, old caretaker in an ancient castle who shuffles around, day and night, guarding the halls of your unconscious. His job is to inspect your behaviors and make certain that nothing around you changes. For him, *not changing* means that "all is well."

Your caretaker feels comfortable clinging to the status quo. He sees to it that you do everything in the same way that you have for years. He is like a dog sniffing a tree to find a familiar scent: Unless he recognizes a precedent for your actions, he won't sanction them.

His beliefs are absolute! Even if your life patterns have made you a perennial loser, he is quite satisfied to have you continue in your unsuccessful rut.

This caretaker, your ego, speaks in the eerie symbolism of your dreams. "If you change," he says, "something terrible is going to happen to you . . . and what's worse, I will lose my lifetime of service and be put out of a job. Listen to me. I've kept you safe all these years, haven't I? It may have been awful, but at least you're alive.

"Beware! If you change . . . you will *die!*

"The proof is that you are already having anxieties, uncomfortable feelings and maybe even dreams about you or someone you love dying. So stop listening to that Kassorla woman because something dreadful will happen if you change!! And even worse—you'll lose your faithful, loyal helper—ME! Be sensible and do it the same as you have all this time . . . the family's good old way."

If you challenge his message and complain that you have been a loser and that you've had too much pain and too little fun, the old man will have a pat answer for you.

"I agree that your life hasn't been all roses, and that you have felt inadequate, worthless and unsuccessful," he will acknowledge condescendingly. Then hc'll pound away with his warnings: "But we have survived all these years doing it like this. And you've been safe with me right here advising you. Besides, you *know* what we have now, but you *don't know* what will happen with that winning stuff. Why take a chance? Why take the risk of changing to something unproven? It's far too dangerous!"

THE OLD CARETAKER IN THE NEW REGIME

It is your unconscious guard who is causing most of your fears and confusing dreams. His ploy is to frighten you so much that you will NEVER change. Don't listen to his voice.

In spite of his ominous warnings, as soon as your caretaker sees that he is powerless to stop you from changing, and that your new behaviors are becoming firmly established, he will quickly relinquish his endless tyranny and join you.

When you give up feeling worthless and inadequate and begin learning how to receive praise, approval and more compliments, it will be a strain on the old man. As a last-ditch effort to frighten you back into "Loser-ville" and complacency, he may throw in a few other symptoms, such as backaches, nausea, sweating palms, hot flashes, blurring eyes or pains in different parts of your body such as your neck, arms or legs. Whenever he thinks he is about to lose his job, he will make you ache and groan.

While I always recommend contacting a medical doctor about any persistent pains or physical problems, I want you to be aware that you may experience signs of apparent physical discomfort, temporarily, as you begin winning. These negative body signals are common psychological reactions to the stress of being successful and the fear of change. They become evident when you dare to disobey your caretaker and work toward winning.

Once you move into action and make the psychological "buy" that you deserve to enjoy more happiness, your fear of success WILL DIMINISH and so will the physical symptoms. But you will need to keep an eye out for that ancient caretaker acting up and trying to pull you away from being motivated and achieving. Remember, he wants to get back to the comfortable loser castle that was *his* familiar place, just as strongly as you want to take *your* place as a confident, successful and joyful winner.

THE CONSTANT VIGIL

Let us imagine that it is several months from now. You have conscientiously digested the theories and exercises in this book, and are experiencing more success. The caretaker has reluctantly joined your new regime, and you are enjoying rewarding new family, business and interpersonal situations.

YOU STILL NEED TO STAY ON GUARD!

Because of your long-term fears of success, it will not be easy to completely shed your old ways. Whenever a significant new win occurs, there will be a tendency for your fears to mount and for you to undermine your own progress. You may even try to sabotage yourself and slip back.

Don't worry: This, too, will be temporary. Keep your eye on your goals. Don't be detoured from your winning route.

THE SABOTAGING "KLEPTO"

Mimi, a forty-year-old woman, came to see me for therapy because she was afraid she couldn't stop herself from shoplifting. At regular intervals since she was a teenager, she had stolen small items from various shops.

She looked troubled as she said, "I knew I had to get help, fast! I'm afraid I'll wind up in jail!"

After eight months of therapy, the shoplifting seemed to have completely subsided. At last Mimi felt free of her compulsion. She discontinued her sessions with me and I didn't hear from her again until she phoned for an appointment a year later.

"I can't believe I did it again," she said, sobbing. "I'm still a crazy kleptomaniac! All this time I haven't had even the *slightest urge* to steal . . . until the other day. Then, before I knew it, I was walking out of a store with a scarf under my coat . . . a scarf that I don't need, don't like, and that isn't even a color I can use. I must be going totally berserk!"

When Mimi stopped crying, I asked her to explain what had happened during the period of time that she was out of therapy. What had led up to this theft?

She explained that a year before she had taken a part-time job selling cosmetics house to house. "I love my work and I'm good at it!" she told me. "I did so great. My sales started soaring and I ended up with the firm's top award for a part-time salesperson. It was a big, fat bonus. I was ecstatic! At last, I had made a success of something on my own!"

Driving home the day she received the bonus, Mimi had been looking forward to telling her husband her good news, thinking, "I'm so happy! This money will pay for our vacation this year. Wait until Jim sees this check!"

As she told me about the events that followed, Mimi started crying again. "I'd like to forget what happened from that point on. I decided to do a little shopping. Before I realized it, I was driving home, frantically checking the rear-view mirror, with my heart pounding and a stolen scarf stuffed under my coat!"

When Mimi finished her story, I explained to her that doing something that was self-destructive and frightening was an escape route from the unfamiliar success and happiness she was experiencing with the bonus and her job. She had "overdosed" on winning and had knocked herself back to the frightening "good old days" of feeling crazy, miserable and inadequate.

Next I quickly and emphatically reminded her how well she had done since I had last seen her. "You went an entire year without a *single incident of shoplifting.* That is a remarkable record. Be proud and give yourself a kiss for that . . . a whole year! You will get right back to tolerating your new success and probably never have the urge to steal again."

I also reminded Mimi of the irregular course that the learning curve takes. "If you were a computer, you could just work away at your new winning behaviors and never make a slip," I said. "But you are *not* a machine . . . you are a dear and valuable human being who is making real progress toward being highly motivated and effective.

"When you spend a lifetime fearing success and then get a windfall, it is understandable for you to become emotionally rattled and slip back. But don't forget you *earned* your success. You *deserve* it.

"Stop worrying and go to work at keeping your excellent sales record," I reassured her. "Your next big success will be easier, and so will the next . . . because before long you will expand your tolerance for success and become accustomed to winning. Being an effective achiever will get easier and easier. With practice, winning will be more familiar and comfortable for you."

* * *

HARRIS WAS ONLY TRYING TO HELP

The fear of success dons many cloaks. Each of us wears these fears in unique ways that relate directly to our childhoods. Even when we are fully grown, we tend to respond to success by using the destructive skills that we learned long ago.

The problems of Harris and Beth, a couple I treated, resulted from repeating these same kinds of early patterns. Beth complained one night in group therapy about an incident with Harris that had enraged her.

Throughout their twelve years of marriage, Beth and Harris had both held executive positions with companies they loved. A few weeks before, after being with one firm for all that time, the company changed hands, and Beth was fired. She was hurt and angry. Beth hated to start job hunting. It was a difficult time for her.

Months passed before Beth finally landed another position. It was not easy for her to adjust to the new environment. At first, she felt awkward and out of place. But after a short time she began making friends, and felt pleased with the rapport she had established with several people.

Beth went home from work one evening feeling very excited. Bubbling with energy, she greeted Harris: "I feel great! I think my new job is really going well. Everyone there seems to be so friendly. And my boss is really easy to work for."

Beth continued her story to the group, "As I spoke to Harris, he shook his head and looked troubled. Then he said, 'You don't know *everyone at work* well enough to make generalizations. And after you have been there awhile, your boss may not look so good to you.' "

Undaunted, Beth had continued happily, "The view is gorgeous, and all the offices are so elegantly decorated. It's a pleasure to work there."

Harris's entire face then contorted into a frown, and he had begun shouting: "Don't get so excited! You don't know how you're going to feel a month from now. We live in a big city, and there are plenty of other great jobs in this town!"

Beth started shouting, too: "What's the matter with you? Can't I get excited about my new job without you putting me down?"

At this point in Beth's story, I turned to Harris. "You *were* putting her down," I said. "Is something frightening you about her work? Overreacting usually stems from some kind of early hidden fear. Think back to that night and see if you can get in touch with your feelings about Beth's excitement or success. What pops into your head now?"

"I was only trying to soften the blow in case it turns out that they fire her after a trial period," Harris answered. "When her last job folded, Beth felt so disappointed and beaten that she was depressed for weeks. Her reaction frightened me. I can't stand it when she gets so low . . . then I get lonely . . . and I actually feel like a deserted little kid. I don't want her to be devastated again if this one should fall through. I was trying to protect her. If I can cool her excitement about her new position, it won't be so tough on her if she ever loses it."

While Harris sounded like he was putting Beth down, he was actually trying to help her! Parents do this, too. They interject these same destructive kinds of remarks when attempting to *protect* their children from being discouraged. They respond to their youngsters' success stories with comments like "Don't get so excited or you'll bust a blood vessel . . . Take it easy! This isn't the most important thing in the world" . . . or "You'd better watch

out or you'll get a fat head." They don't understand that by step-
ping on the small twigs of successful performance in their children, they prevent these behaviors from growing into giant oaks.
By dampening a child's feelings of pride in achievement whenever he is doing well, parents are assembling the building blocks
for the fear of success later in life.

As adults, like Harris, we tend to make the same mistakes with
our children and the people we love the most. We don't understand how we're killing their incentive to achieve . . . we are not
aware that we are reinforcing them to be mediocre. Perhaps
worse, we are blind to similar ways we inhibit *ourselves* from
attaining the rewards that lie within our reach.

* * *

Much of our fear of success stems from our terror of failure. This,
too, is deeply rooted in childhood, when most of us are taught that
failure is the dreaded enemy, to be avoided at all costs. As a result
of such training, some people would rather sacrifice the possibility
of achievement, wealth and fame . . . than risk making any mistakes.

FAILURE IS A TEACHER

To become successful adults, we all need training in problem
solving techniques and in how to fail. I discussed failure in Chapter
2, "Blowing the Whole Thing." Now I want to underline in your
thinking that:

FAILURE IS A TEACHER.

From each of our unsuccessful efforts, we can learn something
valuable about ourselves and our behaviors.

Acquiring the ability to cope with failure is an important part of
growing and maturing. You have heard the old adage "An apple a
day keeps the doctor away." Well, I would like to change it to "A
little failure a day keeps the Dr. Kassorlas away!"

Most parents hope to raise capable children. Yet they don't
realize that frustrations and let-downs need to be introduced
early, and in small doses. When this becomes a normal part of
living, youngsters can develop their abilities to contend successfully with adversity. When given that opportunity early, by the
time they mature their coping skills are well established.

When a body-builder is starting to train, he works out first with light weights. Then very gradually he increases the poundages until he is able to lift incredibly heavy barbells. In the same way . . . children who are exposed daily to small amounts of stress and disappointment by supportive, watchful parents . . . will build strong anti-frustration muscles. The resulting endurance in dealing with setbacks will help them handle huge amounts of anxiety and pressure when they are finally exposed to difficult problems as adults.

People who have been raised to handle "a little failure a day" have healthy survival skills that build and ripen over the years. Whenever handicaps do occur, they aren't easily ravaged like straw huts in a storm. They are able to stand strong against an entire hurricane of distress.

Many psychologists hold that experiencing a setback or failure frees you to take more risks. Once you have discovered that you can survive, there is less to lose. Ralph Waldo Emerson expressed the same idea somewhat more poetically:

> A man's success is made up of failures, because he experiments and ventures every day, and the more falls he gets, moves faster on . . .
> I have heard that in horsemanship he is not the good rider who never was thrown, but rather that a man will never be a good rider until he is thrown; then he will not be haunted any longer by the terror that he shall tumble, and will ride whither he is bound.*

When children are allowed to make mistakes without suffering severe disapproval, they feel comfortable experimenting with trial-and-error behaviors and taking more chances. Win or lose, their next confrontation with problems will be easier, and the next will be easier still.

Do you *use* the information from your mistakes as valuable tools to help you? Or do you abuse yourself with negatives about your errors and waste precious time in scolding yourself?

Falling short of your objective can be very disappointing. It hurts. Most of us have been bruised in this way. But it can also make a positive contribution to your body of information. It is how you deal with an unsuccessful try that counts.

DON'T ABUSE IT, USE IT.

Failures can be signposts . . . clearly marking what you want to

* Fredelle Maynard, "Turning Failure into Success," *Reader's Digest* (December 1977), p. 126.

avoid. Watch out for them. Then they will become guidelines of instruction about where "not" to go next time.

As family therapist Virginia Satir has said, "Every person has the right to fail."*

This is your right, too. By daring to throw away your fear of failure, you will simultaneously be casting off your fear of success.

FAILURE = LEARNING = WORKING = SUCCESS

IS SUCCESS UNFEMININE?

Research indicates that fear of success can be an even greater problem for women, because many of them grew up learning that it is unfeminine to be assertive or push ahead. Psychologist Matina Horner, president of Radcliffe College, demonstrated this in a 1968 study at the University of Michigan. In observing sophomore women who were high achievers and had backgrounds that could be considered conducive to success, she found that the learned stereotypes that women "should be passive" and "shouldn't win" forced these young women into conflicts whenever they did begin to achieve. As a consequence, they unconsciously avoided success.**

Without question, in our culture, being successful has traditionally been considered a male trait. From earliest childhood, boys hear about the value of winning. By the time they reach grade school, they have been indoctrinated with sayings like "Winners never quit and quitters never win," or "Show me a good loser and I'll show you a loser."

If a boy acts discouraged or feels overwhelmed, he is usually attacked for his lack of courage and manliness. He is forced by threats of ridicule or ostracism to stay in a competition until he either fails or wins.

The importance of winning is particularly emphasized in the male-dominated world of sports. Great athletes are worshipped in this country. Too often, even scholastic achievement is esteemed less than success in sports. Coaches and athletic superstars become heroes whose words set the standard for masculinity, and they articulate the value and pleasure of winning again and again:

It's only a game when you win. When you lose it's hell.
                    —HANK STRAM, Former Coach Kansas City Chiefs

* Ibid., p. 124.
** Laura Shapiro, "Did 'Fear of Success' Fail?," *Mademoiselle* (July 1977).

Ultimately, the "may the best man win" philosophies that children hear when growing up leave no room for girls but encourage boys to learn to be competitive. This early training spills over into the adult world of business. Then the thrust toward winning practiced in boys' competitive games is transferred to adult goals of success, fame and fortune.

Even many expressions used in the working world originated in competitive, male-dominated athletics. Business people speak of "a whole new ball game," "grabbing the ball and running with it," "Monday morning quarterbacks" and "taking a turn at bat."

WOMEN FINALLY ENTER THE WINNER'S CIRCLE

The idea that competition is "for men only" is nonsensical historical mythology. Now, in the 1980s, we live in an era of progress for women. The feminist movement of the last few decades is one of the important sociological phenomena of this century, and our society as a whole has become more accepting of the idea that women can achieve as much as men. Women are now entering the winner's circle and incorporating more winning skills into their behavioral repertoires.

All of us already know successful women who were *not* affected by the traditional dogmas dictating that competition and winning are "not for girls." I have often found that the early conditioning of high-achieving women was similar to that of boys. They were encouraged to compete, to be athletic, to actively pursue good grades and participate in school activities, and to win.

One of my patients, who earns a quarter of a million dollars a year as a corporate vice president of a manufacturing firm, told me, "My mother didn't distinguish between boys' activities and girls' activities. She never used the word 'unfeminine.' I was good in sports and I was always voted captain of the team, because I tried harder and practiced longer than the other kids. I was never told that playing baseball, climbing trees or driving a motorboat was manly, so I was a great center-fielder, loved to climb trees and raced a lot of boats. Now my husband, our children and I race boats together.

"My mother always pushed for the best. If I had brought home a 'C' on my report card, she would have had a heart attack!

"It wasn't until I became an adult and heard about the problems other women were having in competitive situations that I realized there *were* women who had conflicts about their desire to get ahead.

"When the women's movement gathered momentum and there was so much attention given to the lack of opportunity that so many women suffered . . . I hardly noticed. I was so busy struggling up the corporate ladder, earning as much as any of the top men in the company, it never affected me.

"I didn't know that a woman 'shouldn't do' this or 'couldn't do' that. *I did everything.* I had gone to a good college, which put me on a par with the men in my firm. I worked longer hours than most of them. That's why I succeeded; my sex didn't matter.

"When I *did* become part of the women's movement and started going to meetings, I began to realize how much my upbringing differed from that of most women. In a sense, I had been raised with 'male values.' "

My patient was able to become a corporate vice president because she had practiced the so-called "male values" since childhood and could easily embrace them without conflict. She could deal with competition by working diligently and persistently, while taking pride in her achievements. And none of this detracted from her life as a wife, a mother and a very feminine woman.

* * *

Dianne Feinstein, San Francisco's first woman mayor, is another accomplished woman with a confident attitude about competition:

> . . . I don't look at failure as being anything other than a part of my chosen career. If I were overcome by losses I wouldn't be a good mayor . . . so you learn not to take defeats personally. A good politician has to have a bit of the phoenix in him or her.

Feinstein has been competing for years, undaunted by the idea that politics is a "man's world." In a recent interview for a forthcoming book, Feinstein explained that she was able to survive in this "man's world" because her father had conveyed to her a positive attitude about competition. At home, she was rewarded for striving and being aggressive.

Clearly, the capacity for achievement and excellence does not depend on gender. The person who rises to the top is the one who gets the necessary training, expends the time and energy required to get the job done and maintains a sincere dedication to doing his or her best.*

In these pages, you've read about the experiences and ideas of several women who have enjoyed success and national prominence, among them Dianne Feinstein, Margaret Thatcher, Mary Wells Lawrence, Paula Meehan, Diane Von Furstenberg, Jessica Savitch and Judianne Densen-Gerber. Observing their luminous careers offers a persuasive argument for the positive effects that winning can have on a person, regardless of gender.

The archaic stereotypes that have encouraged women to be passive and to fear excelling are unrealistic and unsubstantiated. Women who are high achievers in business can also be thoroughly happy as wives and mothers.

In a recent article written for *Cosmopolitan* called "Career, Husband, Kids . . . Can You Have It All?" Mary McHugh interviewed me and twenty-nine other "success stories all . . ." who had "flourishing marriages or relationships, terrific children, challenging careers." All of these women, including myself, said they enjoyed the "deeply rewarding business of combining career and family."**

As a psychologist, I have seen many vital and exciting women whose activities cover the whole spectrum of human accomplishment. They are happy and fulfilled women being achievers, being aggressive, being competitive, being feminine . . . being *everything!*

HAPPILY EVER AFTER

Losers believe that people who are successful are free from problems. This is like the "get married and live happily ever after" myth. In a loser's mind, once you reach the top, you never have to worry or be frightened again.

The reality is that winners experience problems and a great deal of fear, but in spite of them, they keep working and doing their best. Sometimes, however, they struggle through difficult periods during which they seriously sabotage themselves.

• This happened to the prima ballerina . . . the international star of the company . . . whom I treated. Periodically, on the day of a

* Kathy MacKay, "Success," *Working Woman* (August 1980), p. 11.
** Mary McHugh, "Career, Husband, Kids . . . Can You Have It All?" *Cosmopolitan* (January 1983).

performance, she would go into a rage during which she would tear off her ballet slippers and quit eating. Although her dressing room overflowed with 250 pairs of toe shoes, on these occasions, she would find it difficult to locate a single pair that fit.

• A renowned opera singer with whom I worked sometimes felt his throat close just as he was preparing to go on stage. When this happened, his heart would start pounding at a frightening rate and his body would become flooded with perspiration.

• I also treated a famous athlete whose ability to function was periodically reduced by back problems. Sometimes the pain would be so great that he could hardly walk. Yet X-rays revealed no physical irregularities, and doctors could find no internal or structural causes.

• Another patient was an internationally known beauty and a fine actress. Posing for close-up photographs was part of her daily activities. At times, however, she was unable to appear in front of the camera because of a recurring acne flare-up. Her embarrassment about her skin condition was so emotionally debilitating that she was unable to work.

In treating all of these highly successful people, I found that their shoe, throat, back or pimple symptoms coincided precisely with certain events. They occurred *only* after an outstanding win: a success in their individual careers that was lauded by audience and press alike. It was at these triumphant moments that they became enmeshed in their emotionally spawned dilemmas.

In their individual sessions, these patients and I discussed how their inability to tolerate success caused them to develop these debilitating problems. As we worked together, they came to understand that *they* were the saboteurs who destroyed their own wins. Before therapy, none of them realized that they unconsciously targeted the precise body part that was crucial to their successful functioning. They had all found a physical excuse to lower their effectiveness and thereby reduce their performance and their probability of winning.

These famous patients were all extremely intelligent adults, yet none of them was aware that his pain was self-inflicted, until our discussions. I explained to them that through the use of their symptoms, they were hurting themselves with the same intensity and frequency that they had experienced from scoldings and chastisements as children. Year after year they were repeating the same amounts of pain they suffered in childhood. But now *they* were administering the punishments and acting as their own cruel parents.

It is difficult to change and to feel at ease with great acclaim when you have spent most of your developmental years as a "garbage can" kid, a human catch-all for criticism and punishment. You become so accustomed to abuse, it serves as a comfortable old friend. Because you overdose on negatives as a small child, the resulting feelings of inadequacy and low self-esteem will keep you struggling and unconsciously seeking out pain for the rest of your life.

In therapy, I instructed these people that when their physical problems appeared, they were to stop their self-flagellation. Instead, they were to be their own kind and loving parents and give themselves kisses and support. Each of them had worked hard for many years, studying and polishing his skills. They had earned every bit of their successes.

I helped them understand that there is no ceiling on success and no limit to happy experiences. After good can come more good . . . after triumph can come more triumph.

Once they had made the "emotional buy" that they were good people who deserved their wins . . . and *more,* they *were* able to learn how to be kinder to themselves. Then their symptoms disappeared and they could discontinue treatment and learn to tolerate and enjoy more success.

* * *

When you have attained recognition for your talents, there is still another way that the fear of success can be manifested. Having struggled with the fear of winning on your way up, you may now worry that you won't be able to stay "on top" and continue achieving. You may live with the terror that you will never be able to match the level of excellence you have already attained.

I'LL NEVER BE ABLE TO DO IT AGAIN

It was 3:00 A.M., the morning after the Academy Awards presentation. I was awakened by the doorbell. Struggling out of a deep sleep, I groped my way to the door. Outside I could hear the loud voice of one of my patients, pleading, "Irene, please open up. I'm freezing . . . it's me!"

Recognizing the voice, I quickly released the latch. I was surprised to see Klaus standing there in a tuxedo, tears spilling down his cheeks. He was waving an Oscar over his head. "I know I'll never be able to do it again," he cried. "Everyone is going to find out I don't deserve this thing. Soon they'll all know that I'm a fraud."

I invited Klaus into the kitchen, where he poured out his feelings to me. We sat and talked . . . and drank tea until morning.

Tearfully Klaus explained that he was terrified that his success was the result of "accidentally being in the right place, at the right time, with the right talent behind me." He didn't know how to accept that he had earned his Oscar with years of schooling, talent and hard work. Even though his peers had recognized this when they voted his cinematic achievement the best in its category . . . he didn't believe how exceptional and creative he was.

Klaus was too frightened even to acknowledge his own achievements. He was certain that his future projects wouldn't measure up. He imagined that every move he would make in the industry from that day forward would be judged negatively compared to his work on the Academy Award–winning film.

"How can I ever do it again? When everyone is watching me and expecting perfection, I'll be so self-conscious that I won't be able to function. The only way to go after this is down!

"Receiving this prize is no prize," he said, looking at his Oscar. "It is like having a huge monkey on my back. It represents too much. I'll never be able to relax. Every minute I'll be thinking about living up to this last film."

"Nonsense!" I said. "Everyone is *not* watching you. They're too busy struggling and striving for what they want themselves.

"I know it is a frightening responsibility to be a high achiever," I said. "But that is part of your excitement. You will probably *always* be doing excellent work, because you are a dedicated man who loves working long hours every day. As for mistakes, you know there is no way to get around them . . . except in a cemetery.

"People who are willing to experiment and to fail are the world's creators," I reminded him. "And most of them make lots of mistakes. You have been going through the process of being frightened, trying harder than the next fellow and succeeding since you were a child.

"Winning awards is nothing new for you," I pointed out. "It doesn't matter if you ever receive another Oscar, because whatever you do, you will always be a winner."

ENJOYING THE JOURNEY

Whether you are laboriously inching toward your cherished goals or you have already arrived, you will be more of a winner when you can experience yourself and your life *joyfully.*

Find *pleasure* in your work as you go after the things that add up to success for you. *Stretch* to the limit of your abilities and feel *proud* to put forth everything you have. You can turn failures into an advantage by enjoying the *excitement and fun* of playing with your unique style of life. This can be the big win for you . . . and for everyone.

Smile at yourself more and appreciate the humor in the absurdity of your foibles, failures and manipulations. Watch out for the saboteur inside of you, and don't take your adult role-playing too seriously. Then you can have more fun observing the drama of your striving for a richer life.

When you can accept and believe that all of us have stamped visas . . . that no one is getting out of this beautiful world alive . . . you will learn to savor every hour.

I believe that a healthy way to get your revenge with death is to truly experience every *sweet moment* of your life now . . . with feelings of *gratefulness and wonder.* It is a fascinating journey you are taking. Winning or failing, you win by just being here on this wondrous planet.

WINNER SCORECARD #16

The paths of winners and losers diverge significantly at the very point when success comes within their reach. At this juncture, fears of the unfamiliar prompt losers to cling to their comfortable old self-defeating ways. Winners push through these fears and move ever closer to their goals.

LOSERS	WINNERS
1. When losers abandon an old, self-defeating style of behavior, their unconscious fear is that their new, successful ways will drive them into some vague and unforeseeable jeopardy. In order to alleviate these fears, they quickly stop their own progress.	**1.** As winners improve their capacity for succeeding, various physical symptoms and fears manifest themselves, but they ignore them and forge ahead. They stay with their new winning skills and eventually become more comfortable with success.
2. As losers experience more success, they often become so anxious that they are relieved when they slip back into their old habits. At this point, they decide that winning is just too costly, too difficult and too inaccessible, and they resume their old behaviors.	**2.** When winners fall back into an old negative pattern after a period of success, they remind themselves of the length of time that they *were* able to maintain their winning behaviors. Then they get right back to their new course of action.
3. Losers try to reduce the excitement of successful achievements of the people they love. By doing this they believe it will soften the blow if failure should follow. When someone relates a success story, they say things like "You're getting too big for your britches," or "You'd better watch out or you'll get a fat head."	**3.** Winners reinforce the accomplishments of friends and family members. They freely offer them uplifting praise and congratulations, anticipating that the future will be fine and that the new winner will sometimes experience failure as part of their overall picture of success.

4. Losers think they are sheltering their children from adversity by teaching them "Be careful; watch out; avoid errors; never fail."

4. Winners know that failure is a teacher, so they don't protect their children from small doses of frustration and disappointment. Their youngsters learn how to deal with problems, and by the time they mature, their coping skills are well established.

5. Losers are so afraid of failure that they would rather sacrifice the possibility of achievement, wealth and fame than risk making mistakes.

5. A winner's philosophy allows latitude for trial-and-error behaviors. Because he knows he can survive setbacks, he feels free to take risks and try new things.

6. Some women are losers because they have been taught that being competitive is for men only. They believe that successful achievements require them to be overbearing, scheming and crass, and that a truly feminine woman would never display any of these qualities. Because of their conditioning, such women are afraid to be winners.

6. Winners don't concern themselves with gender. Women who are winners know that both sexes can rise to the top, and can embrace the so-called "male" values about success without conflict. They get the necessary training and experience and work hard. They expend the time and energy required to complete the job.

7. Losers believe that once people become winners, they "live happily ever after." In their minds, successful people never have to worry, strive or be frightened again.

7. Even after they have achieved a significant measure of success, winners continue to strive. Sometimes they may unconsciously undermine their own efforts and cause their own failures. But by getting to work and actively trying, eventually they get back to winning.

LOSERS	WINNERS
8. Losers are so worried that they'll never be able to maintain a high level of achievement that they find a way to sabotage their own success.	**8.** Winners are anxious about their ability to remain successful, too, but they are dedicated to tirelessly trying. By virtue of the hours they put in and the experience they gather, they continue winning.
9. Losers believe there is a limit to happy experiences. They think that after good comes bad, and that after triumph comes despair.	**9.** Winners know there is no ceiling on success. They make the "emotional buy" that they are good people who deserve their wins, and can work for even "MORE!"

CHAPTER 17

Boldness Has Genius

What you can do, or dream you can do,
Begin it,
Boldness has genius, power and magic
In it.

—GOETHE

Both winners and losers have daydreams. But too often losers spend a lifetime with their fantasies, conjuring up images of fame and glory . . . and *never doing anything* about them. Winners are more pragmatic. They move into action, climbing boldly toward their goals. They haven't time for unproductive dreaming because they are determined to turn their hopes and aspirations into tangible realities.

Winners may work at something for years, finding the most sensible and practical routes to push themselves ahead. They learn, through trial and error, how to catapult themselves forward, leapfrogging over the opposition with their "never-say-die" attitude that gets the job done.

Winners develop enterprising courage and the hardiness to survive whatever confronts them. Applying an undaunted and innovative spirit, they forge new pathways and are resolute in withstanding disapproval.

THE BOLDNESS TO WITHSTAND DISAPPROVAL

A significant attribute that winners share is confidence in their own abilities, in spite of what "others" might say. Examining the early lives of celebrated personalities reveals that some of them suffered painful discouragement and disappointment from their teachers, judges or peers. Often rejection came in the very pursuits that they were later to dominate.

Many of them were told they would never make it, or that they simply didn't have the necessary talent. But they wouldn't listen! They remained firm in following their own beliefs.

Do you recognize any of these names?

Woody Allen, Academy Award–winning writer/producer/director/actor, flunked motion picture production at New York University and the City College of New York and failed English at N.Y.U.

Malcolm Forbes, editor-in-chief of *Forbes* magazine, one of the largest business publications in the world, did not make the staff of *The Princetonian,* the school newspaper at Princeton University.

Leon Uris, author, scholar and philosopher, flunked high school English three times: "It's a good thing English has nothing to do with writing," he says.

Liv Ullmann, two-time Academy Award nominee for Best Actress, failed an audition for the state theatre school in Norway . . . the judges said she had *no* talent.

Geraldo Rivera, TV journalist, had to take remedial courses in English and math before he could be accepted by the Maritime College of the State University of New York.

Barbara Jordan, U.S. Representative from Texas, was defeated in an election for president of her freshman class at Texas Southern University.

Dr. Richard L. Mani, neuroradiologist at Veterans Hospital, University of California, San Francisco, flunked neuroanatomy cold his first year of medical school. He now teaches the subject.

Dr. Albert Einstein, physicist and Nobel Laureate, whose theories were the foundation for nuclear energy, flunked his college entrance exams and was a poor student in mathematics.

Dr. Theodore Maiman, physicist and inventor of the laser, flunked his Ph.D. orals at Stanford and had to take them again.

These noted achievers refused to be held back by defeat, failures or even the well-meaning but negative advice they received from others. Instead, they reexamined the judgments laid down by those in authority and, disagreeing with them, they ventured forward boldly.

Some two thousand years ago, Socrates counseled that reexamining long-established ways of thinking and being before accepting them was a necessary quality of maturity. Winners dare to question authority figures and rigid policies. Their creative imaginations and their boldness give them the latitude to fearlessly initiate new ways of moving up through the ranks. They are not shackled by binding standards that their mentors may have blindly adhered to in the past.

NORMAN LEAR DOES IT HIS WAY

Norman Lear, one of the dominant talents in television today, was at one time a shoe salesman who aspired to become a Hollywood writer. He tried all the conventional avenues to get the attention of agents and producers, without any luck. The standard methods of breaking into the comedy field just weren't working for him.

Then he boldly initiated a fresh approach for presenting his talents. By using his ingenuity and asking friends for help, he was able to find the home phone number of a well-known Hollywood comedian.

He called him right away. The minute he recognized the star's voice on the other end of the line . . . without so much as a "hello" or any introduction . . . Lear announced, "You'll love this. This is a great joke." Then he recited a very funny short sketch he had written. When he was finished, the comic laughed uproariously at the unique presentation, the brashness and the gag.

During their ensuing conversation, the star asked Lear if he had ever done any television work. The spunky shoe salesman, who had never so much as set foot on a television set, answered without missing a beat, "Sure!"

The famous comedian was especially pleased with this outrageous caller who was not only a good joke writer, but had television experience as well! By the end of the conversation, Lear had been offered his first writing job . . . working on Danny Kaye's Christmas TV special.

Needless to say, he accepted!

HIS BOLDNESS LASTED A YEAR!

Jerry Weintraub now enjoys the prized position of being one of the top manager/producers in Hollywood. His client list contains a long roster of superstars, including Neil Diamond, John Denver, Wayne Newton and Herb Alpert.

Jerry told me the story of his biggest challenge . . . trying to win the opportunity of promoting the most exciting star on the musical horizon at the time, Elvis Presley.

In those days, everybody wanted a piece of Elvis. Being involved with him meant millions for the people who produced his concerts.

One morning Jerry Weintraub woke up and shared a dream with his wife, Jane Morgan:

"Last night I saw something wonderful! It was a huge marquee that read 'Jerry Weintraub presents Elvis Presley.' "

The moment Weintraub arrived at his office that day, he telephoned Colonel Parker, Elvis's manager. He hoped to create some interest in a deal to handle Elvis through his firm, Management III.

The Colonel turned him down flatly, but Weintraub wasn't deterred. He had a bold plan . . . he would unrelentingly pursue the Colonel with daily phone calls. And he did! He spoke to Parker about Elvis every day for an entire year. In spite of constant rejection, he persisted.

"Why should I do this for you?" the Colonel would ask him. "I owe so many people favors, and I don't owe you anything!"

Weintraub had a firm and confident answer: "Because I'm so good at what I do. I can do the best job. Give me a shot!"

Finally the Colonel contacted Jerry and said, "If you get over here with a certified check for one million dollars, we'll start talking."

The Colonel, who was well practiced at being bold himself, had no difficulty coming up with his outrageous demand. At the time, there was no precedent for his million-dollar request.

Weintraub persuaded a businessman in Seattle to invest the enormous sum of money he needed. Like Weintraub, whose tenacity paid off on every front, the moneyman, too, was bold.

Weintraub met with Elvis's manager in Las Vegas and presented his ideas, along with his ticket of entry . . . a certified check for a million dollars.

Colonel Tom Parker quickly took the money. Throwing it on his desk, he shook Jerry's hand and said, "You have a deal!"

Elated, Jerry hurried back to his associates, shouting, "We've got Elvis!"

When he told his lawyer about the deal, the attorney inquired about the contract. Jerry answered, "I don't have one."

"Well, what are the terms?" the lawyer asked.

"I'm not sure," Jerry replied, "but I know we've got him."

A year later, after Weintraub had promoted Elvis in concerts across the country, Colonel Parker returned the million-dollar check. It had been in his desk drawer since the day he had received it. When Jerry asked him why he hadn't cashed it, Parker's reply was "I wasn't interested in the money. I just wanted to see if you had what it takes to play with the big boys!"

THE NEW INTERN GOES TO WORK

Stories about boldness are exciting to tell. I would like to share an incident from my own life when bold action produced very rewarding results for me.

In 1970, I returned from my studies at the Institute of Psychiatry at the University of London with my doctoral diploma in hand. I had already been treating patients for three years in England. With this background, and four additional years as a therapist in the early sixties at UCLA, I was surprised to find that I wasn't licensed to do psychotherapy in California. I was still required to spend a year doing a post-doctoral internship in an institutional setting.

In London, I was a well-established media personality. I not only had a thriving private practice as a psychologist, but I appeared regularly on BBC radio and television. Having to start all over again as an intern in this country was disheartening. But in order to get licensed in California, there was no alternative.

When I arrived for work on my first day at the hospital where I would serve my internship, the head of the Psychology Department told me I could choose my office from one of three empty spaces.

First he showed me a large, sunny room with no furniture except for a desk and two metal, straight-backed chairs. My other two alternatives were very small rooms, so cramped they looked like cells. One of them didn't even have a window. However, they were both adequately furnished.

Because I conduct large therapy groups with as many as two dozen people at a time, my immediate choice was the largest room . . . even though it was practically empty.

I had heard that the entire south wing of the hospital had been closed for over a year. Since my room was so barren, I decided to take a look and see if there was anything lying idle in the vacant ward that I might be able to use.

As I walked through the main door into the silent, deserted hallways of the closed ward, I had an eerie feeling. It was like entering an Egyptian tomb. The rooms were filled with treasures: comfortable couches and chairs, tables, lamps, filing cabinets . . . everything I needed was right there before me.

I couldn't believe that all of this had been gathering dust for so long when the Psychology Department was still inadequately furnished! I had noticed that even the head psychiatrist's office wasn't well appointed.

Quickly, I went to work. I pushed couches, chairs, desks . . . the works . . . from the south wing to my office. Because the floors were highly polished, it wasn't difficult to do.

The notion of whether it was permissible to take the furniture never crossed my mind. This was my logic: The entire hospital, including the Psychology Department, was owned by *one* organization. I needed furniture, and the south wing was full of it. I reasoned that I was simply transferring needed equipment from one section to another. It didn't make sense to have a busy ward *without* furniture, when an empty ward housed *all the things I needed!* It was all accessible, so I took the initiative and did something about it.

Picture me, dressed in a very conservative English suit and weighing a full one hundred pounds, nonchalantly propelling an overstuffed couch through the hospital corridors. Then, imagine me pushing the additional pieces of furniture through the long corridors, one by one, into my office.

Various nurses and attendants approached and questioned me as I whisked by. They looked at me almost flabbergasted. "Where are you taking that couch?" . . . "Why are you moving those lamps?" . . . "Do you have permission to remove those chairs?" . . . "No one ever goes into the south ward . . . it's closed!"

In every case, my answer was a smile and a friendly nod as I quickly moved on. I didn't speak or try to explain . . . I was afraid I'd be sidetracked. I needed the pieces I had appropriated, and I was determined to have them.

People tend to back off when confronted by someone who acts with authority. By displaying an attitude of smiling, friendly assurance, I conveyed the idea that I must have been granted permission from above. It appeared that I knew exactly what I was doing . . . and even more . . . that I was supposed to be doing that very thing!

By the end of an hour, my room was transformed! It was completely appointed. I had done it! My heart pounded with pride as I looked around, admired the results and smiled with delight.

THE THREAT OF DOOM

Ten minutes later, one of the doctors walked into my palatially appointed office looking very troubled. The entire hospital was buzzing with the news of the mass furniture transport! He didn't understand why I had brazenly "taken over" like that. He solemnly announced that Dr. Selden, one of the most influential members of the hospital board, had heard about my unauthorized requisitions.

He warned me, "He will be in to see you at the end of the day!" His grave proclamation felt like the order for my execution.

From that moment until Dr. Selden walked in at around 4:00 P.M., I did very little breathing. Throughout the afternoon, my stomach churned.

Though I was frightened, I thought to myself, "If this man is smart enough to be such a power on the board, he is also smart enough to understand the absurdity of the situation. It would be foolish to have two dozen patients sitting on the floor in the north end of the hospital while there is furniture lying idle in the south end."

When Dr. Selden finally arrived at the end of the day, my knees were shaking, but I walked up to him and shook his hand firmly. With a big smile, I said, "I'm so pleased to have company in my new office!"

Assuming the grace and ease of a hostess welcoming someone to her stately mansion, I invited him to sit down. (This was certainly no problem now, as the room was quite stuffed with furniture!)

"You know, you are my first visitor," I said warmly. "I'm so happy that you took time out of your busy schedule to stop in to see me. How kind of you!"

Dr. Selden started laughing. The hearty sound filled the room. He slapped his knees several times and just kept laughing. Finally, he said, "You're something else. That furniture has been sitting there for ages gathering dust, and no one had the imagination to go and get it. Here you are, in your first hour in the hospital, and you're already moving things around!"

Then he began laughing again. "I really like the way you get the job done," he continued. "Tell me about yourself. I heard you did therapy on television and radio in London. That's pretty special for an American student."

Dr. Selden sat with me for over two hours, as we talked about my research studies in England. He was an interesting person to be with, and I was happy that he wanted to hear about the work I did with psychotic patients. He also inquired about my plans for my one-year internship at the hospital.

Answering his questions about my media experience in Britain, I explained that it was through my television and radio exposure that my research had become so well known in England. I suggested that I could make his hospital famous and probably double the outpatient population if he would allow me to take time off my normal duties as an intern to appear on the local media. I proposed that I could talk about the large family therapy groups I would be conducting and invite the public to participate.

I also wanted to visit PTAs, Rotary and Kiwanis clubs and other civic groups. I could let them know about the hospital's outpatient and in-patient services and my focus on family therapy.

I told Dr. Selden that my first plan was to organize a weekly mothers' group of approximately sixty women who would discuss their child-rearing problems. I said I was also eager to start a large married couples' group, consisting of fifteen or twenty couples. I was willing to stay late and work with them in the evening.

I concluded by suggesting that I would be much more valuable reaching out to the community and increasing the hospital's patient population than just pursuing a formal internship.

Dr. Selden was very supportive of my proposal. He liked my ideas, and we started planning how I could begin to implement them.

He wanted to know if there was anything I needed in the way of stationery, supplies or other equipment. "Absolutely!" I responded. "I'll make a list. I'll also need a staff to help me handle the workload. At least one secretary to start with."

Looking shocked, he said, "Don't you realize that there are only *two* secretaries for the entire Psychology Department? And there are twenty-two doctors who share those two secretaries? You want me to give *one* secretary to only *one* Dr. Kassorla?"

"Of course!" I said simply. "I'll double the intake here, and I'll need hands to help me."

Dr. Selden looked puzzled as he examined his watch and got up to leave. Then he turned back abruptly. He started laughing again, pointed his finger at me and said, "You'll have your new secretary by noon tomorrow."

My bold actions resulted in a windfall: I received permission to carry on the work I love to do on radio and television; I got my own private secretary; my office looked wonderful; and this important board member was prepared to support my ideas so I could work with large groups of families.

By the end of the month, I had already put some of my suggestions into action. I had lectured at the local PTAs and had been interviewed on television and radio several times.

And I made good on my promise. At the close of three months, I had doubled the Psychology Department's outpatient intake. A few months later I had tripled the hospital's psychiatric patient population. Even more exciting, I was conducting large therapy groups daily with families and their small children, some of whom were only three years old.

When the number of patients doubled, I opened my paycheck to find a note from Dr. Selden that read, "Great job!" Along with his encouraging words came a salary increase, which in 1970 seemed like a fortune to me.

My boldness really did pay off, and boldness will pay off for you, too. Keep in mind the advice of New York psychiatrist Dr. Jack Chernus:

> Take firm action to solve your problems. Others may contradict you or try to sidetrack you, but don't give in. Stick to the plan you think will work.

IN TIMES OF CRISIS

The bold tactics illustrated in these three stories demonstrate some of the advantages of fearless, persistent action and thinking. During normal times, these attributes can be a tremendous asset in your approach to living. But in times of crisis, mustering an attitude of boldness not only helps solve existing problems, but may be instrumental in creating new opportunities.

The ancient Chinese understood this concept. The wisdom of their culture suggests that a crisis can be a good time for advancement and progress. In fact, in their written language, the character for "crisis" is a wedding of two symbols, one meaning "danger" and the other meaning "opportunity."

In a crisis, winners not only try to solve problems but make an effort to improve even the most discouraging situations. They are the iconoclasts who dare to explore new ideas and creative methods.

EVEN PRESIDENTS EXPERIMENT

During his tenure as President of the United States, Franklin Delano Roosevelt was confronted with two of this century's major crises . . . a devastating worldwide financial depression and a global war. The address Roosevelt delivered at Oglethorpe University in 1932 illustrates his strong resolve to attack problems:

> The country needs, and unless I mistake its temper, the country demands boldness, and persistent experimentation. It is common sense to take a method and try it. If it fails, admit it frankly and try another.

Living up to his words, Roosevelt initiated innovative programs and social reforms. His bold trial-and-error approach did indeed result in some failures, but it also led to successes that had an impact around the world.

Few of us will have the opportunity to lead a nation. But each of us can introduce more boldness, persistence and experimentation into our everyday lives. For example, here is how one of my patients kept pursuing alternatives until she scored the win she was seeking in her business.

SHERRY WOULDN'T LET GO

In England, I treated a dynamic woman named Sherry, who for ten years had successfully managed her own antique importing company.

One day, when Sherry returned to her showroom after lunch, she was told that a Mrs. Avery, who was scheduled to see a new shipment of furniture from Holland, had cancelled her appointment. According to Sherry's secretary, the client had a conflicting appointment with her dentist.

Annoyed, Sherry asked her secretary, "While you had her on the phone, why didn't you try to arrange another time for her to be here? I don't want to lose Mrs. Avery. She is eager to buy Dutch antiques, and if she doesn't see our furniture soon, I'm worried she'll find another dealer. You know my philosophy . . . a 'no' means you try harder."

But Sherry's secretary said Mrs. Avery had been emphatic about not wanting to book another appointment. "I did try, but she wasn't interested," she said. "I know when somebody sounds really cooled off, and I decided not to push it. She sounded a bit angry and kept repeating that she was just too busy."

Sherry knew that her secretary was reliable and she trusted her impression about the phone call. But she wasn't going to just let the matter drop. She picked up the phone and called the customer herself. Her style was to aggressively approach a problem with all of her resources.

After offering a warm greeting, Sherry began to talk about her own fears of the dentist. She related a story about herself when she was only eight years old, and hid in the closet from her mother to avoid seeing the dentist. She acknowledged that, like Mrs. Avery, she never broke dental appointments now because she was so eager to get them over with. She made a few jokes about herself and how anxious she still felt when she was in the dentist's chair.

Sherry felt that just picking up the phone and pushing for another appointment with a client who was uninterested would meet with rejection. Her success in business was only partly related to her vast knowledge and experience with European antiques. To a larger extent, her business was thriving because she really liked people. She was understanding about their problems and sensitive to their moods.

Because Sherry genuinely cared about her customers, she had learned when to be a businesswoman and when to be a person who could share her own difficulties. She knew how to listen to the problems of others and when to interject her own.

Some time into her conversation with Mrs. Avery, Sherry began talking about the fun that she and her staff had experienced uncrating the magnificent old pieces that had arrived from Amsterdam. Then she made a positive prediction, almost as though it were a reality: "Wait until you see all the treasures!" she exclaimed. "I'm certain you will be as excited as all of us are here."

Continuing to be optimistic, enthusiastic and directive, she added, "Knowing your excellent taste, I think you're going to have a difficult time choosing what you want to buy, because every item in this shipment will be perfect for you. Why don't you get your appointment book? I have mine in front of me. We can put our heads together and find a two-hour spot that will work for both of us."

By being undefensive, understanding her client's needs and showing a sense of humor in identifying with her, Sherry had created a comfortable atmosphere in which she and Mrs. Avery could chat. Then her boldness in suggesting "You're going to have a difficult time choosing . . ." transformed Mrs. Avery's attitude from annoyance and disinterest to eagerness to arrange an appointment. As Sherry suggested, Mrs. Avery got her date book, and they discussed setting up a meeting.

Then several other problems arose. First, Mrs. Avery explained that she had to pick up her daughter Caroline every day after school, so afternoons were out. Then she said her mornings were spent at her own job. Weekends she traveled to the country. She kept presenting obstacles that seemed almost impossible for Sherry to overcome.

But Sherry persisted. She offered to have her secretary drive Caroline from school to the showroom, in order to give Mrs. Avery more time to view the antiques. Each time her client presented another difficulty, Sherry was equally helpful and encouraging.

As a result of Sherry's bold perseverance, Mrs. Avery finally made an appointment. And as Sherry had predicted, she was delighted with the entire shipment and bought several items.

*   *   *

How would you have handled the situation with Mrs. Avery? Would you have given up when your secretary said your customer had cooled off completely? Could you have reestablished contact and a friendly rapport with your client? Are you saying to yourself now, "Sherry really forced that woman to make an appointment through her aggressive tactics and manipulative flattery"?

This simply isn't true. Sherry was an honest woman. Everything she said was genuine, including her empathetic remarks about the dentist and her positive comments about Mrs. Avery's excellent taste. It wasn't flattery . . . it was a matter of sincerely understanding and caring about her client's problems, coupled with bold and decisive actions in pursuit of her own objectives.

Was Sherry aggressive? Absolutely!

WINNERS *DO PUSH* FOR WHAT THEY WANT.

And the results are often rewarding for everyone involved. In this case, remember that in the end there were *two* happy women: the satisfied client who *loved* her purchases, and the shop owner who was doing what she loved, too . . . buying and selling antiques.

DEDICATED TO SURVIVING

To become a winner, it is important for you to learn how to push on during difficult times. In order to encourage winning opportunities, you must be dedicated to surviving the emergencies and problems that come up. As long as you actively work on your dilemmas, you will have the chance to find out where new pathways may lie.

> Success seems to be largely a matter of hanging on after others have let go.
>
> —WILLIAM FEATHER*

The following exercise outlines some major points that you can review when you need to move into action. In a crisis, it will help you find a way out of your predicament. And even if this is a happy and contented time for you, the pointers will still serve as guidelines for you to work on and become even more successful.

EXERCISE 16: HOW THE BOLD SURVIVE

Every day, people are forced to do battle with emergent crises and weather severe economic or emotional storms. We hear about businesses failing, untimely deaths, tragic accidents and errors in judgment that have irreversible consequences.

However devastating the circumstances, through trying and failing and continual practice, winners cultivate personality characteristics that allow them to survive situations that might cripple others.

If you want to develop the capacity to outlast a crisis (and deal

* "Don't Give Up," *Glamour* (August 1978), p. 224.

better with whatever hardships are confronting you today), you can learn to incorporate these winning skills into your life:

- *The more trying the times, the harder you need to try.*
  Quitting too soon only adds to your problems. In the face of serious setbacks, keep going . . . double your efforts and rate of production. Make the decision to survive and then, through sheer will and raw determination, stick to it until you do.
- *Be realistic.*
  Assess the extent of your crisis realistically. Don't discount the seriousness of the problem. If you deny the gravity of the situation, you will be ill-prepared to go to work and change it.
- *Don't hold back.*
  Put forth every bit of energy you have. Don't worry about becoming depleted. Winners do too much, and after that, they do even more. They don't think about fatigue or exhaustion.
- *Follow your hunches.*
  Once you have decided that you want to forge ahead, listen to your intuition as well as your intellect. Resist pressure from family and friends. Take a position and stand up for what *you believe in.* Right or wrong, it is time to trust your *own* judgment and believe in your *own* wisdom.
- *Get in touch with your anger.*
  It is normal to feel angry when unfortunate circumstances force you into a crisis. While it is important for you to understand how you may have helped to create your difficulties, you still have the right to be furious that so much of your time needs to be spent dealing with the problem now.
- *Take one step at a time.*
  After a major crisis, or something as serious as the death of someone close to you, be content to take one small step at a time until your emotional strength returns. Don't try to be superhuman and tackle all your problems at once. Choose one manageable task and do only that. Each small experience of success will increase your energy and positive outlook.
- *Let others comfort you.*
  In good times and bad, losers are constantly complaining. Because of their chronic negative attitude, when a crisis does occur, they are rarely believed or comforted. Their situation is similiar to that of the boy who cried "Wolf!" But if you are a positive person and normally manage your life well, be sure to share your remorse and

fear during hard times. Give others the opportunity to comfort you. You deserve this support and can feel good about asking for it.
* *Keep experimenting.*
The solution to a crisis may not be easy to discover. However, if you relentlessly pursue new channels and are willing to experiment when the probability of success is low, you *will* find a way out.
* *Translate your liabilities into assets.*
Keep your mind alert and your eyes open for opportunities that may lie within the core of the crisis or difficult situation. Rather than focus on the extent of the calamity, hunt for threads of hope and positive directions to take. Even in the midst of turmoil or disaster, an original idea could develop that will lead you to a profitable new venture.

LAUREEN JUMPS IN

Winners are committed to achieving. They have their antennae alerted for opportunities in every situation. They are actively communicating and interacting in any way they can . . . regardless of whether it's social or business. By their bold actions, they turn casual remarks or vague invitations into fruitful openings.

Here's how another patient took the initiative and created a major professional alliance.

Laureen is a songwriter whose words have been on the lips of people all over the world for years. Her colleagues in the music publishing business would certainly label her a winner.

I remember a story she told me that clearly illustrates how winners boldly grasp every possibility for success.

Laureen was introduced to a well-known recording artist at a cocktail party. After several minutes of conversation, he mentioned to her that he was thinking about recording a song about loneliness.

The minute he let this idea drop, Laureen picked it up. "I have so many feelings about loneliness!" she said. "It's such a rich topic to write about. Dealing with the whole subject interests me! Right now, as we're talking, all sorts of words are running through my head. I'd just love to write the lyrics for you!"

The famous recording artist didn't seem particularly interested in her suggestion, but as he was leaving, he gave Laureen his card and said, "Maybe we could talk more about this one day."

Although his parting remark was vague, Laureen went into action. Like a winner, she ignored the indefinite nature of his "one day" and boldly picked up on his suggestion that they might work together.

The very next morning, full of energy and positive thoughts, she called the singer and said, "I could hardly sleep last night, because so many phrases about loneliness were spinning around in my mind. I have a whole song sketched out, and I can't wait to show it to you. When can we get together?"

Laureen's last remarks were directive and bold . . . she *assumed* they *would* get together and collaborate on the song. The recording artist liked her enthusiasm and invited her over. The happy result was they worked together and the song became a big hit.

Laureen learned later that his original indecisive response to her had been a product of his extreme shyness. He wasn't being vague or uninterested with her . . . just awkward socially.

If Laureen had been a loser, she would have gone home from the party and spent a sleepless night angrily going over what she should or could have said to the songwriter. By daybreak, she would have concluded, "He thinks he's too big and famous for me. The heck with him! I won't beg for work where I know I'm not wanted. If he's not interested in me . . . I'm not interested in him. Handing me that card was just part of the phony insincerity I find everywhere in this town. Who does he think he is, saying he would like to 'talk more about this one day'? I don't need charity from him or anyone else!"

Winners think differently. They work on the tiniest thread of hope, or possibility to enhance their careers. When they get even a hint of an opportunity, they are off and running. If a door is slightly opened, they seize their chance and push it the rest of the way.

YOU WON'T MAKE IT EVERY TIME

You will not necessarily be successful every time you act boldly. In fact, according to some of my most successful patients . . . *real* winners are people who may lose as much as 70 percent of the time, but they keep trying when their efforts fail or they receive "Nos."

Diane Bennett, the music critic for the *Hollywood Reporter,* is a bold and successful woman who shared this thought with me one evening:

I'll take a million "Nos" and keep going, because all you need to make it is only one "Yes."

WINNER SCORECARD #17

Both winners and losers fantasize about what they hope to achieve one day. For losers, fantasy is usually as far as it goes. Winners discover how to push themselves ahead and reach their objectives. Among the traits that carry them forward are the courage to withstand disapproval, the strength to endure disappointment and the imagination to create new pathways. You, too, can discover the boldness within yourself that can transform your grandest imaginings into realities.

LOSERS	WINNERS
1. When losers suffer rejection from teachers, judges or peers, they decide they don't "have what it takes." They get too discouraged too fast, and give up their hopes for success too soon.	**1.** Winners have confidence in their abilities. When they believe in themselves and are told they don't have talent in their field of interest, they try harder, redouble their efforts and move boldly ahead.
2. Losers are afraid to challenge the status quo. If a way of doing something isn't standard procedure, they avoid it.	**2.** Winners dare to question established methods and fixed policies. They fearlessly initiate alternate ways of looking at life and getting things done. When they are thwarted, they discover innovative ways to reach their goals.
3. Losers often become immobilized in times of crisis. They are so preoccupied with their fears that they miss seeing opportunities that could turn their problems into advantages.	**3.** When faced with a crisis, winners not only work on resolving it, but try to find something beneficial in the situation. In the midst of chaos, they manage to discover that fine vein of positive thinking that can lead to new chances for success.

LOSERS

4. At critical times, losers become so overwhelmed with anxieties that they stop the very trial-and-error behaviors that could lead them to success. Instead, they quit in despair.

5. Losers don't want to appear too aggressive, so they accept "Nos" without question, resigning themselves to whatever explanations are given. They live with disappointment and discomfort, because they are too frightened to try to change their situations.

6. Losers wait for definite proposals or promotions to materialize. When vague suggestions or job possibilities are presented, they ignore them and wait to be courted. Terrified of rejection and suspicious of kindness or compliments, they pass up opportunities to improve their personal and professional lives.

7. Losers are willing to make an effort only occasionally, when something is easy to achieve. They look for guarantees of success. Rarely finding them, they seldom act to help themselves.

WINNERS

4. Winners hang in when the going gets tough. Actively dedicated to surviving, they continue struggling with a problem until they find a solution or uncover new information.

5. For winners, a "No" means they need to double their efforts, or perhaps move in another direction. They push boldly ahead, trying and experimenting until they reach their goals.

6. Winners go to work at the slightest hint of an opportunity to enhance their careers. If a door is slightly ajar, they seize their chance and push it open the rest of the way. If they are rejected, they will try to change the situation and alter the circumstances in their favor.

7. Winners have many successes, because they are so active and try so many new projects. Knowing that many of the things they attempt will end in failure, they are optimistic, positive and keep trying!

AFTERWORD

It's Time to Say Goodbye

Goodbyes have always been difficult for me. I'm never quite sure how to say them and I'm never really ready to begin. Finishing this book is like closing a very important and precious chapter in my life. As I sit here at my desk, my eyes are filling with tears and the words are blurring before me.

Why do I always find myself sobbing when I write the last pages of my books? Why? Perhaps it's because I've spent these three years living so close to you through the pages . . . perhaps it's because I've put so much of myself between the covers that I don't know how to separate now . . . perhaps it's my own unconscious fears about success that frighten me. I am forced to confront them whenever I finish a major project that is as much a part of my life as is this book.

I was thinking to myself, "How would I comfort this Kassorla woman and her tears if she were my own patient? What would I do?"

Then I answered me, "First, I would hug me, be very gentle and say, 'There now, dear one. I understand your tears . . . they are related to the pain you feel in separating. But don't worry . . . you will be back with your readers someday soon, you know.'"

Next, I would hold Irene's hands in mine and say, "Kiss them all goodbye now, Irene; finish your last pages . . . and dry your sweet, sad tears."

* * *

At the beginning of this book, I asked you to take my hand. I wanted you to feel safe, because I know how frightening it is to try to change when you are all alone.

I'm proud that you trusted me and came along. Now it's time for you to trust yourself and take the last part of your journey without me.

You are ready, dear friend.

The rewards are all out there waiting for you. Reach out for them . . . grab on to your life . . . RISK.

GIVE YOURSELF THIS OPPORTUNITY.

Set out on your own, and experience the amazing adventure of you. Embrace the exhilaration of your successes.

If you are willing to put forth effort, you, too, can be energized working happily and effectively. But remember to be ready for failures. You *will* fail some along your road to winning. When you do . . . be encouraged! This will be evidence of your trying harder. Good!

And when you do fail, pick yourself up and . . .

GIVE YOURSELF A KISS

and try even harder. Experiment! Be active and productive. Get acquainted with exploring new pathways. Become familiar with trial and error behaviors. Learn how to be disappointed and yet try again. Then you will know success and the drama, the excitement and the euphoria of winning. Find out just how much fun you can have experiencing your wins during the priceless allotment of time you are given on this, your magical planet.

You have all the tools now with which to move your destiny ahead. You can design an individual formula for your unique lifestyle, bearing your personal signature for living. If you want to be successful, it will include perseverance and the courage to develop yourself to the fullest extent possible.

I want you to forge ahead with your own miracles and transformations. Squeeze out every precious drop of your mosaic of creativity and excellence. Become the person that you can admire and respect . . . the person you truly want to be.

Begin now.

You have it all inside you . . . THE POWER TO GO FOR IT AND MAKE A WIN OF YOUR LIFE.